A Stranger and Afraid

Billy Connolly: The Authorized Version
Gullible's Travels
That was Business, This is Personal
The Underworld

Duncan Campbell

A Stranger and Afraid

The Story of Caroline Beale

MACMILLAN

First published 1997 by Macmillan

an imprint of Macmillan Publishers Ltd
25 Eccleston Place, London SW1W 9NF
and Basingstoke

Associated companies throughout the world

ISBN 0 333 69146 6

1 3 5 7 9 8 6 4 2

A CIP catalogue record for this book is available from
the British Library

Typeset by SetSystems Ltd, Saffron Walden, Essex
Printed by Mackays of Chatham plc, Chatham, Kent

I would like to thank everyone who agreed to be interviewed, without whom this book would not have been possible. I would also like to thank the staffs of the New York Public Library, the Colindale Newspaper Library, the *Guardian* Library and the *New York Daily News* Library. My thanks also to Robert King, Ronan Bennett, Tony Walton, Gen LeRoy, Joanna Malloy, Mark Dowie, Scott Malcomson, Ruby Crystal, Harriet Stewart, Luciana Bertolino-Zan, Niall Campbell, Ian Katz, Catherine Hurley, Hazel Orme and Clare Thomas for their help in different ways. I am very grateful to the *Guardian* for giving me the time to complete this book.

Prologue

In September 1994 Caroline Beale, a thirty-year-old civil servant from Essex, was arrested at John F. Kennedy airport in New York and charged with the murder of the baby to whom she had given birth a few hours earlier in a New York hotel. No one – including her family and the boyfriend she had lived with for eight years – knew she had even been pregnant. She was locked up in America's largest jail and held there for eight months. She eventually stood trial in March 1996.

Like most journalists, I had been aware of the story, although I never worked on it at the time. Tales of young women held in foreign jails – in Thailand, Brazil, Morocco – are not uncommon but usually the women have been arrested for drug smuggling and mostly they are guilty of the offence with which they have been charged, however pitiless the penalty may be. Caroline Beale's case seemed different because there were still many unanswered questions and when I was asked if I would be prepared to work on a book on her story I was curious to meet her.

We met on a summer's day at her parents' home in Chingford. Her father, Peter, made coffee and pointed out a poem she had written, which was framed and on the wall. Caroline was smartly dressed in white shirt and jeans and looked very different from the terribly distressed person I had seen on television news bulletins and documentaries of her case. But it was clear that she was still very bruised from what

1

had happened to her in America and in a note I made of the meeting I wrote that her eyes filled with tears as she spoke. We parted without agreeing whether or not the book would happen and I felt that she might well decide not to go ahead with it and that that might be the wiser course for her. Journalists can often persuade vulnerable people to tell their tales by suggesting it will help other people, that their side of the story can be finally told, that they owe it to themselves. Sometimes we may be proved right and the reliving of horrors is justified: an injustice is exposed, a record is set straight. Sometimes we just reopen a wound and depart leaving the subject puzzled and bewildered.

Caroline and I met again a couple of weeks later at an Italian restaurant on one of those rare English nights when you can sit outside and eat. She described some of her experiences in court and in jail, the people she had met, attorneys and crack dealers, prison chaplains and detectives. I liked her. I thought she was – quite literally – painfully honest and that if she did decide to agree to the book, it might be possible to tell the real story behind what had happened and, yes, to see an injustice exposed.

This is that story.

Chapter One

Alex Velez calls it The Look. He learned it as a military policeman in the Marines. He has used it as a security guard spotting shoplifters at bookshops in Manhattan. He is quite proud of it.

'I gave her The Look. You give The Look and they figure – Does he know? I'm telling you, as a cop, they're all psychological games out there on the street,' says Alex, as he contemplates the taco on the paper plate in front of him in the café near the ferry docks on Staten Island. 'You want to win the game all the time. And that time I did because I psyched her out. The scenario was perfect. I was there in uniform, so she couldn't back up.'

Alex is thirty-seven, a slim, wiry Puerto Rican, born in Manhattan, brought up in the South Bronx. He joined the Marines in 1978 – he still wears their snappy red windcheater – and served with them for four years as a tank driver in the desert in California and as a military policeman. He had moved east, found work as a security guard and met his wife at the Barnes and Noble bookshop on 14th Street and Eighth Avenue where he gave The Look to the panhandlers and the light-fingered brethren of Greenwich Village. Ten years earlier he had become one of the 1200 officers attached to the Port Authority Police, which handles the policing of the main transit terminals in New York and New Jersey. For the past five years Velez had found himself at John F. Kennedy airport watching for bag thieves who prey on preoccupied passengers, spotting EDPs (emotionally disturbed persons) who try to board flights, checking out people who think they can take home to Texas a handgun they bought in Brooklyn, working with the armoured trucks that protect aeroplanes from hijacking, acting as back-up to the security teams that search travellers and their luggage. And giving people The Look.

'It was a crowded night and I was real tired. When you're working shifts you're always tired because your body never gets used to it. I thought I saw a bag thief who was acting suspicious but I lost him in the crowd. I was working at the screening point behind a glass divider. I was watching the people going to the screening point. I'm looking to see if there's any bag thieves waiting for people kissing and hugging goodbye so they can snatch a bag. I was talking to a security guard, a friend, about this bag thief that I lost and as I watch people coming in I watch people's faces. When I was in the military I was trained and when I worked in security on shoplifting detail I learned: always look at people's faces. If they're going to do something wrong, they're going to look at you and you're going to know.'

Into his line of vision at Gate 30 came a young woman, fair-haired, casually dressed, one of dozens heading for Air India flight 102 to London Heathrow. The travellers were a mix of Indians on the first leg of a journey back to Delhi or Bombay and young British travellers taking advantage of budget fares on the Palace in the Sky and airline meals less anodyne than the normal bland offerings. The cops were wary of odd goings-on in that patch because it adjoined the departure points for both El Al and Pakistan International, both airlines with good reason to be security-conscious.

'I happened to glance over and this woman had a frightened look, like as if she did something and I was there for her. I thought she was pregnant. She had a coat and what looked like a big belly.' He saw one of the women security guards checking her out. 'Now I looked again at her and at her belly

4

and I looked at the security girl and she looked at me. We looked at each other – as if to say there's something wrong.'

The security officer at Gate 31 was Clara Tejada of Aviation Security. Neatly turned out in her brown uniform, she had been watching the young woman as she put a tapestry-style bag on the stand to be X-rayed. She noticed that she had a bulge under her coat and thought it was probably a money-bag. Tejada gestured at her stomach and told the young woman that she would have to have the money-bag X-rayed. 'I'm pregnant,' said the young woman.

'You're not,' said Tejada. 'You must place the bag on the machine.' She started to check out the bulge and pressed it with her fingers. 'It's too hard,' she told the young woman.

The young woman said, 'Forget it,' and started to walk away from the security area towards the women's toilets. Tejada gestured Velez over and told him, 'She said she's pregnant but she doesn't look like she's pregnant.' Even if a woman is pregnant, she can still go through a metal detector without harming the baby. Velez wondered if this was someone who wanted to be caught.

Velez told Tejada to take her into a side room, where the boilers were, to check her out. He was suspicious. Perhaps she had drugs, although the typical smuggler would be bringing stuff into the United States rather than taking it out. At first he assumed she was travelling alone. 'I didn't realize she was with her boyfriend. I lost focus because my threat level was high, thinking that she might have a weapon, although she didn't look like that kind of person.'

Clara Tejada called her manager, Patricia Alvarez, to ask her to assist in the search. At this stage, the feeling was still that the woman must have a weapon, drugs or drugs proceeds. Tejada asked the young woman to take off her coat and her shirt. Underneath they saw a checkered bag with the words Canal Jeans on it. They asked her to open it. She looked at them and said, 'I don't want my friends to know.' She asked them to close the door to the boiler room, telling them, 'I don't want him to see me.' She told them there was a baby in the bag.

Patricia Alvarez ran out of the room, astonishment written on her face. 'She has a bag there, she says she has a dead baby in the bag.'

Velez told her, 'You gotta be kidding.' It was near the time for his break and he was peckish and he thought Alvarez was fooling around with him. He asked if she was serious. The look on her face told him she was. He called his station on his police radio to say that he had a problem: 'You don't give details over the radio because you have people in the news media listen in on a police scanner. From the tone of my voice they can tell I want back-up.' He then rang on a fixed line and told his supervisor what was going on and said he would check it out. 'I've dealt with a lot of EDPs and I wanted to make sure she wasn't an EDP with a dead puppy in her bag that she was calling her dead baby.'

The young woman was sitting down shaking uncontrollably. He tried, he says, to put her at ease: 'How you doing, miss? Is everything OK? Is there a problem? Is there something in the bag I should know about? Is there a baby in there?'

He opened up the plastic bag carefully. 'I went to my wife's birth so I know how a new baby smells. I saw the little baby's hand. That was enough for me to confirm that it wasn't a dog or a cat or a doll.' He radioed again. 'We don't say "dead body" over the radio because of the scanners. I just said, "We have confirmed DOA" [dead on arrival]. I closed the bag. I've seen fatalities which were kind of gruesome. One time I see a man slumped in a van on the highway at the airport, I figure he passed out. When I get there, the guy's head has exploded in the van, they had to shovel up the brains and put them in a bag. I had nightmares every time I saw a white van but after a couple of months it was OK. I didn't eat Italian food for a while. I'd seen fatalities but never dead babies.'

A Stranger and Afraid

Alex Velez asked her what had happened. 'She said the baby's dead. I said, "How did it die?" She said the baby was born dead. I had to coax it out of her. She said she had the baby last night in the bathroom at a hotel in Manhattan. I had to calm her down. She always kept saying, "Don't let my boyfriend know." That was the one thing she didn't want. So now we have a body.

'She said her boyfriend didn't know she was even pregnant. I said, "How come he doesn't know? You've been here for a week, don't you fool around with the guy?" She was real thin, but how she hid it I don't know.'

Police procedure is that anyone believed to be emotionally disturbed is handcuffed from behind before they are taken away for further questioning. The young woman became even more distressed as they tried to put the cuffs on her. 'She said "My boyfriend will see."' Velez said he would allow her to cover the handcuffs with her coat. He asked her what she was going to do with the baby when she returned to London, 'to see if she said, "I'm going to take it to the doctor to see if he can make her feel better." All she told me was "I don't know – don't let my boyfriend know."'

The young woman was put into a police ambulance to take her to hospital and handcuffed to one of the stretchers. Detectives at the downtown precinct responsible for the hotel where the baby had been born and members of the murder squad nearest to the airport, based at the 113th Precinct in Queens, were alerted. It transpired that she had been travelling with three young men and detectives arrived to interview them.

The young woman was taken down to Queens General Hospital while the detectives from 113th Precinct and the duty District Attorneys from Queens arrived to interview her. Alex Velez was asked to stand outside the curtains round her hospital bed and listen to her answers to see if she changed her story. There is a slight edge between the Port Authority Police and the New York Police Department, 'New York's Finest' as they are called, sometimes sincerely, sometimes with irony. In the same way that the Metropolitan Police feel that they may be a cut above the British Transport Police and have a more glamorous image, the NYPD know that no one makes television series about the PAP. Alex Velez was anxious that the credit for the arrest should go to his team although, because the PAP have no murder squad, he had to surrender his charge. The young woman told the detectives the same tale: 'She said her boyfriend went out drinking and she went to the bathroom, the baby came out, she cut the umbilical cord with a pair of scissors. She said the baby came out, she saw it wasn't breathing and she put it in a plastic bag, wrapped it up, put it next to her bed. She saw her boyfriend when he came back. They went on a tour the next morning to see New York City, the river, whatever. She said she had the baby on her person so we had, say, twenty-four hours of the baby being in a bag. This girl kept it good and hidden.'

The young woman was detained as an Emotionally Disturbed Person and taken into custody for her own safety and for unlawful removal of a body. The penalty for the latter offence would have been, says Velez, a 'slap on the wrist, maybe just a fine'. The baby was taken to the medical examiner for a pathologist's report on how she had died. Velez reckoned that the young woman must have been suffering from the 'baby blues': 'My wife had it mild – we have a little girl who's three now – but this woman had it to extremes. She was a nice girl. I don't know what made her crack and go crazy. She couldn't have been so crazy because she had a boyfriend and if I had a girlfriend that was crazy I sure as hell wouldn't be going out with her. My fatherly attitude was, how can you do this? But my personal thing is she had the baby blues. But I'm not a medical doctor.

'If I wasn't there in uniform and looked at this girl, she probably would have just left the baby in the bathroom,' says Alex Velez contemplatively, wiping his fingers on a paper napkin and looking around the Taco Bell at the teenagers who have come in for lunch and are joshing around the soft-drinks machine. They are well behaved. Staten Island is a popular place for cops to live because it has a relatively low crime rate. It has few of the tensions of the Bronx or Brooklyn or the wilder parts of Manhattan. 'It happened to be a miracle that I was there otherwise she would have been in London and no one would have been any the wiser. It would have been a mystery. I just happened to be there at the right time. And I gave her The Look.'

Chapter Two

Caroline Ann Beale was born in Oldchurch hospital in Romford, Essex, on 20 June 1964, the first child of Peter and Daphne Beale. Peter was from an East Ham family. His father had been badly wounded and shell-shocked in the First World War and later ran a sweet and toy shop with Mrs Beale in Forest Gate, east London. There were two elder brothers, Roy and Stan, both of whom died relatively young, the former having been a member of both the Palestinian and the Metropolitan Police and the latter an airman and engineer. Peter was a boy during the war – 'in East Ham when they dropped the sky on it' – was evacuated to Norfolk but brought back on occasions by a determined mother and present for some of the heaviest bombing. After leaving school he had worked briefly in an office before joining the RAF for his National Service. He extended his time in the Air Force to four years and served as an instruments technician in Aden, Cyprus, Malta, Egypt and Iraq. After he was demobbed, he took a job in mechanized accounting and then in computers with International Computers and Tabulators. He liked the job, worked long hours to keep up with the developing technology and during the course of it met the woman who was to become his wife.

Daphne Edmunds, one of five brothers and sisters from a family in Hillingdon, west London, worked in a local shop after leaving school and then in the accounts department of British Railways in Baker Street. It was there that she met Peter and they found they had much in common, sharing a love of gardening and walking and a desire to start a family. They married in 1962 and lived with Peter's family for two years before buying their own home in Harold Hill. Caroline arrived in 1964 and Stephen two years later. Daphne was very ill with chest pains when the children were small and had to stay in hospital for long periods. Stephen was cared for by both sets of grandparents, and by aunts and uncles while Caroline was looked after mainly by her father and a neighbour. In 1972 the family moved to Chingford, to a neat, well-kept house with lavender and snowdrops outside and a back garden large enough for Peter and Daphne to pursue their interest in bonsai. It was on a steep road just down from the local police station and the parish church in King's Head Hill. The air seemed clearer and Epping Forest and King George's Reservoir were within walking distance. The turmoil of inner-city life seemed a thousand miles away.

The children had been happy enough at Harold Park primary school and Peter still remembers with pride how one of the teachers had told him how he wished that all the pupils were like the two little Beales. Caroline learned to swim, joined a local swimming club and eventually competed in the breast-stroke at borough level. 'She was a normal, healthy, happy little girl,' says her mother.

It was a conventional English upbringing: the Beales were respectable, law-abiding, anxious to instil into both their children the virtues of study, honesty, decency and hard work. Holidays would be in the village of Mundesley in Norfolk and there were trips at weekends. Voices were not raised in argument, there were no family feuds.

It was not a church-going family but Caroline attended Sunday school and both children were encouraged to say their prayers before they went to bed at night, although neither are now religious, Stephen saying he would describe himself as an atheist 'because there is so much badness in the world'. Caroline was a keen Brownie and a Girl Guide with an armful of badges for everything from swimming to flower-arranging. She went to ballet classes. After the family moved, Caroline went to Chingford Church of England Primary and Chingford High where she was remembered by teachers as well behaved, neither brilliant nor notably underachieving. Academic work, with the exception of history, did not interest her much and her exam results were disappointing.

Caroline and Stephen experienced the fairly typical frictions of a small brother with a big sister who had to take him round the shops and put up with the usual behaviour of little boys. Her friends would stick up for her as she would try to find excuses not to have to take him with her.

Stephen turned into a sportsman and an accomplished wind-surfer, eventually competing at national level. Peter Beale would drive him to competitions all over the country with Caroline occasionally going along in support. Friends say that Caroline was in her brother's shadow at this time, that her achievements never seemed quite to match his.

When Stephen left school he taught wind-surfing and outdoor pursuits briefly before joining the Marines where he stayed for a few months, feeling that he had gone in too young when he saw what his contemporaries were doing in their lives. With Peter Beale's assistance, he bought himself out. As Caroline and Stephen grew up, their relationship improved, especially after he had started going out with the woman who became his wife in 1992, Caroline – known in the family as 'Caroline Two'. After initial coolness, the two Carolines became firm friends. Stephen had met his wife, an outgoing young woman from a big Coventry-Irish family, after they had spoken on the phone when he was working for a computer firm and she was in a related firm and had liked the sound of his voice. 'We got talking and then a friend said, "Let's go and meet them," and now I've got two kids,' says Stephen. They appear devoted to each other.

Caroline One made friends both at school and among the

neighbours, with some of whom she is still in touch twenty years later. Clare Warby, now Webb, a nurse in Suffolk; Mandy Goff, who works with people with learning difficulties for social services in Suffolk; Susan Tinkler, now a graphic designer in Winchester; Marilyn Doughty, who runs a card shop in Leeds; and Lesley Warren, who lives in Bromley and works for London Electricity and whom Caroline has known since the two girls were taken for spins and sweets in a neighbour's sports car.

As her teens arrived Caroline started going to a local youth club called Spicer Hall, played badminton and, as a Ranger Guide, hung out with boys from a local Venture Scout group, going hiking in the Lake District, staying at youth hostels and attending sedan-chair rallies. At the youth club they played records – Wham! and the New Romantics – and ran their own discos. 'We were terribly well behaved – we ran a Brownie pack and did the Duke of Edinburgh's award.' Friends were struck by how well Caroline got on with children and how at ease she was with them. She took up the guitar and started taking lessons, both classical and rock; friends still recall her brave renditions of 'Greensleeves'.

'She was a bit of an ugly duckling, I don't mean that unkindly,' says Mandy Goff, who has known her since they were twelve. 'But she wouldn't wear the latest fashions and she was a little bit on the plump side and didn't have a grand hair-do and I don't think she made much of an impression on people. But as she started to work and got money to buy nice clothes and got out of her parents' hair she blossomed into this gorgeous woman with a wonderful figure and she slimmed down and filled out in all the right places and really was quite stunning.'

There were occasional forays into London to see bands like U2 but essentially the most exotic trips were to Walthamstow Market. The West End of London, although less than an hour away, was a foreign country. The group seemed relatively

13

untouched by the world of joy-riding, speed-taking and casual sex of some of their contemporaries. The family's only experience of the law was when Stephen was caught speeding in his car and when, as he left school, he made friends with young police officers in south London. The only tragedy to afflict them was the death of their uncle Roy, whom Stephen hero-worshipped. The children did not attend the funeral and were conscious of being protected from it.

After failing to get any O levels at Chingford High, Caroline went to Loughton college in Debden in 1981 to take a course in community care. There she passed three O levels in English, history and sociology. 'I didn't want to be at school but I didn't want to be at work. At sixteen I wanted to be an adult but they treat you like a child.'

Her friends, Mandy Goff and Clare Webb, were at the same college. Clare and Caroline took the same course and did voluntary work together in Leytonstone House and Grange Farm with teenage mentally handicapped people, helping them to wash and reading to them as part of the practical side of their course. After achieving her certificate in community care, Caroline briefly considered a career in nursing but she was not selected for the course. As she applied for jobs she worked in a local sports shop on Saturdays and, briefly, full time. Friends worked in the nearby Spar. It was a social time.

Her first interview was with the Department of Health and she 'just sunk into doing that'. In 1982 she started work, dealing with ministerial correspondence at the DoH in the Elephant and Castle, a ninety-minute daily journey, during which she would read magazines or Jackie Collins novels. There would be letters from MPs to put on the computer and assign to different departments where officials would draft replies. She did this for a year and a half before working in the liaison division dealing with health authorities and monitoring their work, drafting replies to letters from individuals in a different office at Euston Towers. She was transferred into community services as a promotion and then attached to the Social Services Inspectorate, where she stayed until 1992 arranging conferences with local authorities on issues like the Children Act and the Community Care Act.

She liked to party and had started to drink and smoke. Her friends remember that Peter Beale was the most protective of the parents, the father who would phone up to ask where his daughter was and when she was coming home. 'He didn't like Caroline drinking and smoking,' said one friend, 'so she used to come round to our house to have a fag.' For the most part the girls in the group were independent-minded and wanted a career before they settled down. There was not much talk of marriage or babies. 'None of our group was very maternal,' says Clare Webb.

Caroline's first real boyfriend was James, who was at college with her. One friend remembers him as something of an eccentric who rode his bicycle in his pyjamas. He played keyboards in a punk band called Vicious Bootlace and the friends would go together to watch him perform. After a while he and Caroline parted and she started going out with Peter, who came from Surrey, worked for British Telecom and whom she had met through Venture Scouts and Ranger Guides activities.

She started holidaying abroad with groups of friends: Corfu, Ibiza, Tenerife. They were good, carefree times, beaches and bars, a Club 18–30 holiday during which they spent their time hiding from the reps who wanted them to take part in 'various awful things like Tarzan and wet T-shirt competitions'. On one occasion in Corfu Mandy Goff contracted chickenpox and had to be smuggled in and out of their apartment as she was meant to be in quarantine; Mandy would chase Caroline's Peter, who had not had chickenpox, up and down the road threatening to hug him and infect him. There seemed to be few clouds on the horizon.

Work was fine, if unexciting. There would be Friday night

get-togethers in the pub and trips to watch a colleague who played in a band at the Hand in Hand pub. Caroline was the life and soul of leaving parties and although her colleagues knew she did not find her work completely fulfilling, she was liked for her ready wit and general amiability. 'My life,' says Caroline, 'was very normal.'

Meanwhile, she had met Paul.

Chapter Three

Paul Faraway was a handsome, tall, shy young man who worked as an actioner making sporting rifles for the gunsmiths Holland and Holland, a job in which he had been interested since he was a teenager. One of four brothers from Highams Park, he was the son of Michael, a judge's clerk who worked at Redbridge Crown Court, and Maureen, an art teacher. Paul was the second son; the eldest, Julian, was a mathematics professor in America, the third, Dominic, known as Dom, was a graphic designer and the last, Sam, was a student of graphic design. The three youngest were close, more like friends than brothers.

Paul had been part of the sociable crew that hung around in the Chingford/Walthamstow area, drinking together in pubs on a Friday night, going out for late-night curries, heading off for rock concerts and festivals together or having weekends in Brighton. For a year or so he went out with Caroline's friend Clare Webb, who was fond of him but found him 'shy and anxious'.

Jenny Bloor, who now works in Walthamstow for the Health Service, knew Caroline and Paul then and was going out with a printer friend of Paul. She had been away at music college studying the oboe – she now plays bass guitar in a band – but had returned and met up with the group. The crew of around seven or eight of them would meet regularly at one of the local pubs, the Cuckfield or the Reindeer, for drinks or to dance. They liked rock rather than disco music and a few were into the tail end of punk. The pub world was not as flash as the local Charlie Chan club but it suited their musical tastes and their pockets better. They would lark around by the canal, build campfires in Epping Forest and sit around them drinking cider. Sometimes Paul would get out his rods and go fishing at Waltham Abbey or Broxbourne. When someone's parents were away for a weekend there would be a party. 'It was a full social life,' says Mandy Goff. Paul was one of the first in the group to own a car, a battered white VW Beetle – 'with old kebabs stuffed down the backs of the seats,' recalls one friend – and used to get lumbered with driving the others around. 'He was a nice bloke,' says Jenny. 'He wasn't an extrovert but he had a nice quiet sense of humour.'

Caroline and Paul finally got together at the Cuckfield, one New Year's Eve. 'He was very attractive, lovely chap, super manner, quite shy and regarded as quite a catch,' says Mandy Goff. For their part, Caroline and Paul were attracted to each other – the song they referred to as 'our song' was Eric Clapton's 'Wonderful Tonight'. They felt at ease in each other's company, although Paul was said by friends to be more reserved than Caroline until he had had a few beers. They were different in other ways, too. While Caroline was a snappy dresser, Paul was a 'jeans and sweaters man', and while she liked to cook and entertain, he was happy with 'Beans, beans and beans on toast,' said one friend. At the time he was sharing a flat with three other men – 'They were worse than *Men Behaving Badly*,' says a mutual friend cheerfully.

'Caroline decided she wanted to go out with Paul,' says another friend. 'She was very determined.'

Neither set of parents seemed overjoyed about their child's choice, a situation not unfamiliar to millions of couples all over the world. 'It was very much a case of "He's not good enough for our little girl,"' said one friend. The Beale family found Paul monosyllabic when he visited and he seemed only too anxious to get out of the house in Chingford as soon as he had arrived. There were occasional, awkward family meals but they became rarer and rarer and when Caroline visited her parents she tended to come alone and infrequently, even though she did not live far away.

Meanwhile Stephen and Caroline Two had moved first to south London and then to Sheringham, a village with a green, three pubs and a Greek restaurant on the Norfolk coast where they now live with their two children, Josh and Amy, whose godmother Caroline is. They met Paul but never became close to him.

Caroline did not meet the Faraway parents until she had been going out with Paul for four years and, according to one friend, 'Caroline felt very strongly that Mrs Faraway disapproved of her and thought her strange and awkward. Neither of them knew the slightest thing about each other at all.' Caroline, however, became close to Paul's grandmother, who was very fond of her and made her feel welcome. She became the member of the Faraway family to whom Caroline felt closest. At Christmas, there would be gatherings of both families with Paul and Caroline spending Christmas Day with one family and Boxing Day with the other.

The lack of parental excitement over the relationship had little effect on the couple, and when Carline was twenty-three they moved into a rented ground-floor flat in Wanstead. Although her parents came from a generation that would have been happier if the couple had been married before they started living together, they accepted that all of Caroline's contemporaries were doing the same and raised no objections.

'There wasn't much point in objecting or saying they should get married,' says Peter Beale. 'I remember asking Paul if he cared about Caroline and he said yes, so I said to Daphne, "There's not much we can do." We accepted it as the norm.' Marriage seemed likely in the future although it was not a subject that they brought up. 'Paul is a very, very shy person whose shyness inhibits him. Having been extremely shy myself I think I recognize many of the symptoms,' says Peter.

Caroline and Paul stayed in the flat for three years and it became a base for friends to drop round. Caroline was the home-maker, friends said, whipping together pasta for late-night visitors while Paul played the amiable host in charge of the drinks. It was a happy, carefree existence, both were busy with their work and surrounded by a fairly tight circle of friends, with Paul driving them to see Genesis at Shepton Mallet or bands like AC/DC and Van Halen at the Lyceum in the West End. There were trips to Bisley, too, the headquarters of the shooting world, where guns on which Paul had worked would be on display. Paul was out at night more often and although initially Caroline accompanied him to the rock concerts he attended, she gradually preferred to stay at home.

When property prices started to drop, the couple went house-hunting. The second house they saw, in Leytonstone, they bought for £76,500 with a £70,000 mortgage. This meant they paid £300 a month each, a sizeable chunk from Caroline's £14,000 annual salary. Her parents helped with the deposit. Caroline had always wanted an old house and set about carrying out the decorating herself, lavishing particular care on the bedroom.

Colin Brosnan, who had met Caroline at the Spicer Hall youth club in Chingford and is now a manager in construction services at Hackney Council, recalls the period fondly. 'Caroline was as much the life and soul of the party as anyone,' he says. He found Paul honest and easy to get along with 'although he wasn't into football – he supports Queens Park Rangers!' He thought Paul and Caroline were well suited and relaxed with each other.

'We were thinking about getting married at one stage and I think we would have done eventually,' says Caroline. They did get engaged and had a party to celebrate at the Wanstead hospital social club where Colin Brosnan's mother worked and where Caroline, Clare and Mandy had had their joint twenty-first birthday party. There was a DJ and dancing and friends queuing up to congratulate the happy couple. Both sets of parents attended. 'It was more a declaration of their commitment than "We're getting married in seven months' time,"' says Jenny Bloor. 'They were committed to one another and they were formalizing that. She had steady boyfriends at a young age and she very much wanted to settle down, make a home, make a nest. Paul was a reticent kind of person, who would just go with the flow. A typical English bloke, not without depth but not one to say, "Come on, let's get married next week."'

The couple went to see a local minister because the families wanted a church wedding but he indicated that he would like to see them in church regularly over the next six months if he was to marry them. They both decided that to put on such a performance would be hypocritical.

Paul, anyway, preferred the idea of a more casual wedding, perhaps carried out on a beach somewhere hot and far away, in the Caribbean even. Mandy Goff would tease them: 'When are you going to get married? How are we going to get out to the Bahamas if you get married there?' The Beales and the Faraways had one meeting to discuss the wedding but it was, by all accounts, rather stiff with talk circling around who would pay for what and how big it would be. The matter was allowed to drop.

'There was certainly talk about getting married,' says one of Caroline's friends, 'but it was mostly to do with what she was going to wear and it never got close to booking a place for a reception or anything like that.'

When Araminta Thorne, now twenty-five, appeared at Euston Towers as a young newly arrived Zimbabwean to apply for a job, the 'brisk and efficient' person who met her at the lift was Caroline Beale, who became one of her closest friends in Britain. Now, seven years later, Araminta is still in England, still in the ground-floor council flat in Kentish Town, north-west London. As a colleague and friend of Caroline, she was privy to the way the relationship was going.

'When she wasn't coming to work and saying Paul was the greatest thing on earth and her darling sweetpea, he was a total bastard and all men were bastards. The biggest problem was that he was never as affectionate as she needed him to be because he was a very self-conscious kind of guy. I found him pleasant, mild, shy in an endearing kind of way.' In December 1993, Caroline, Paul, Araminta and friends went to Calais to buy wine and cheese and to stock up for the festive season. Paul was not in a good mood and was complaining much of the time. 'The next day she was saying, "See – see what I mean, see what he's like!"' says Araminta.

Paul had gone into business on his own but had run into financial problems and was facing possible bankruptcy. Caroline and he had discussed children briefly but felt that it was not the right time to start a family. Soon, though, they were both to be engulfed in something that was to dominate and define their lives.

Chapter Four

Alison Taylor was a year older than Caroline and the two had known each other since Alison started going out with Paul's younger brother, Dominic, with whom she shared a flat in Tufnell Park in north London. Alison was a strikingly attractive woman, slim with short, dark hair, whose extrovert nature made her friends wherever she went. Caroline soon became one. A swimwear designer based in Islington in north London, Alison had come south five years earlier from near Leeds and had retained her Yorkshire accent. Her widowed father still lived in the north as did her younger sister.

She was artistic, a skilful illustrator and line-drawer who led a sociable life, going to see live bands and comedy acts at places like the Comedy Store in Leicester Square and the Market Tavern in Islington with the rest of her crowd of friends. She liked the theatre and had particularly enjoyed *The Rise and Fall of Little Voice*, starring Jane Horrocks, in the West End. She would go away with Caroline and Paul and Dom for weekends to bed-and-breakfasts on the south coast. Caroline saw her every week: 'She was someone you got on with right away. She was very open and direct.' She was active, too, taking kick-boxing classes and going riding at weekends. The two women became close, with Alison, as one friend saw it, acting as a bulwark for Caroline against the Faraways. They shared confidences and clothes and enjoyed each other's company. Everyone who met Alison seemed to like her: 'Alison was a real bubble, full of life, bursting with energy. You took an instant liking to her,' says Daphne Beale, who had met her at Caroline and Paul's engagement party.

Then, in 1991, Alison told Caroline that she had a lump in her breast. She went to the Royal Free hospital in Hampstead where she was operated on and was assured by the hospital that there was a 90 per cent chance of a complete recovery. Caroline remembers how Alison reacted at the time: 'She was really positive and we weren't worried at that stage.' The cloud seemed to have passed.

But in July 1993 it gradually became apparent to her friends that her illness had returned. 'She was getting backache the whole time and was always very tired,' says Caroline. One weekend Caroline, Paul, Dominic and Alison had gone to Mandy Goff's home in Ashfield Green near Diss in Suffolk. The local Crackfield Poacher pub was holding a 'beach party', an all-day affair with a barbecue. 'She was great, tremendously good fun,' says Mandy. 'She had had a fair bit of treatment but she was full of life.' Alison complained of feeling unwell but it was thought that it was because the caravan was so hot – 'like sleeping in a microwave'. In fact, she was by now very ill. She returned to the Royal Free.

At first the doctors said that she might be suffering from sciatica. 'Then things got worse and worse. She was losing weight. She couldn't walk up the stairs of their flat so she was taken into hospital.' She was put on a course of chemotherapy and was in and out of hospital, gradually becoming weaker.

'We knew by Christmas-time that she was not going to recover but she was unaware of that and she was still optimistic,' says Caroline. 'We had a juicer and she would put carrots in it and say that she was going to drink lots of healthy juices and get better. I think she knew all along, really, but when we would go on walks to places like Hampstead Heath, she would say things like "I'm going to beat this cancer."'

Alison's health began to deteriorate fast. In September, she was readmitted to hospital. In the spring of the following year she was told that her ovaries would have to be removed. This was painful for her, because she had always wanted very much to have children and Caroline was acutely aware of how difficult this was for her. In May 1994 Alison was moved to the Marie Curie hospice in Kentish Town. It was a harrowing time for her close friends, none of whom had experienced the loss of someone so close to them before. Caroline found it distressing to see the friend she adored lying with her mouth open and her eyes staring at the ceiling of the hospice but she continued to visit her. 'Her legs were as small as my arms,' she says. Alison died on 16 June 1994.

Both Caroline's friends and her family noticed how much Caroline was affected by Alison's illness. 'I remember asking Caroline if she had seen Alison and she said, "I just can't cope with it, Dad,"' said Peter Beale. ' "She can't even see properly, she doesn't even know who we are." I noticed that Caroline would shake as she spoke about her.'

Araminta Thorne saw the change in Caroline. 'She was in a terrible state about Alison and was very affected. She was very withdrawn and upset at this time. If you asked her why she was so distraught she would explain it in terms of Alison. We were very worried about her because she was in such a fragile state.'

Other friends noted that Caroline seemed under pressure to give support and comfort to Paul and Dominic but to be receiving little herself. 'She said "I can't take much more, everyone's putting all their burdens on me,"' says her friend Lesley Warren. 'Everyone who knew Alison was coming round to the house expecting Caroline to take it all on. She just couldn't take it, she would phone me at dinner-time and she would be in tears and saying, "I just can't take it."'

Caroline spoke daily on the phone to Caroline Two, who was also aware of her distress at Alison's illness: 'She would just cry sometimes. She was brilliant really and put on a brave front.' Brother Steve says, 'Everyone would be round at the house crying and saying, "What are we going to do, Caroline?" and putting the pressure on her. Once Caroline saw a counsellor but seemed to gain little from the experience.

Alison was cremated at a humanist ceremony. It was a highly emotional event for all the young people there. Caroline agreed to act afterwards as one of the drivers ferrying people from the crematorium to a hotel where a group of them went for a drink.

After Alison's death, Caroline had 'visions' of her in her bedroom in the house. She saw her in her dreams. She also had nightmares in which all her teeth flaked off in layers. She found herself sleeping for up to eleven hours a night.

'The death took a lot out of us all,' she says. Paul had cried for the first time since she had known him. He also became closer, as Caroline saw it, to Dominic and Caroline felt excluded. She believed that no one had much time for her.

For his part, Paul had already started to notice that Caroline would retreat to her bed early, pull a blanket over her and go to sleep. He would stay up late, watching television, and left early in the morning for work. They had stopped having sex and he barely saw her without her clothes on. Paul had told friends that he and Caroline were having a lot of difficulties in their relationship and they were going on holiday to try to get over Alison's death and to sort themselves out.

At her workplace, colleagues were concerned. David Lambert, a short, stocky, genial man, was Caroline's boss at the Social Services Inspectorate at the time. Sitting in his office in Hannibal House opposite the Tabernacle at the Elephant and Castle, he speaks with warmth of Caroline – 'a delightful and a very popular young woman' – who was the same age as his daughters. He says that all of her colleagues were conscious that she was under great stress. She was told that she could take as much time off as she needed in compassionate leave while Alison was ill.

Another colleague, Arnold Sobdogjor, a Ghanaian who

had known Caroline as a colleague since 1992, was also concerned. He valued Caroline's organizational abilities in the team, describing as his 'only strength' the ability to make people happy doing work they did not want to do. He was worried that Caroline was clearly in such distress but again felt that her sadness over Alison was the sole cause. All her colleagues felt that perhaps the holiday would ease what seemed to have become an intolerable burden. Caroline herself did not want to go away but felt unable to say so.

In July, Caroline had visited Lesley Warren in Beckenham to do some shopping at Ikea in Croydon. Lesley was surprised by her behaviour: 'I thought it was strange because Caroline doesn't normally eat and she ate this big meal in McDonalds and came back with an Indian takeaway and I thought, Caroline, you don't normally eat this much . . .'

Araminta Thorne recalled seeing Caroline for lunch at Babushka's, a vodka bar near Caroline's work: 'It surprised me that she had an orange juice rather than her usual glass of wine. She said she was keen to talk but she didn't come out with anything. She was quite excited initially about going to America and there was a sense of relief that it had ended for Alison because she had been suffering so much. I remember one elderly messenger who loved her to bits and the evening before she was due to leave for America she gave him a hug goodbye and burst into tears on his shoulder.'

Over the August bank holiday weekend, Caroline and Paul went to Mandy Goff's house in Suffolk for a barbecue. It was a large, jolly do, with bicycle polo and baseball in the paddock – Mandy is an accomplished horsewoman and has played horseball to international level – with loudspeakers blasting music out of the windows of the house and plenty of food and drink. Mandy remembers Caroline arriving wearing a baggy T-shirt, leggings and a black quilted jacket: 'The first thing she did when she got out of the car was grab a beer, light a cigarette and wedge a chicken leg in her mouth as we were chatting away.' Later she and Paul went off to the Poacher for a drink and got lost on the way back, before spending the night in sleeping bags in the lounge. There were a lot of hangovers in the morning and a general reluctance on Paul's part to go up to Sheringham for the christening of Caroline's niece, Amy.

A video of the christening shows Caroline looking drawn and tired. Caroline Two thought that perhaps Caroline and Paul had had a row: 'You could tell that something wasn't right,' she says. As her sister-in-law climbed into the car to drive back to London, she gave her a hug.

What none of her colleagues, friends, parents, brother and sister-in-law or Paul knew was that, as she set off for her first visit to America for the holiday that was to help her and the Faraway brothers rebuild their lives, Caroline Beale was nearly nine months pregnant.

'I had realized I was pregnant in March but I didn't tell anyone about it and I didn't go to see the doctor. I know it sounds really weird but I didn't think about it. I just put it at the back of my mind. Obviously I didn't look pregnant but I didn't really make any great effort to hide it. No one really made any remarks about it although Paul said that he thought I was putting on weight. No one asked any leading questions. No one ever said anything.

'Around the time that Alison was dying, she was told that she would never be able to have children. I just didn't want to talk about it at all. And then just after Alison died, I was sure the baby was dead. There had been some movement right at the beginning and then there was nothing. I had to cope with all of that and with Alison. I had seen her in one of my dreams and she said she was lonely and wanted the baby for company.

'I couldn't tell anyone. It wasn't that Paul and I weren't speaking but we were going through a bit of a rocky patch. I didn't want to go to work, I didn't want to go out, I didn't want to do anything. I didn't really want to go to New York

28

and I said that, but I just went along with it. I didn't know what to do. And so I found myself sitting on the underground going to Heathrow and not being able to tell anybody what was happening.'

Chapter Five

A photograph of Zayed Ali's grandfather, pictured outside his business in Cairo in the 1930s, hangs in the breakfast room of the Off SoHo Suites Hotel in Rivington Street near the Bowery on the Lower East Side of New York. Beside the grandfather, staring inscrutably at the camera, is an elderly retainer. 'Someone said they could have sworn they saw him in the Bronx,' says Zayed Ali laconically. This would mean that the elderly retainer was not only by now about a hundred and ten but had also found his way to the United States. 'I suppose,' adds Ali, with a New York shrug, 'anything's possible in this city.'

The Off SoHo Suites Hotel was originally intended by Mr Ali's father as a condominium building but had been hit by the recession of 1990 and became, when it finally opened in October of that year, a downtown hotel aimed at European travellers who would be less concerned with the neighbourhood's somewhat flaky reputation than Americans would be: 'The first European hotel that brings the charm of Little Italy, SoHo and the East Village to your own backyard,' its literature proclaims somewhat optimistically. Its clients come mainly from Germany, the United Kingdom, France and Switzerland, budget travellers attracted by the fact that they can stay in a suite with their own bathroom and kitchen for less than a hundred dollars a night.

Immaculately clean – Mr Ali periodically books into one of the forty suites unannounced to keep the staff on their toes

– it distinguishes itself from the rather mildewed old hotels around the Village with which it competes for foreign trade. Young bands on the make and not yet able to afford a suite in the more fashionable Paramount or Royalton stay here and their photos adorn the walls of Mr Zayed's back office beside the giant Japanese fan and the picture of the breaking waves. 'Who's that band? The Four of Us from Ireland. Don't know what happened to them.' Unlike many competing hotels, who know that every square foot should be turned into lettable accommodation, the hotel has a small café. Behind its counter are a series of warnings and a poster helpfully instructing staff in Heimlich's manoeuvre by which a choking diner can be saved by having his chest squeezed from behind. The most prominent sign, however, warns expectant mothers about the dangers of taking alcohol when pregnant.

Caroline did not notice such warnings when she and her three weary companions checked in at the desk, whose clocks tell the time in Cairo, Paris, Moscow, London and New York, on 14 September. She was already certain that the baby she was carrying was dead.

Dom Faraway – who had been in New York on business about six months earlier and liked the city – had booked the hotel and, with three healthy young men in the party, they were not put off by the area's reputation. (The *Rough Guide to New York* warns: 'This part of town can be a little tense – you may want to make use of the hotel's discount cab service at night.')

They were shown to suite 101 on the ground floor. It was spacious with a double bed in one room, a fold-out double sofa-bed in the kitchen-cum-sitting room, a fridge, television, and a grey-tiled bathroom with bath and shower. Caroline and Paul had the bedroom, Dom and Sam the sitting room. It was a humid, sticky, New York night and the four went out for pasta in Little Italy. Sam Faraway noticed that Caroline seemed detached: 'She seemed to be exhausted and not very hungry and less interested in being in a new place.' She retired early.

Inside, the hotel was a clean, elegant haven but outside its front door, it would be the Off rather than the SoHo that would strike the visitor: the hotel sticks out like a gold tooth in a rotting gum. It is not a pretty area and Caroline found it disappointing and forbidding. Catering stores, selling giant toasters and woks big enough to stir-fry a moose, jostled beside the bargain retail warehouses, a massive cut-out Marlboro Cowboy bucking the country's anti-smoking conventions against the Manhattan sunset, and a few joints with Runyonesque names like Jimmy Jazz and Little Charlie's Clam Bar. Round the corner was the Bowery, best known still to most Europeans for its 'Bowery bums', who still feed pigeons and slump peacefully on benches in Sara Delano Roosevelt Park. The usual salad of New York flotsam was around: elderly women with thick stockings and plastic bags filled with oddments, people of a size not seen anywhere else in the world, who look as though they have been poured into their clothes and forgotten to say, 'Stop.'

'People thought we were insane when we first opened,' says Zayed Ali, of his hotel. It was then a high crime and drug area but is gradually being turned round: young City workers see its potential for coverting disused warehouses into apartments. 'My father taught us at a very young age to make friends with people around us,' he says, sitting behind his desk in the president's office at the back of the hotel. 'He would say, "Always make friends," and we've tried to carry over this concept. We try to treat our guests the same way although I didn't go into the hotel business, I "stumbled" into it.' He remembered the Beale–Faraway party well. His wife – 'Doctor Mona', as he refers to her – had said that they looked like a nice party. She was always happier with European than with American guests.

On the morning after their arrival the quartet headed off

32

on the first of their sight-seeing expeditions, visiting, as Caroline recalled vaguely, 'all those tall buildings'. There were trips to the Empire State Building, the Twin Towers and to Chinatown, against the constant background 'whuh-whuh' of the NYPD's sirens.

Caroline found the city daunting, but much as she had anticipated from films and television programmes, and already she was low: none of the excitements of the Village or Manhattan could change her mood. The holiday that had been aimed at cheering them all up merely deepened her depression and reminded her of Alison's death. While the brothers went out to the bars in the evening, she went to bed, not even bothering to channel-hop through the thirty-odd stations on the suite's television.

The three men all found Caroline detached and moody. Paul later described her as 'a bit of a pain all week'. He told her he was tired of her depression and that it was time she started to try to put Alison's death behind her. He felt that she wanted to tell him something but could not get the words out. They rode the subways where almost every train carried the advertisement: 'Accidents happen. Call 1800 GOOD LAWYER.'

Sam and Dom sympathized with their brother. Sam said, 'There were many attempts to get Caroline to be more enthusiastic and join in with everyone but all were unsuccessful. We suggested different explanations for her lack of interest in life in general. Maybe it was because of Alison's death, maybe she was ill. We could not get Caroline to say what was wrong with her.' He wished she could have become what he described as her 'normal happy self', but she remained low throughout the week.

Dom said, 'From the first night in New York, I noticed how quiet and unhappy she seemed. However, despite every attempt to find out what the matter was, she said she was fine. She stayed in every night and just wanted to sleep or watch

TV. She ate very little and found it very tiring during the day. I talked to Sam about the problem but we just thought she was dull and had no interest in life. We both felt sorry for Paul because his relationship with Caroline didn't seem very happy. Because Caroline kept saying she was fine when asked, we dropped the subject.'

Caroline found it hard to concentrate: 'It was as if I was in a dream, a daze the whole time. I could have been anywhere, it was as though I was in another country but not.'

She sent a postcard of Central Park and Fifth Avenue to her parents:

Dear Mum and Dad, Hi, got here OK. The weather is v hot and humid but at least there is air conditioning in the apartments. Have been up the Empire State (107 floors up) and round the Statue of Liberty all in one day. See you soon. Paul and Caroline.

There seemed no hint of anything untoward.

Chapter Six

At the end of the two hour boat-trip round the islands that lie off New York's coastline, which the four took on the last day of the holiday, around five p.m. on 22 September, Caroline began to feel unwell, with stomach cramps and nausea. She knew that the pain was related to the baby. She returned to the hotel where she lay down and felt slightly better. As it was the last night, the men wanted to go out for a drink. Caroline declined but encouraged them to go, saying that she would be all right on her own. They headed off to St Mark's Tavern, a jazz bar on First Avenue.

Caroline was about to give birth.

'On that final day, I can remember just bits of it. I can remember being on a boat, being in a restaurant but the bits in between, they're just not there. I can remember being in a cab but not who was with me. It's frightening that you can block things out so totally that they almost don't exist. I know I must have been doing other things because the times just don't add up.'

Alone in her hotel room, the pain became intense. By around eleven it was intolerable. 'I thought I was going to die. Someone asked me later why I didn't get someone, why didn't I dial 911, the emergency number. I didn't know the number, of course, but the thought of going to get someone didn't even enter my head. Logically, you would have done something but I can't explain it, I didn't even think about it.

'I remember either saying or thinking, "Please, God, help

me." I had one bath and felt a little bit better and went and lay down again. Then I had this really, really bad pain and that's when I thought I was going to die.' Her waters had broken. She got back into the bath up to her waist. 'The whole room was grey. It was like one of those old black-and-white photos. I know it sounds bizarre but it was like you were outside yourself, detached from yourself. It's like looking at something else, almost like watching something on TV. I don't think anyone can understand.

'I think I might have passed out. The baby's head was coming out. I knew she wasn't alive. Then I was awake again. I was so scared because I thought I was going to die as well. I just didn't know what to do. There were scissors on the sink so I just cut the cord with scissors and left her in the bath while I went to the loo. The afterbirth came out. The water was still in the bath and the baby was floating. I was like on automatic pilot. I took her out of the bath and I didn't know what to do. I put her in a bag because I didn't know what else to do. I knew I had to get her back to England, somehow.

'I lay down, I was exhausted. I remember my hair was wet and I was wet. There was blood on me. I didn't care. I tried to go to sleep. Then Paul and the others must have come home. It's just so completely irrational.

'The next day we were going to come home and we were going to stores and they were buying jeans and presents. Walking around was as if I was in a tunnel, as though I had blinkers on, I couldn't see anything that was happening on either side of me. I remember being somewhere where there were red and white tablecloths, somewhere down in Manhattan.'

They stayed out until around five p.m.

When he had left the room at around ten thirty that morning Paul had noticed that Caroline had done her hair strangely. Her make-up, with which she usually took care, was messy. But when they stopped in a SoHo bar on their final trip to buy souvenirs and have some pancakes for lunch, Caroline had two beers and, thought Dom, seemed quite chatty: 'I put it down to relief that we were on our way home because she had seemed unhappy from the moment we landed at JFK.'

The following day Zayed Ali checked the four out because the manager was away. He noticed nothing untoward but his wife remarked on the group and said that the girl had seemed cheerful. Mr Ali noted that Caroline had gone into the room behind reception to leave her bags. Later, when she collected them, she had closed the door behind her and had spent an unusually long time in there. It seemed a little odd to him but he assumed she was changing for the flight as many travellers did. He headed back into his office without giving it another thought.

After the guests' departure, the Off SoHo Suites housekeeper, Janina 'Olga' Piwowrska, a forty-four-year-old Polish émigré, went into suite 101 to clean it. The room seemed in a reasonable state to a woman used to clearing up after the excesses of rock bands, but she noticed a pile of ten towels in the bathroom. One had been spread out to wrap up the other nine, all of which were wet as if they had been washed out. Three were heavily bloodstained and she reckoned that a guest must have had a heavy period. She decided that the towels were so bloody they were not worth trying to wash and threw them into the garbage.

The hotel had called a cab for the four for five thirty p.m. It arrived at JFK airport at about six forty-five. The three men were anxious to fit in one last end-of-holiday drink in the bar before departure and were carrying their souvenirs and hand luggage. Caroline was carrying the body of her child.

Chapter Seven

Robert O'Donnell could have been smuggled out of an episode of *NYPD Blue*, the hard-boiled television series about New York's Finest: the loose tie and the unbuttoned blue shirt, the belly that has, perhaps, seen too many of the New York's detective's favoured fast food, the humble doughnut. A gun is stuck in his belt and his thick grey hair is swept back. He wears a prominent ring on the right little finger. The Brooklyn-born-and-raised cop with thirty-three years on the force is clearly at home in the sardonic hey-buddy atmosphere of 113th Precinct on Blainey Boulevard in Jamaica, Queens, which was opened in 1971 by John V. Lindsay, the charismatic mayor of New York whom many believed would one day be President of the United States.

Upstairs on the first floor, in the rackety detectives' room, hangs a banner stretching the length of one wall: 'Remember, it's just another day in paradise.' A slightly crumpled Stars and Stripes covers another. It is a high-crime area with drug-related killings and larcenies aplenty. There are wanted posters and reward offers, cluttered desks with opened bags of candy, ringing phones. 'Who does he want? O'Donnell, O'Connor or O'Sullivan?' asks one young detective of a colleague.

Sitting reflectively in a bleak, fly-blown interview room that almost smells of the despair of its previous occupants, O'Donnell recalls the case of Beale, C. He remembers it well. Although his precinct handled around twenty murder cases in the first nine months of 1996 and an average of forty-five a year, the Beale case is one he won't forget and he has not had to look up the file to jog his memory.

On the night of Caroline's arrest he had been contacted as the duty detective by the Port Authority Police. He spoke to Alex Velez and to security guard Clara Tejada. 'We were brought to an alcove where Caroline Beale was and also this sack. We opened up this tote bag and found the baby, wrapped in a couple of plastic bags.'

Caroline recalled O'Donnell equally vividly: thick grey salt-and-pepper hair, gold-rimmed glasses, blue-striped shirt and blue tie, tweed jacket, charcoal grey trousers, a badge and that big ring on his little finger. The ring was to haunt her.

'He said to me, "What do you think we should do with you – chuck you in jail and throw away the key?" I was in tears and he said, "Don't cry, you're breaking my heart." He was so sarcastic. He took my fingerprints. He took my clothes and shoes.' She was handed a paper suit that prisoners are given to wear when their own clothes have been taken for forensic examination. The top didn't fasten properly and she was embarrassed because she had on nothing underneath. She was photographed in the traditional American suspect pose, holding a number and standing by a board that indicated her height.

'They kept asking, "Do you know where you are?" There was a big sign across the top of the room which said, "Queens General" so I kept reading it out to them.'

She was handcuffed to the bed. One doctor gave her an internal examination, then another examined her and filled in forms about her condition. By now it was around three a.m. and two detectives were with her constantly. She was moved into another bed behind a screen.

Willie Daniels, the duty social work services screening officer, recorded: 'Patient appeared anxious, pulling covers over her face. Patient informed worker that she did not feel like talking to anyone else but did express concern as to "How am I going to tell Paul?"'

Caroline was in a state of confusion. 'One of the officers was really awful and kept putting handcuffs on my wrists. Some of the cops were really nice and came back with cake from the takeaway place. They were asking what it was like in England and what sort of cars people drove there. O'Donnell told me I was going to be charged with murder but I couldn't really comprehend what was going on.'

While Caroline was being taken to hospital and assessed as to whether she was fit to be questioned, O'Donnell set about interviewing the Faraway brothers who were all stunned by what they had been told. They explained that they had been in New York on holiday to lift their spirits after Alison's death. They were asked about Caroline and told O'Donnell that she had tended to go back to their hotel towards the end of the day and seemed listless and depressed.

O'Donnell surmised fairly swiftly that the men knew nothing of what had taken place: 'This did not appear to be any kind of a conspiracy especially as these boys were freely talking about carrying this tote bag about. They mentioned an incident when the strap of the bag actually broke and fell to the ground as they were hustling across a busy intersection. One of the boys sort of scooped the contents of the bag and put it back in the bag and offered to carry it but Caroline said no, she would carry it, and she wound up carrying the bag for the rest of the day.'

Sam, the youngest Faraway, said O'Donnell, was so amazed by the events that he could barely speak: 'His mouth would open but nothing was coming out.' The detective remembered being struck by the size of Faraway's feet, which he found enormous.

The three Faraways made their statements in which they sketched out why they had come to New York and how Caroline had behaved during their time there. They all said that she had not seemed herself but none had had any idea that she had been pregnant.

Meanwhile, at Queens General Caroline was seen by a psychiatrist who deemed her fit to be interviewed, and by the British consular official, Jackie Cerdan, who had been informed, as foreign embassies and consulates are meant to be when one of their citizens is arrested.

O'Donnell saw her again to take a statement from her: 'She said the child had been born in a tub of water and she thought that the child had been born dead because the child didn't make any noise. She had cut the umbiblical [sic] cord and emptied the tub, refilled the tub and got back into the tub, presumably to cleanse herself. Then she took the baby out into another room and put the baby in the plastic bag and then in this tote bag and put the bag at the bottom of the bed and some time later the boys came back and they had a very casual conversation about how their night was and she eventually fell asleep.' He relates the events in a matter-of-fact way, the only odd part being his reference throughout to the 'umbiblical' cord, which gives the whole episode a kind of heightened moral frisson.

'The following morning they left the hotel at approximately ten and went about finishing, if you will, their various shopping chores for souvenirs for themselves and friends. At five in the afternoon they had hired a car and took the cab to the airport and Caroline excused herself and went to the ladies' room and, using the bag that the baby had been in, put it over her shoulders like a bra fashion, if you will, and tucked the bottom of the bag into her waist and proceeded to try and go through this checkpoint.'

The basic facts were passed on to the Assistant District Attorney, who returned to take an audio statement from her. Detectives were dispatched to verify what had taken place in the hotel.

'It was unusual for New York in that – to be honest with

you – Caroline could have placed the baby in any kind of garbage can and we would probably still be looking for the mother. People have miscarriages every day of the week and don't feel that it's a big deal. There are stories on file about mothers who abandon babies in their infancy for one reason or another. It's a sort of everyday occurrence in a big city.

'The thing that bugged me, if you will, is that Caroline Beale is not a young flighty individual,' says O'Donnell, offering some 'American candy'. 'She's an educated girl, she comes from a sophisticated city, she works in what would be the equivalent of a welfare office here and would have seen many instances similar to this. Additionally you have socialized medicine in England and she could have walked in at any time and ended this pregnancy in a legal fashion. Not only that but she went for a period of, she believes, six months but obviously it was nine months and in that time she never saw a doctor.'

Zayed Ali was at home when a call came through from the Port Authority Police saying that they wanted to talk to him about the 'homicide' that had taken place at his hotel. 'I kept telling them that they must have the wrong hotel.' He was told the room number and remembered that four nice young people had signed out. He went from his home to the hotel and met the officers who had been sent from his local precinct to take photos of the scene. By now he knew that Caroline was said to have killed her baby. 'My first response was that she didn't have a baby. If guests have a baby they usually request a crib. Then they notified me that she had given birth in the hotel. So – I'm a New Yorker, nothing is impossible. It was just kind of shocking. Every hotel has incidents but nothing as bizarre.'

The police sought out Olga Piwowrska and a police car was sent to pick her up. Her English was not good so an officer from a Polish family came along as an interpreter. At first the nervous maid thought that she was being questioned over the missing three towels – the ones she had thrown away because they were so bloody. She was reassured that this was not so and told the police her tale.

The press also arrived at the hotel in numbers, news agencies, New York One television crews, British stringers, the BBC. Mr Ali was puzzled that there was such media interest. 'I don't mean to sound cruel but in New York you hear of people killing babies but later I found out there were political aspects to the case.'

The District Attorney's office contacted him and asked him if he would agree to being sub-poenaed so that he could give evidence. They came downtown to visit him. He had already talked the issue over with his wife, who had been amazed as a doctor to discover that Caroline had so recently given birth yet showed such few signs of it, so little change in her colour or manner.

Back with Caroline, O'Donnell was exploring his hunches. He was told by Dom Faraway that Caroline had been seeing another man, a friend from work. That gave O'Donnell an idea: perhaps Paul Faraway was not the father. This would have given Caroline a motive not to have told him about the pregnancy and to have wanted to dispose of the child. He also suggested that Paul had not wanted to marry Caroline and that might have acted as another motive.

There was confusion now. O'Donnell claims that he tried to get Caroline to see Paul but that she 'shut him out'. Caroline remembers nothing of this. The baby was being taken for forensic examination to determine the cause of death. For Caroline the nightmare was continuing apace. No one would tell her what was happening. She felt completely alone.

Chapter Eight

'They had gone out for a walk and I saw them coming back when the phone went,' says Caroline Two, as she sits with her two small children playing at her feet and the new dog curled up on the carpet of their home on the Norfolk coast. She can still picture vividly the call that came through on the day after Caroline's arrest. 'It was Paul's father, who I had never spoken to before. He said, "Is that Caroline Beale?" and I said "Yes." I can remember him saying to me, "Do you want to sit down? I've got some bad news." But I stood up and he said, "You're aware Caroline's in New York . . ."

'I automatically thought drugs, someone had put some drugs on her and she'd been caught coming through Customs. Then he said Caroline had had a baby down the toilet and going through Customs it had been found under her coat. It was all very muffled and confusing. I said: "Whose baby?" I had hugged her at the front door before she went away a few weeks before so I thought, It's not her baby. Then he went on to say, "Have you got a pen and piece of paper? Write this down."' She recorded the numbers of the New York British Consulate, the Foreign Office and the Faraways' number. 'He was very lawyerlike on the phone and I was gobsmacked. I put the phone down and stood for a minute and thought, How am I going to tell them? I went out to the garden where they were sitting and I said, "I don't know how I'm going to tell you this, I'm just going to blurt out what I know." I wasn't crying but I was shaking.'

A Stranger and Afraid

Peter and Daphne had gone to Norfolk for Peter's fifty-ninth birthday. He had taken early retirement from ICT and they had been reflecting on their lives and taking stock during a walk on the Norfolk coast. 'I was saying to Daphne, "We haven't done too bad, really." And then when we came into the garden Caroline came out and . . .' He pauses as he recalls the lightning bolt. 'She said, "You'd better both sit down. Caroline's been arrested for killing her baby." I said, "What baby?" No one knew she was pregnant. It was so unbelievable. To hear that she had been arrested for the murder – the homicide of her baby . . .

'We went into a kind of trauma, the symptoms being that your voice is high-pitched, which stayed with us for months and months like you've been breathing helium gas, your throat's tight.' They were given a phone number for a Detective Peter Lambrizi in New York. The questions flew between the four of them. How can this be? Why is this? Recalling it, more than two years later, the Beales' voices both reach that higher pitch again.

'We phoned this guy who sounded like Kojak and called us sir all the time. He said yes, they had Caroline Beale, they were waiting for the autopsy report and she was in Queens General hospital.' They dialled frantically, constantly coming up against the computerized system that requires a caller to press another number from a menu of choices, all of which added to their confusion and frustration. When they did get through it was to bored, anonymous voices who were unable to help them. 'I don't know if it was my incompetence or their indifference.'

Peter and Daphne left for home at five a.m. To compound their feelings of helplessness, the car broke down in the darkness of the countryside and they were stranded far from anywhere before help could be summoned and a recovery vehicle could rescue them. Now began the long, long haul to try to save their daughter from spending the rest of her life behind bars.

A friend had given them the number of Gary Jacobs, a flamboyant self-made lawyer with a practice in Gants Hill and his own legal-advice radio programme. He had started his career as a solicitor's clerk after he had been wrongly accused of insulting behaviour when he was a hot-dog seller in Petticoat Lane and discovered that he relished a legal fight. Jacobs, who had left school with one O level, has since started a legal-advice column in the *Daily Mirror* called 'Justice with Jacobs'; the paper introduced him to its readers as 'the little solicitor with the big heart'.

'He sounded a wonderful guy on the phone,' says Peter. 'He knew lawyers everywhere and he seemed to have phones coming out of every pocket. He said, "I'll help you." I said, "I haven't got a lot of money," and he said, "Don't worry." He was great. He could have eaten us for breakfast.' Jacobs was as good as his word and, through contacts in the International Bar Association in North Carolina, found an attorney in New York called Robert Krakow.

Krakow rang the Beales and told them that he could take the case '*pro bono publico*' – effectively for nothing. He assured them that there was no case against Caroline. But just as they were starting to feel that Caroline might soon be freed, Krakow rang back to tell them that he had not been allowed to take on the case because he was not on the panel of state-approved attorneys who carry out defence work on a rota basis in Queens. Their spirits fell. They set about trying to find another lawyer, contacting the British Consulate in New York and the Foreign Office. Peter would not leave the house in case the phone rang and he missed a vital call. Steve and Caroline bought him an answerphone which Peter, despite having spent a lifetime in computers and tabulators, was unable to work. 'My mind just wouldn't operate properly.'

Gary Jacobs suggested approaching the media, so that any visit they needed to make to New York would be paid for. Wearing his Dennis the Menace braces, he picked them up in his Jaguar (GARY 1) and drove them to the studios of GMTV for the first of what were to become countless media appearances. The journalists were supportive from the start and the Beales decided at that early stage that they should work with the media rather than against them. Both GMTV and *London Tonight* indicated that, if the Beales would give them interviews, they would pay for their flights to visit Caroline.

By chance the Beales had a copy of the *BBC Family Directory*, a guide sent to interested viewers. They found an entry for the Association for Post-natal Illness, through which they were given the name of Postpartum International in San Diego, California, who contacted Dr Susan Hickman, an expert in the immediate after-effects of childbirth. Peter Beale was also told of Professor Channi Kumar, Professor of Perinatal Psychology, from the Maudsley Hospital. 'I said, "Please, please help us."'

They contacted Paul's parents and found that they were as puzzled as themselves, although they seemed to have greater faith in the American justice system. 'The Faraways had a belief that the United States was a civilized country, that it wasn't as if she was in Iran, and that the courts could be relied on to come out with the right decision,' said one friend.

Lesley Warren had been away on holiday but was back in Beckenham when her policeman boyfriend noted on Ceefax that someone had been arrested with a dead baby at JFK airport. Caroline's father phoned to tell her that the woman arrested had been Caroline. 'I didn't believe it. I was flabbergasted.'

Araminta Thorne was equally bemused and refused to believe it until a friend faxed a newspaper clipping. 'I had the kind of relationship with Caroline in which she could confide in me because I wasn't connected with any other part of her life and she would have a fag break and drag me onto the fire escape and she would talk about all the things which were going on in her life. It brings it home for me how serious it was for her that she didn't say anything about it because she would tell me all the things she didn't confide in her family and wouldn't talk about at work. I wasn't aware at that stage of how much she had cut herself off from her friends.

'For a month or so afterwards it felt as though Caroline had died. It was such a momentous thing, so different from what I had thought was going on and the consequences were so enormous for this person who didn't like having to face up to big challenges and responsibilities to try and realize what it would do to her life. The feeling was one of total devastation and I was grieving. I picked up very soon that everyone expected me to have known and thought I was covering up.'

Mandy Goff heard the news at seven thirty a.m. when the radio woke her up. Although Caroline Beale's name was mentioned she could not accept that it was her friend, as she was certain that Caroline had not been pregnant. She telephoned Caroline's parents, received no reply, then flicked through the television and radio news to try to find out what was happening. 'She never really confided in us and it leaves you feeling quite guilty. Clare racked herself with guilt because she hadn't come to the barbecue before Caroline left because she had a migraine. She felt she would have known but I had no idea and no one at the party did. It was a big shock – we'd been together for so long you assumed that if you had a major problem you could just pick up the phone and jump in the car.'

All the Sunday papers for 25 September carried the story in one form or another. The *People* quoted neighbours of Caroline's as saying they had no idea she was pregnant. The *Mail on Sunday* reported: 'Jet Woman Held Over Dead Baby'. Clare Webb had taken the Sunday papers to a riding show in which she and Mandy were taking part and had read about Caroline but she, too, found it impossible to believe: 'I still don't believe it ever happened.' Jenny Bloor, who was perhaps the most politically involved of Caroline's friends and who had had experience of campaigns through her work at the Royal College of Nursing and from her own interests in Amnesty International and the Campaign for Nuclear Disarmament, was horrified at what was happening: 'I couldn't understand how they could be prosecuting her. If it had been Heathrow airport rather than JFK she would have ended up in hospital not in prison. I found it bizarre to see it unfolding in that way.'

Caroline's female friends, said Jenny Bloor, were immediately supportive. 'I think we realized that it could have been any one of us who had had the breakdown. The blokes were a bit more grey about it all.'

Paul, Dom and Sam had all been released after their interviews with the police in New York and allowed to return to England the following day. Paul felt the same sense of bewilderment as everyone.

'It must have been horrendous for Paul,' said Jenny Bloor. 'I had been angry at him because we had expected he would be banging the drum and saying, "I'm going to stand by my woman," but as soon as I saw him it just dissolved. I felt sorry for him. He was broken and it showed. He was shaky and he looked very drawn.'

Colin Brosnan had asked Paul and Caroline to come with him to the Reading Festival and to Torquay but they had said they were off to New York. 'A girlfriend of one of my mates rang me up and said she had seen Caroline on the local news and she had had a baby in New York and had been arrested. I was stunned and amazed. I sat for an hour going through Teletext waiting for something to come up. I tried to phone Paul but he was round his mum and dad's house. His mum and dad said the first week he was back he was obviously in a state of shock.

'He told me that walking through the airport Caroline was a little way behind and suddenly there was a scuffle and commotion and Caroline was dragged off and it was the first he knew of anything,' says Colin, sitting beneath a Marilyn Monroe mirror in his home in Beckton in Docklands. 'We were all pretty shocked. Paul's a fairly intelligent rational sort of person. He might be a little disappointed and upset but I'm sure his overriding feeling once he got over the shock himself would have been, "How can I help Caroline out?" I know that as a fact. In the months that followed the only thing he wanted was for the situation to be sorted out so that Caroline could come back home. He had the press on his doorstep the whole time, ringing him up, and he was under a lot of pressure himself. The following months he was spending all his energy getting back to work and making sure his job was secure and making sure the bills were paid and to start with that was taking everything out of him.'

Araminta telephoned Paul: 'He was very shell-shocked when I rang him. He was finding it very hard to accept what happened. She had lost his child and he was in a sort of dialogue with himself about what he should feel about it.' She kept in touch with him and met up with him: 'He blurted out that she had been having an affair with someone. He was quite bitter about the whole thing and he was saying, "My child has died as a result of her not saying anything." He was very upset, quite antagonistic towards Caroline, but at the same time very concerned about what was happening to her.'

Detective O'Donnell's suggestion was rattling around in the minds of all the Faraway brothers. Caroline may have flirted with male workmates, as happens in any office, and had after-work drinks that Paul had not known about at the time but both she and her friends are adamant that there had been no affair, that there was no chance that the child was not Paul's. Paul, however, had to deal both with the pressures of the media and with the realization of what had happened. He later told the *Independent*: 'I don't think Caroline knows what happened. She didn't seem crazy to me. If I didn't realize how sick she was, what are a jury who don't know her going to say?' A survey carried out by the school of Human Studies at Teesside University, Middlesbrough, and published in the *Journal of Medical Psychology* in 1996, found that men whose partners miscarry suffer just as much grief as women but feel they have to hide their feelings, and that they show levels of grief similar to that found for other forms of bereavement. What is more universally recognized is that it is not unusual for women to have full-term babies without realizing that they are pregnant and without their close friends or relatives having any such idea. Usually it happens with young and overweight women but middle-aged women who had thought they could no longer conceive have also suddenly delivered a baby to the amazement of themselves and their families.

Caroline Two rang Paul. 'I was cross with him and I do speak my mind so I said, "You've not been in touch. Have you any idea what they're [Peter and Daphne] going through?" But he had been advised to keep a low profile, he said, and the press were everywhere and of course he still cared for her. I got a very positive feedback and I thought, He's going to see it through.'

At Caroline's workplace, too, there was disbelief. David Lambert had read a small paragraph in the *Observer* on the Sunday morning but found it hard to accept that the Caroline Beale arrested for the murder of her baby was the same person who he believed had been looking forward to her first trip to America. 'We all thought long and hard about how she had been in those months before and, with the benefit of hindsight, we could see things. I asked people to set notes down on the four to six months up to the event and she had been very unhappy and on the point of tears. But all that had been put down to Alison who was very ill.

'What stunned people was that they had seen her day in day out – and many of these are mothers – and no one had any idea that she was pregnant. There was the guilt and uncertainty. Why didn't she tell us, why were we not insightful enough to see? It took a long time to sink in.' There was a series of meetings with staff, some of whom were offered counselling by the welfare services. 'People were emotionally confused about what had happened and our part in it.'

Her workmates were almost universally supportive. 'There was never any question of any person acting judgementally or in a distanced way,' said Lambert, who kept Caroline's job open for her. 'I refused to fill the post because I thought it might send out the wrong signals.' The backing appears to have gone all the way up the department even to the extent that the then minister in charge of the department, Virginia Bottomley, indicated her own support and made it clear that Caroline was not going to be cut adrift by her employers.

Kevin Mansell, with whom Caroline had worked in the Social Services Inspectorate, said: 'It was completely baffling. No one could understand it.' Arnold Sobdogjor, to whom Caroline had been 'like a little sister', was also wondering whether her colleagues could have done anything to help her. With hindsight there had been signs: 'She would wear her coat in the summer and she would come in and sit down before taking it off and putting it on a desk behind her and I would say, "You lazy girl, hang it up." But nobody noticed. Also we had all known about Alison so we thought that was what was making her lose contact with real life.' He still remembered the news item in that day's *Observer*: 'It was only an inch high. The reaction was one of total shock.'

Chapter Nine

Caroline became aware that two young women were at her bed in the hospital. They introduced themselves as having come from the District Attorney's office. She remembered thinking that one – Lori Ann Fee – had a pretty name and that the other, dark-haired, neatly dressed, in her mid-thirties, had a remarkably persistent manner.

There are, as Goldie Hawn remarks in the film *The First Wives' Club*, as she asks her cosmetic surgeon to pump her lips full of collagen, only three ages for women in Hollywood: 'Babe, District Attorney and *Driving Miss Daisy.*' On one level, Marjory Fisher might have appeared the classic model for that middle role: cool, tough and elegant. And, as far as she was concerned, investigating another murder.

Born in Ohio, Marjory Fisher had studied law at George Washington University National Law Centre before embarking on a career as a prosecutor; she has never been a defence attorney. Married to a lawyer in private practice and with two small sons, from her arrival at the Brooklyn District Attorney's office in 1983, she appeared to colleagues and police officers alike to be going places. Some police officers describe her as 'one of the best', a compliment from a body who are not always over-impressed by the efforts of the prosecution to press for a conviction. She worked her way up through the Grand Jury, Criminal Court and Sex Crimes bureaux and was promoted to the post of Homicide Bureau supervisor and Supreme Court Bureau deputy chief before she joined the

Queens DA's office in 1992 as Bureau Chief of the Special Victims Bureau. The SVB handles all cases where the victims are seen as particularly vulnerable because of their gender or age, dealing with around a thousand cases a year although only around forty come to trial; around 25 per cent of those accused confess in the course of their videotaped interview.

There are 310 lawyers at the DA's office in Queens, their annual pay ranging from $34,000 to $100,000, much less than a successful attorney in private practice but their salary is assured and they do not have to hunt for work. There is no shortage of willing recruits: about thirty of 'the brightest and the best' are hired from around 1400 who apply each year.

But behind the bare statistics lies another story. Tom Wolfe in *The Bonfire of the Vanities*, his rich tale of New York City life, wrote:

> The Homicide Bureau was the elite corps of the District Attorney's office, the DA's Marines, because homicide was the most serious of all crimes. An Assistant DA in Homicide had to be able to go out on the street to the crime scene at all hours, night and day, and be a real commando and rub shoulders with the police and know how to confront defendants and witnesses and intimidate them when the time came, and they were likely to be the lowest, grimmest, scurviest defendants and witnesses in the history of criminal justice.

Marjory Fisher was enthusiastic about her work: 'If you don't have the "heat", if you don't believe the victim, or don't care, the jury will know it ... I love this work. There are unexpected benefits. For instance, I tried the case of a young rape victim and she said, "You know what was the most important thing? You're the only one who ever said I was smart."'

She had also been outspoken on the role of the rape victim.

In the quarterly journal of the DA's office, she was quoted in a round-table discussion on her bureau's work: 'Lots of people are still operating under the same misconceptions as they had years ago. For instance, the belief that women have to be injured to prove rape. Women are consistently held to a higher standard than other complainants.'

She regularly prosecuted rapists and sex abusers, became a member of New York State's children's justice task force and of the mayor's committee on child abuse, author of the prosecutor's manual on sex crimes, a regular speaker at both professional and lay forums on abuse. So when Marjory Fisher entered the Queens General Hospital room where a wide-eyed young Englishwoman lay handcuffed to the bed, she was already on her way up in the hard school of New York prosecution. She was also, as one journalist who knew her observed, normally regarded as 'on the side of the girls'.

She was no stranger to high-profile cases. In 1987, she had successfully prosecuted an emotive murder case of an eighty-seven-year-old man who had been killed by two men who had also attacked his wife. In 1989, she was the DA in the first case in which a woman had pleaded guilty to manslaughter for failure to protect her children. During her eight years in Brooklyn, she dealt with over fifty rape and murder cases, and in 1994 with the case of a woman student raped by a neighbour.

Caroline had no idea who she was or of the influence she wielded: 'I thought I was just going to tell this woman what had happened and that would be it. The cop who was on guard said I would be home by Thursday, home in a few days.'

Caroline only dimly remembers the first interview conducted by Marjory Fisher and Lori Ann Fee although she recalls her confusion as to who all the people were who kept arriving and asking her questions. The tone of how the interrogation was conducted, and how Caroline gave her first account of what had happened in the hotel, is perhaps best conveyed by the transcript of part of that interview, on which it is noted that 'The subject did not wish to take a videotape because she felt it would be televised.'

FEE: Ms Beale, I understand that you wish to make a statement concerning the incident that occurred, on September 22, 1994, at the SoHo Hotel in Manhattan. Is that correct? Before you make a statement, I am going to advise you of certain rights that you have, OK? You have the right to remain silent and to refuse to answer any questions. Do you understand?

BEALE: Yes.

FISHER: You must speak up. Speak up just a little so that the machine can pick it up.

FEE: Anything you say may be used against you in a court of law. Do you understand?

BEALE: Yes.

FEE: If you cannot afford an attorney, one will be provided for you without any costs. Do you understand?

BEALE: Yes.

FEE: If you do not have an attorney available, you have the right to remain silent until you have an opportunity to consult with one. Do you understand?

BEALE: Yes.

FEE: Do you remember the date?

BEALE: 22nd of September.

FEE: That was yesterday. Which date did you come here?

BEALE: 14th September.

FEE: And were you travelling by yourself?

BEALE: No. I was here with my boyfriend and his two brothers.

FEE: What are their names?

BEALE: Paul Faraway, and Sam and Dom Faraway.

FISHER: Can you speak up just a little?

[They take her through her penultimate day in New York and her return to the hotel.]

FEE: Did you say anything to Paul or Sam or Dom about your stomach pains?

BEALE: Yes, I said to them we have to get back to the hotel because I did not feel well. And Paul said we can have a lay down. And then we can go out later. So we went back to the hotel and I had a lay down and then we went out for dinner and I did not feel very well going out for dinner so Paul said we'll get a taxi back to the hotel and you can stay there and we'll go out for the evening and if you lay down then you'll probably feel better again. So I say yeah. But then at about eleven or twelve o'clock or so I just felt really really ill. So I was . . . can I have a bath to try and make your stomach feel better? So I . . .

FEE: What time was it when you got into the tub the first time? When you got into the tub the second time? About . . .

BEALE: About quarter past one.

FISHER: When the water came down your leg, was it like a lot or a little?

BEALE: A little.

FISHER: And did it smell funny to you?

BEALE: No.

FISHER: What did you think happened?

BEALE: I don't know.

FISHER: You didn't know?

BEALE: Well, I sort of knew . . . what was going to happen . . .

FISHER: At that point, what did you think?

BEALE: I was scared.

FISHER: But what did you think was going to happen? When you felt that water coming down your leg, what did you think was going to happen next?

57

Duncan Campbell

BEALE: I thought that the baby would come then.

FISHER: 'Cause the water was breaking.

BEALE: In the bath . . . It just came out in a straight way in the bath, and it was just there and it was just . . . was not moving or anything. And I did not know what to do.

FEE: What did you do?

BEALE: I just got the scissors and cut the thing and then I took it out of the bath and it was not moving so I put it in the bag and I went to the loo and . . .

FEE: What happened when you went to the loo?

BEALE: That stuff came out.

FEE: What kind of stuff was it?

BEALE: Just like . . . like . . .

FISHER: What color was it?

BEALE: Red.

FISHER: Big, like a steak? It came out?

BEALE: Yes.

FISHER: Did that hurt?

BEALE: [unintelligible]

FISHER: When the baby came out, how did that feel to you?

BEALE: Well, it hurt a bit, but I thought it would hurt because it would make you, really . . . It was worse before than when it actually happened.

FISHER: When the baby was coming out, were you pushing it out?

BEALE: It just seemed to do it automatically.

FISHER: Right, but did you feel like your body pushing that baby out? Like an urge, and you pushed, and the baby just popped out?

FEE: Could you answer the question?

BEALE: Yes.

FISHER: Yes, so you felt that push. Why don't you tell us when the baby came out? Where was the baby? In your hands?

BEALE: No, in the bath.

FEE: How much water was in the bath?

BEALE: About the same as before.

FEE: So you filled the bath about eight inches. Where were
          you? Were you sitting in the bath? Was your bottom
          on the bottom of the tub?

FISHER: She is not answering!

BEALE: Yes.

FEE: And were you sitting in the tub?

BEALE: Yes.

FEE: And your bottom was resting on the bottom of the
          tub?

BEALE: Yes.

FISHER: How were your legs?

BEALE: In front like now.

FISHER: Straight out, spread out?

FEE: Ms Beale, when the baby came out you said it was
          face up, right? You have to answer me.

BEALE: Yes.

FEE: Was it underneath the water?

BEALE: Some of it was. But it was in the water. But . . .

FEE: What part of it was in the water? What part of the
          baby was in the water?

BEALE: All of it.

FEE: What part of it was not in the water?

BEALE: None of it. It was all in the water, because the water
          was there and it was just in the water.

FEE: So the baby was submerged in the water. Then what
          happened after that?

BEALE: It wasn't moving, that's all, it just wasn't moving. I did
          not do anything. It just wasn't moving.

FISHER: And what happened after you cut the cord?

BEALE: It wasn't moving so I just . . . I did not know what to
          do. So I took it out of the bath and it still wouldn't
          move so I put it in the bag that . . . from the hall and I
          put it in the bag and then I went to the loo and the

59

stuff came out and then I went into the bedroom and I just put it by the side of the bed.

FISHER: Let me ask you this: from the time that baby came out until the time you cut the cord, do you know how much time passed?

BEALE: About six or seven minutes. Ten, something like that.

FISHER: Seven to ten minutes.

BEALE: Something like that. I don't know.

[They then took her back to the time she first realized she was pregnant.]

FEE: Did you stop having your period? When?

BEALE: January.

FEE: Did you think anything was wrong at that point when you stopped having your period?

FISHER: Yes or no. You have to answer.

BEALE: Yes.

FEE: What did you do?

BEALE: Nothing.

FEE: What did you think was wrong?

BEALE: I knew.

FEE: What did you know?

BEALE: I knew that I was pregnant.

FEE: Did you go to the doctor?

FISHER: Yes or no.

BEALE: No.

FEE: Did you tell anyone? Why not?

BEALE: No, I don't know.

FISHER: Why do you think . . . What about it bothered you that you didn't want anyone to know?

BEALE: I was just scared, I guess.

FISHER: Scared of having a baby? Are you an only child? Do you have other kids in your family?

BEALE: I have a brother.

FEE: After – I am going to jump ahead a little bit, OK?

After the baby was born, after the baby came out. Did
you call anyone? Why not?

BEALE: I don't know. Because I was scared and I panicked and
I did not know what to do because it was not moving
or anything.

FEE: Did you try to help the baby?

BEALE: No.

FEE: Did the baby make any noise when it came out. Yes or
no?

BEALE: No.

FEE: Did you look at the baby?

BEALE: Briefly.

FEE: Briefly. How long?

BEALE: Just, I looked and I saw that it was not moving so . . .

FEE: What kind of baby was it? Was it a boy or a girl?

BEALE: Girl, I think . . .

FEE: OK and after . . . What time, if you could remember,
did you put the baby in the bag?

BEALE: About two in the morning.

FEE: Then what did you do after you did that?

BEALE: I went to bed.

FEE: Did you fall asleep?

BEALE: No.

FEE: What did you do?

BEALE: Just laid there.

FEE: What did you feel like?

BEALE: Terrible.

FISHER: Physically how did you feel?

BEALE: Ill.

FEE: Ill in which way, stomach, head, what?

BEALE: Stomach, head and what had gone on.

FEE: What do you mean what had gone on?

BEALE: Well, about what had happened . . .

FEE: This is continuing the interview with Caroline Beale.
Caroline, you mentioned that you felt ill, right, about

61

it happening. What were you talking about when you said it happened?

BEALE: About the baby and it not moving.

FEE: Did you think to call anyone?

BEALE: No, I did not know who to call. I did not know what to do. When it did not move I just panicked.

FEE: It wasn't making any noise you said. Was it moving?

BEALE: No, I didn't see it move at all.

FEE: Were you looking at it the entire time?

BEALE: I didn't look at it the entire time, but all the time I looked at it, it wasn't moving.

FEE: You said you were panicked, right. Now, after you put the baby in the bag, you said you felt ill, it was about two in the morning?

FEE: So Paul came in about three. Did you say anything to him when he came in?

BEALE: Did you have a nice time?

FEE: So you were awake?

BEALE: Yes.

FISHER: Did he wake you up or were you already awake at the time?

BEALE: He woke me up, I think I was already awake but I think that he . . .

FEE: Can you speak up a little?

BEALE: I think that I was already slightly awake, but he took the phone . . .

FEE: Did he make some noise and that woke you up?

BEALE: Yes.

FEE: Did he say anything when he came in?

BEALE: I think he was a bit plugged. [Caroline thinks she probably said 'pissed'.]

FEE: OK, but do you remember him saying anything?

BEALE: No.

FEE: And what did you say to Paul?

BEALE: I said, Did you have a good time?

FEE: Did he answer you?

BEALE: Yes. He said, Yeah.

FEE: Then what happened?

[They moved back to the arrest at the airport, when Caroline was initially challenged by the security officers.]

FISHER: What exactly did you say?

BEALE: I said it was a baby, and she said . . . and I said can we go and she said yes and then they called the policeman again, and they put me in those things and put me in the ambulance with these things all tight and they brought me into this place, and they had me handcuffed to . . . and there were these awful people in there.

FISHER: How come you were taking the baby?

BEALE: I don't know.

FISHER: Why do you think that you hid the baby and took the baby shopping and everything?

BEALE: I don't know, I don't know.

FISHER: Do you have any idea at all? Were you going to tell Paul about it? Or show Paul the baby or something?

BEALE: No, I was going to tell Paul. I was . . .

FEE: When?

BEALE: I was going to tell him when we got back home about being pregnant, and I was going to tell him.

FISHER: Were you planning on . . . if you could have taken the baby with you to London?

BEALE: Yes.

FISHER: You were going to take it on the plane with you? What were you thinking about doing with the baby once you got to London?

BEALE: I don't know.

Shortly afterwards, the interview was concluded and the two women left.

Meanwhile in London, Paul's father, Michael Faraway, had contacted the consular department at the Foreign Office who, in turn, had alerted the British Consul in New York. At this stage the information was that Paul's wife, as Caroline was described, had been charged with child homicide. Peter Beale also phoned the Consul's office. Caroline had been 'looking like a beanpole' when she left, and, he told the Consul's office, he thought there must have been a mistake and his daughter must have suffered a miscarriage.

The Consulate's role in New York is to look after the estimated 250,000 Britons there and in the neighbouring states of Connecticut, New Jersey, Pennsylvania, and in Puerto Rico and the US Virgin Islands. Business is brisk. In 1995 they issued 631 emergency passports, catered for the sixty-eight citizens in local jails and dealt with 30,000 phone calls from the 3.5 million British visitors who come through JFK airport every year. They are used to being contacted by the American police but the offences are usually connected with drugs; often the British citizens arrested have lived in the United States for many years and have no real need of help from the Consulate. It soon became clear to the Consul, Michael Carter, a relaxed and experienced diplomat with experience in Accra, Athens, Moscow and Tunis, that this was no ordinary case. The Vice Consul, Jackie Cerdan, who had been sent to the hospital, had been struck by Caroline's distress when she first saw her surrounded by police officers in hospital. 'She was incoherent. There were no charges at that point because they were still awaiting the autopsy but she was in a very vulnerable state.'

About four hours later, Marjory Fisher returned with another member of the DA's office, Frank Carterisano. The time was now seven thirty p.m., the night after Caroline had been arrested and less than forty-eight hours after she had given birth. Marjory Fisher reminded Caroline that they had met earlier and told her of her rights and that anything she said could be used against her in a court of law. Carterisano had difficulty in hearing what she said and Marjory Fisher told him that Caroline spoke very quietly. Caroline agreed to answer any questions.

FISHER:	OK, Caroline, we spoke at length about the circumstances involving your baby. Remember this afternoon. And you were given your rights before that and you told me that when the baby came out, the baby came into the water, is that right?
BEALE:	Yes.
FISHER:	When you were in the tub?
BEALE:	Yes.
FISHER:	And, if I'm correct, you told me earlier in the day that the baby didn't move when the baby came out.
BEALE:	Yes.
FISHER:	OK. Did you hear anything from the baby?
BEALE:	No.
FISHER:	You know how an autopsy was done this afternoon on the baby. And the doctor looked at the baby, and made some determinations. And it is clear from what the doctor saw during the autopsy that there is no question that when the baby was born this baby was alive and breathing.
BEALE:	It was in the water, I had it in the bath.
FISHER:	The baby, based upon the findings . . .
BEALE:	I am telling the truth, honestly. And it wasn't moving in the bath at all.
FISHER:	Well, according to the findings in the autopsy, if the baby had gone directly into the water there would be no air in the baby's lungs.

BEALE: But it was.

FISHER: There was no water in that baby's lungs or in
              that baby's stomach, none, zero.

BEALE: But it was in the bath. Go take a test on the
              bath. I swear to you that is what happened.

FISHER: If the baby had been submerged right away as
              you said and had gone just right in the water,
              there would have been water in that baby's
              belly and there would have been water in the
              lungs.

BEALE: But it was in the bath. Honestly, that is what
              happened. Why would I have had a bath?
              Because my tummy was hurting and that's why
              I was in the bath.

CARTERISANO: Did you ever see a movie, for example, about
              babies being born? Did you ever see the
              pictures when the baby holds . . . where the
              doctor holds the baby up and slaps it on the
              butt? Did you do that? Did you do anything
              like that? Like to slap the baby awake, or
              anything like that?

BEALE: No.

FISHER: So when you first looked at the baby and you
              are looking at that baby face up, did you
              notice at that point that the baby was a girl?
              OK, yes or no. OK, you are looking at the
              baby and the baby is in the water.

BEALE: It was just still. It was just laying in there. I . . .

CARTERISANO: It's OK, take your time.

BEALE: I thought it was dead, so I put it in the bag and
              it didn't move, honestly. It really didn't move,
              and I didn't know what to do, so I just put in
              the thing, like I told you, and it didn't move or
              anything.

CARTERISANO: What kind of bag was this?

BEALE: It was a black bag with two black and white bags.

CARTERISANO: Plastic?

BEALE: Yes.

FISHER: Did you put it in the bags right away? Or later?

BEALE: No, I put it into one bag and then I put it into the other two bags when I was carrying it . . .

CARTERISANO: Just so you understand, we came back to ask you some questions. Ms Fisher came back to ask you some questions together with me, just based on what we have been told from the doctors. We just wanted to clear up with you the fact that what you told Ms Fisher earlier, and the other young lady that was with her, and what we are hearing from the doctors, do not exactly match up, do you understand what I mean by that? Do you?

BEALE: Yes. You mean what I say isn't true.

CARTERISANO: Well, that's up to you whether it is true or not.

BEALE: But it is true, that is what happened, I swear to you.

CARTERISANO: All I am trying to tell you is that, according to what the doctors tell us . . .

BEALE: It was in the water.

CARTERISANO: Do you understand what I am saying?

BEALE: Yes. You can go and take the test on the bath.

CARTERISANO: Just think about that for a while while I ask a couple of other questions, OK? The bags that you had, where did you get the bags from?

BEALE: From the jeans shop.

CARTERISANO: From the jeans shop. You had been shopping earlier in the day?

BEALE: Yes.

[They return once again to what happened on the night.]

CARTERISANO: So you went – you got up from the bathtub and you went to the toilet, and you left the baby in the water?

BEALE: Yes.

CARTERISANO: So now, before you went from the bathtub to the toilet, and the baby was in the water, did you slap the baby to see if the baby would move, or anything like that?

FISHER: Did you touch the baby at all?

BEALE: No.

BEALE: But it was in the water.

FISHER: If it was in the water there would be water in the baby.

BEALE: But it was in the water, it was floating in the water.

FISHER: Floating.

BEALE: It was in the water, and I picked it up and it wasn't moving or anything and I put it in the bag.

CARTERISANO: Our understanding is that if the baby had been in the water, there would have been water in the lungs.

BEALE: But there would have been water on it. Couldn't you test the bag to see that there's water on the inside of the bag or something?

CARTERISANO: We are talking about what they did with the baby, not the bag.

BEALE: But it's true, I swear to you, it's true.

FISHER: You've never talked about having children? I mean he [Paul] was out drinking that night.

	You've had a good time on vacation. Is he somebody who you think would have been happy about the idea about having a baby, or unhappy about having a baby?
BEALE:	I imagine he would have been happy, if he would have known. But I am telling you the truth, honestly, what happened, it was in the bath and it was – like I took it out of the bath and put it in the bag. That is all, honestly, I swear to God that is what happened.
BEALE:	You believe me, don't you?
CARTERISANO:	Well, it's really not a question as to whether or not we believe you, as I said that is not, we did not come here from the viewpoint as to whether we believed you or not. We felt that since what you said earlier today, do not match up with the medical findings.
BEALE:	But . . .
CARTERISANO:	Since you been here, we figured we would come back to let you know and see if there is anything else you remember based on that, anything else you want to tell us, based on that.
BEALE:	What's going to happen? Are you going to throw me in jail?
CARTERISANO:	That is the discussion we need to have with the detective when he comes back.
BEALE:	But you know, don't you, you know?
CARTERISANO:	We don't know.
BEALE:	Well, that's what the policeman said.
CARTERISANO:	Well, that's the police officer trying . . .
BEALE:	They say, the police, that they got . . . all the newspapers are downstairs. They are waiting

for you to come out, you two to come out and
that they are probably downstairs.

CARTERISANO: I don't know anything about that.

BEALE: But it's all over the TV and everything.

CARTERISANO: That is my understanding at this time.

At 8.01 p.m., the interview finished. Marjory Fisher and Frank
Carterisano departed. They were about to decide that Caroline
Beale would be charged with second-degree murder.

As the DAs had explained to her, Caroline had a right to
be represented. At this stage she was unaware that her father
was already desperately seeking legal advice in England and
she was assigned an attorney who, as part of the homicide
panel, was given the case on a rota basis.

Paul Vladimir is a tall, dignified man who walks, shoulders
back, with an almost military bearing. He is bald, wears
bifocals and slightly flashy ties, and has a dry metropolitan
wit. One of Queens' most experienced attorneys with forty-
three years in the business and with his own office high in
Silver Towers on Kew Gardens, he found himself that September day assigned by the court to the case of Caroline Beale.
Lawyers in this position have a right to turn down a case and,
since the fee is – by legal standards – very low at $40 an hour,
many do. Vladimir found it a strange case and decided to
handle it.

Caroline remembers her first meeting with him when he
gave her a mint and a hug. 'He was very friendly and said his
daughter-in-law came from England.' Vladimir recalls, as does
almost everyone of their first encounter with Caroline at this
time, her immense distress. 'Marjory Fisher was indicating that
this was the crime of the century but I frankly felt that we had
a defence.'

On 24 September, Caroline Ann Beale was charged with
murder in the second degree. On 29 September she appeared
in front of a grand jury, which decided she should stand trial

for the crime of murder in the second degree in that 'under circumstances evincing a depraved indifference to human life [she] recklessly engaged in conduct which created a grave risk of death of her newborn baby girl by giving birth in a place other than a medical facility, by failing to call for medical attention after the child was born and continuing in a course of conduct which caused the death of the child due to suffocation'.

Chapter Ten

'We called her "English" and "Blondie". We liked the way she talked – she would say "fag" for cigarette and talk about her "jumpers" for sweaters. But she cried a lot at first. She was very frightened when she first came to Riker's.'

Sherain Bryant is a strongly built young woman with a gap between her front teeth and her hair pulled back. She was born in Harlem, but her home is the Bronx – if she can call a place 'home' that she will not be allowed to see until 2020. She is doing a twenty-five-year sentence for the killing of her daughter. She well remembers her first encounter with Caroline Beale inside the jail on Riker's Island.

Riker's lies in the East River to the southern edge of the Bronx, to which it belongs, appropriately enough since so many of that borough's poorer residents end up there. Its original 87 acres of flat land were owned by the Ryker family, descendants of a settler who moved to Long Island in 1638. The City of New York bought it in 1884 as a prison farm and opened a prison there in 1932. Since then it has cast its baleful shadow over the city, the largest jail in America, regarded as one of the grimmest and most unforgiving of the nation's penal institutions, much in the way that Wandsworth and Strangeways in Britain were once rated by inmates as high on the abandon-hope-all-ye-who-enter-here scale.

In 1954, landfill was added to the island to enlarge it to 415 acres by the dumping of old metals, refuse, cinders and dirt from subway excavations and for years subterreanean fires smouldered, giving the island a genuinely hellish feel. Until 1996 a ferry from the Bronx took the prisoners there, when the sheer numbers of inmates and staff made it imperative to build a three-lane bridge of 4200 feet long.

The prison population is the size of a small town: 20,600 inmates in total of whom 2,050 are women; 57 per cent are black, 35 per cent Latino, 7 per cent white and 1 per cent 'other', mainly Chinese, Taiwanese and Korean. There are 10,700 uniformed and 1500 civilian staff. Since it is mainly a remand prison, a giant warehouse holding defendants while they await trial, the average time spent inside Riker's is only forty-four days before people are either shunted to a long-term institution or, less frequently, freed. Thus, around 70 per cent are awaiting trial while the rest are serving sentences of around a year. There were three suicides in 1996.

On the island, there are eleven separate 'jails': eight for men awaiting trial, one for convicted men, one for women, which had been built for 800 inmates and is now housing more than double that number, and one for youths aged between sixteen and twenty. The island has its own bakery, laundry, print shop, power plant, hospital, methadone detoxi-fication unit, AIDS infirmary and the largest venereal disease clinic in the city. There used to be a piggery, producing a thousand pounds of pork a week. The inmates, weary of their current dull diet, still lament its passing.

In the United States today, the name Riker's has the same bleakly emotive pull as Alcatraz and Sing-Sing had in the past: on news reports it is often referred to as 'notorious Riker's Island' and it has become a byword for penal despair and hopelessness. Sid Vicious, the English punk rocker from the Sex Pistols, who killed his American girlfriend Nancy Spungen in a drug-fuelled frenzy in the Chelsea Hotel in 1978, was held on Riker's Island until he was granted bail and was treated hellishly. As Jennifer Frankel wrote in the Observer, 'Here, too, the name that John Lydon [Johnny Rotten] had bestowed on him came back to haunt him. 'Vicious are you, punk?' asked the cons, then raped and beat him again and again. 'I saw bruises on that guy,' said Jerry Nolan, the drummer of another band, the Heartbreakers, 'where you don't get bruises.' The day Vicious was released, his mother Ann, now dead from an overdose herself, gave him the heroin that killed him in February 1979. 'He chose death over the US prison system.' Faced with the possibility of spending the next twenty-five years in such conditions, his decision is understandable.

So it was to Riker's that Caroline Beale, whose closest encounters with the penal code had been on a Guides' visit to a police station and when a friend was briefly hauled in by the cops for shouting, 'It was me!' late one night outside a police station, was taken at eight o'clock that night.

She was stripped, given a white sheet, told to have a shower with the other new arrivals and then searched by a female officer. This was followed at around two a.m. by a visit to the prison doctor for a urine test and internal examination. The doctor was unable to raise the vein in her arm for her blood test so took instead a sample from the back of her hand. She was then taken to a pen with a stainless-steel toilet open for anyone walking past to see and given a regulation blanket and a green plastic cup. She lay down and tried to sleep.

The housing area to which she was assigned was a long narrow room with single cells on the ground floor and six-bed dormitories above. There was wire all round the balconies so that people could not jump off. 'At first I was in with these real crazies and they were screaming all night. I remember being incredibly frightened because they were going cold turkey. There was a black girl called Henrietta who spread deodorant all over her face and she used to snort Tylenol [aspirin].'

Prisons in America often split along racial lines and Caroline was asked by Mary, a forty-year-old drugs offender from Brooklyn with deep furrows in her arms from mainlining heroin, to move into one of the predominantly 'white' dormitories. Caroline agreed and her early days inside passed in a blur: 'The first week all I did was cry.'

The authorities decided she was a suicide risk and she was assigned a Suicide Prevention Aide. 'They shine a torch on you to wake you up every half an hour and make sure you are still alive.'

In the dormitory, apart from Mary, was Ann, also from Brooklyn and also in for drug-dealing; a big Puerto Rican girl called Anna, who had been charged with holding up a store; Wanda from the Bronx, in for arson – high on crack cocaine, she had started a fire by lighting a joint; and Holly, a seventeen-year-old from the Bronx, also in for drugs. There were the six beds and one toilet, graffiti scrawled on the walls in black ink. Coloured pens were forbidden because, the women were told, it was feared that they could be used to draw escape plans. Cockroaches were their constant companions. The smell of the toilet, cheap disinfectant, vomit and central heating was such that Caroline learned to breathe through her mouth.

But at least she had companionship, and when she was briefly moved from the psychiatric wing into the general population of the prison, Mary passed a message through a friendly guard to tell her to inform the doctors that she was planning to hang herself so that she would be moved back to join them. Caroline followed instructions and was reunited with her roommates. They taught her the conversion rates for the American currency she would use for buying cigarettes and sweets from the store and introduced her to previously unheard-of delicacies like Bear Claws (Danish pastries) and Cheese Doodles (crisps), which she would buy as treats.

Her education was swift. Cigarette butts could be rolled in pages torn from a Bible to make a new cigarette. Packs of cigarettes could be smuggled in her bra. She was taught the '241' loan system, which meant paying back two cigarette packs for one borrowed. 'You had to pay or you got beaten up.' Fights were a regular part of the day, sometimes inmate against inmate, sometimes prison officer against inmate. Some of the guards, she found, were sadistic bullies, happy to take advantage of their hapless charges. There were fist fights over what programme should be shown on the communal television on the ground floor and scuffles when one inmate thought another had stolen her shampoo. On Tuesdays she and her roommates went to the commissary for cakes, biscuits, soda and deodorant. They were given 'state soap', which brings the skin out in a rash – 'It was as if it had sand in it.' If you spoke in line you were not allowed to buy anything and had to wait another week. Sometimes she felt so depressed that she did not bother getting up all day.

She met other prisoners: Sherain, who had seen news of Caroline's case on television, who knew what it was like to be stigmatized as a 'baby-killer' and who became a firm friend; Velma, who had killed a man who had raped her and burned her with a cigarette lighter – she had whacked him over the head with a bottle and he had died in a fire; Christine, from Pennsylvania, who was inside for persistent 'panhandling' or begging, and would be back and forth between the streets and jail throughout Caroline's time inside. She had a sideline as a prostitute, picking up her often violent clients at the Port Authority terminal. She was not well, suffering from both HIV and cirrhosis of the liver from too much booze. Caroline liked her spirit: 'She was about my age and she had run away from home when she was eleven and got in a truck heading for New York. She's going to be in and out for ever because there's no one to help her. She didn't want to go back to Pennsylvania because she was worried about what her mum was going to say.' Charlotte Cicerao, a Native American Indian, who was in for drugs became another friend.

Food punctuated the day. As in many prisons around the world, the meal-times are eccentrically out of kilter with normal life: breakfast was at five thirty a.m., lunch at ten and dinner at four or five. In the morning, the wagon would arrive with its large stainless-steel drums and the inmates would be alerted 'on line for meal' by the CO or Correctional Officer. The automatic locks on the door of the dormitory block would open, although the women had already discovered that they could be jammed ajar by the clandestine insertion of a book of matches.

Breakfast was frosted flakes, a banana, milk and watery coffee, or oatmeal with prunes, on big yellow trays with plastic knives, forks and spoons. For lunch there was Koolaid spiked, it was rumoured, with saltpetre to cut the sex drive. The food would be rice, potatoes, hot dogs – usually cold by the time they were served – sauerkraut and 'what they claimed was goat stew'. 'Chicken day', which came once a week, was anticipated eagerly. Puddings would be of instant, Angel Delight variety. Different diets were catered for: a blue ID card ensured kosher meat, and vegetarians would be given rice and potatoes. Although meat, fruit and fresh vegetables were scarce, there was an ample supply of bread, which meant that many of the women became obese. In telephone calls to her parents, Caroline would refer to meals as 'feeding time'.

There were other landmarks in the day. At eight a.m., the women would be given their medication. At first Caroline took two Zoloft anti-depressants and Benodril as a sleeping tablet. 'I must have got a bit dependent on it because when I was off it for a week because the doctor was away and had forgotten to prescribe in advance I felt terrible.' There was exercise but if the women went to 'rec' in the yard where there were basketball hoops they missed their medication because the times coincided.

'We used to do impressions of each other to entertain ourselves, silly things like jumping off a bed and saying, "That was Wanda jumping out of the hotel window."' At night, when the lights were off, they played true confessions.

There were regular suicide attempts: women would set fire to mattresses in an effort to burn themselves to death, use shoelaces to try to hang themselves by swinging off the bunk or off the top of a locker. One woman threw herself backwards off a locker, cracking her head open.

But they found other, less depressing ways, to pass their time. Caroline was sent draughts, Mastermind and Connect Four by a friend in England. They played card games constantly, mainly one called Zap. Caroline drew a lot, using smuggled coloured pens, which were hidden from the fortnightly searches in the middle of a toilet roll. When her pencils were stolen, her friends would turn over a suspect's cell to find them. Magazines were sent in and there was a regular supply of scandal sheets like the *National Enquirer* and the *Star*.

Jackie Cerdan from the British Consulate brought books for her. Kevin Mansell, her colleague from London, sent a *Breakthrough* French course, which she practised with the help of a Haitian prisoner 'although it was a weird kind of atmosphere to be asking for help with your French verbs. Everyone kept sending me Dickens novels, for some reason, and all the others were reading steamy Jackie Collins books. I got lots of copies of *Martin Chuzzlewit* – it was very depressing because it was about everyone dying and him coming back to England. And I was sent lots of Jane Austen.'

They could study old law books in the library although the women complained that most of the reference books were out of date and thus of little use in the preparation of their cases. Some inmates read the law journals so that they could find out exactly what their fellows were in for and then spread the news.

Caroline learned how to make ashtrays and teddy bears out of soap smashed inside a sock until it had been ground into powder, then mixed with water – or Koolaid to give it a colour – and moulded into the required shape. She also developed a cottage industry making Mother's Day cards, which the others would purchase for a negotiated number of what they, too, by now were calling 'fags'. She was taught how to make glue out of toothpaste for assembling Christmas decorations made of pictures of Christmas trees torn from magazines.

Michael Carter, the British Consul, was aware that it was important that Caroline was not deserted: 'She was a very vulnerable young lady. She talked of suicide and we had to pull out all the stops.'

Jackie Cerdan brought in a jumpsuit because it was getting cold in the winter. 'The central heating was very temperamental,' said Caroline. 'In the spring it was so hot you could hardly move and we would just sit round in our underwear.'

Some of the officers were sympathetic and friendly but others seemed to take pleasure in the inmates' discomfort. 'One would ask if I would "care for a spot of tea" but it was in a spiteful way. And there was another one who, when the other women said I was from London, would say, "Not any more she's not."' Some of the officers with Irish backgrounds would ask her view of the Troubles in Northern Ireland and others would want to know about Princess Diana and the Queen.

Protestant service was on Saturday night in the gym and Roman Catholic on Sunday, which Caroline attended for a particular reason. Some women went to break the monotony and others were clinging to religion. 'I went because Sister Marion was there and she was a great comfort to me.'

It is not difficult to see why this was so: Sister Marion Defeis is a handsome, feisty woman in her mid-sixties who has the indefinable presence that seems to attach itself to a very few people who work unselfconsciously with those at the bottom of the pile. 'When I first saw her,' said Caroline, 'it was like she had an aura around her, she was different from everyone else.' More than one of the prisoners Sister Marion befriended talk of this 'aura', although she would doubtless brush off such references with embarrassment or a joke.

She is employed by the Department of Correction as one of five chaplains catering to the women in the Rose M. Singer centre. There are two Roman Catholic chaplains, a rabbi, the only male who comes once a week because the number of Jewish inmates is very small, a Muslim and a Protestant.

Sister Marion's father was an Italian–American policeman from the Lower East Side and her mother had come to America in the 1920s from Salerno. She had joined the Church – 'at the tender age of eighteen' – and is proud of her sister who is Dean of Seaton Hall law school. A brother works for a law firm in Manhattan and another sister is an attorney.

She is a Sister of St Joseph, an order that was formed at the time of the French Revolution, and had come to America to teach deaf Native Americans who had been affected by the diseases brought over by Europeans. One of the best-known members of the order is Sister Helen Préjean, on whom the film *Dead Man Walking* was based and on whose behalf Sister Marion received an award for her work against the death penalty in Louisiana. Sister Marion had taken a degree in theology at Providence College, Rhode Island, and had taught religion in schools in Brooklyn and Puerto Rico. In 1981 she decided that she no longer wanted to teach. She had met Jane Leggett, another Riker's chaplain, who asked her to visit Bedford Hills prison in Westchester. 'I had a very strong feeling that this was where I belonged.' This led her to apply to Riker's. 'What I was taken with was that they were just so simple, so uneducated, and I thought there's something very wrong here.'

Sister Marion had originally come across the new English arrival when an officer said that Caroline needed to make a collect call. Women can make one free call a day or a collect call from her room, which has been designed not to look like an office. It is surrounded by figurative representations of angels and there is no desk but a table and two chairs, a kettle, some crochet work and artificial silk flowers. NQRX, the classical-music radio station, plays Beethoven and Vivaldi in the background. Sister Marion lives in a convent, a twelve-room house on Coney Island with three sisters, one lay woman and three ex-offenders. Of Caroline, she says, 'She was absolutely devastated, she could hardly speak she was so very, very upset. She was in a complete daze. I had heard something about a woman being stopped at the airport but I wasn't really curious about it, it was just another story I had heard. What surprised me was that she was so tiny, I didn't expect this little thing. She looked about fourteen. I thought, My God. I felt very, very sorry for her.

'They come to me with every problem imaginable. They need to make a phone call, they need to contact their children, or they just need help to navigate through the system.' Some women just come in and ask for a prayer or they have 'really hit bottom and they just want to sort out their lives, talking about what's happened to them, what's brought them to Riker's. I always pray with every woman. That is really important because it distinguishes us from psychologists and social workers.

'Some of them say they are in prison because they've been rescued – they have been heavily into drugs. For some women it's an opportunity to look at their lives and make some real decisions. It's genuine. They're not saying that to impress me because they know they don't have to. A lot of real healing takes place.'

There are few foreign prisoners in Riker's, which was why Caroline was notable, and most of the others – indeed most of the inmates – were in for drug offences. 'What we're doing in our country is warehousing drug addicts. I think that's deplorable.'

Her dismay at the situation of so many of the women led Sister Marion to her involvement with the Correctional Association, a penal-reform body, where she is currently part of a campaign to change the 1973 Rockefeller drug laws under which defendants face a minimum of fifteen years to life for possession of more than four ounces of drugs. Those who do not plead guilty face a far heavier sentence so many plead guilty even when they are not.

She writes about what she sees as the inequities of the laws in Catholic journals and specialist publications like the *Journal of Community Health* where she asked: 'I wonder, if our New York State prisons and jails were populated by 40,000 white middle-class and wealthy black males, whether the study of the legalization of drugs would be thwarted. I also believe that the blindfolded Lady Justice weighing the scales of justice is a sham. I believe Lady Justice sees very clearly. She sees black and white, rich and poor, and judges accordingly.'

She watched Caroline with particular care and noted the changes in her over the months she was in prison. 'She adjusted very, very well. One of the first things she said was she wasn't sure how she would deal with 'these people', the black and Hispanic women, and as time went on it was those women who were so supportive of her and she came to realize that those women are us, we're all the same. She seemed to grow from the experience, she seemed to be more assertive. The officers looked out for her and got a big kick out of her accent. She was such an innocent, this waif, this sweet little person. She brought out the sisterly or motherly or brotherly emotions in people – the male officers still ask after her.'

Sister Marion has worked for twelve years at Riker's, four with male prisoners: 'They are very different. For the women, the first concern is always their children. The men are very concerned about themselves – it was always 'get in touch with my attorney!'

'These women are mostly non-violent and for the most part drug addicts. Some of them are HIV positive. Why are they in jail? It costs sixty thousand dollars a year to keep them on Riker's Island and a residential drug programme is seventeen thousand. The poor use crack because it's a quick high. It's very hypocritical – they treat drug addicts very different from the way they treat alcohol addicts. Five hundred thousand die from nicotine a year, fifty thousand from alcohol, fifty thousand from drink-related accidents and five thousand from drug overdoses. We have what is called the "Vietnam syndrome": you put more and more troops in and you'll win the war, you put more and more people in prisons and you win the "war on drugs". It doesn't work.'

Jane Leggett saw less of Caroline inside because she was not one of her specific charges – the women were assigned to different chaplains depending on the initial of their surname – but she had two vivid memories of her. 'The first was when she was about to be taken to court and was handcuffed and leg-ironed and cried out that she wanted her mother and father. There was nothing to do but put your arms around her.' On another occasion, Jane Leggett recalled, she was picked on by another prisoner who shouted at her: 'You killed your baby.'

Gradually, Caroline became friend and confidante of others facing long sentences. Sherain Bryant is now in Bedford Hills, a penal institution in upstate New York, where long-term prisoners serve their sentences. Visitors are warned as to their mode of dress in a manner of almost Victorian prudery: no bare midriffs, no skintight or see-through clothes, no clothes that show 'private body parts', no short shorts, no Bermuda shorts on adults, 'no short shorts on children who could be mistaken for adults'.

Sherain is dressed in the regulation green T-shirt and trousers because she has none of her own clothes or the money to buy them. She is serving her time for the homicide of her four-year-old daughter, although she protests her innocence. Her husband, a violent crack user who beat her frequently, had attacked her daughter while Sherain was also on crack and she had been accused along with her husband. He pleaded guilty and received an eighteen-year sentence while she pleaded not guilty, having refused a plea bargain that would have left her with a single-figure term, and was jailed for twenty-five years. Like Caroline, she had been reviled as a 'baby-killer' and when she saw Caroline start to get the same treatment she decided she wanted to help. 'When we were in the pen, people would spit at us and throw food and garbage at us.' They were shackled when they went to court because they were CMCs – Centrally Monitored Cases – which meant they had to be under extra surveillance. 'Caroline would cry a lot at first.'

Another friend Caroline made was Venisa White, a small young woman with big spectacles, eagle earrings and the earnest demeanour of a teacher. Like Caroline, she was in Riker's on a homicide charge and was facing a five- to fifteen-year sentence. Originally from Jamaica she had moved, at the age of ten, with her parents to the Bronx.

When she first met Caroline she had not asked her why she was there. 'I don't ask what people are in for because I don't like people asking me but she told me and we became friends.' The women charged with homicides tend to stick together. 'We should all stick together because we're all against the system, but unfortunately it doesn't work like that and the ones who are in for drugs stick together, too, and so on.'

Venisa works as a Suicide Prevention Aide (SPA) now, and remembers how low Caroline had been. 'You have to watch out for any signs, like packing all their things up when they're not going anywhere and telling everyone about how much they love them.' Her own way of surviving was religion. 'I believe in God. I pray a lot and I hope for a miracle.'

Cathy Watkins, a tall, droll, good-looking young woman with a nose ring and a crucifix, her hair braided by herself, is from mid-town Manhattan. She is studying cosmetology – 'nails and hair' – while she awaits trial, also on a homicide charge. 'Caroline was very nervous at first and I remember her writing poems and doing cards. She was unusual because there weren't many foreign girls here and most of them had been in America for a while. Most of the time we would just socialize and play cards and talk girltalk. We liked her because she talked funny.'

Mail flooded in for Caroline. Some came from other people in jail or inmates who had just been released: 'What a pleasure to be able to polish my nails and shave!' wrote Mary, when she was released. 'My sisters couldn't believe how big I'd gotten. I saw my husband. He thought it was gonna be him and me again, but I straightened him out.'

A prisoner from Wakefield in Yorkshire wrote: 'I am writing to you because I cannot sleep, you're on my mind because of an article I read earlier this morning . . . Have you read any Wilbur Smith? His first novel, *When the Lion Feeds*, is brilliant.' He had recently been for an operation: 'I was really embarrassed when I went to the hospital in chains, people stare at you and it makes you feel like a criminal, I'm sure you know what I mean . . . I have found that my budgie likes Vimto, cheese, chips and tuna and I think it's too late to train it.' His next letter enclosed a picture of a cat, in response to Caroline's letter in which she had told him she liked cats: 'I have been in prison for almost two years and the thing I miss most is the smell and touch of a woman.' He explained that he and his co-workers in the workshop had been laid off because they had completed their order of fifty thousand pairs of boxer shorts. A fellow prisoner from Wakefield joins the correspondence to assure Caroline: 'Those damn yankees – I tell you, us Brits are the best lovers!'

There were letters, too, from strangers often with gifts of money, a friendship band or an indication that prayers were being said for her. One hoped that she had 'not succumbed to the temptations of peanut butter and jam sandwiches'. The mother of a stillborn child, who had seen reports on television, wrote to say that, 'I promise you are just a normal young woman who has suffered terribly. The only "evil" woman I saw was the DA.' A retired midwife and lay preacher from Somerset sent a poem called 'Don't Quit'. An 'ordinary run-of-the-mill Irishman with six children', who had written to his MEP about the case, sent her a blessing in Gaelic. A woman from Galway told her: 'There have been a good few times in Ireland where women have been treated in a similar way to yourself.' Many letters came from Roscommon and Tipperary, Dublin and County Cavan, sending prayers, and quotations from Kahlil Gibran: 'Verily, you are suspended like scales between sorrow and joy.' Some said, 'I'm not a great one for the prayers,' but sent words of encouragement and sympathy instead. There was a medal blessed at Knock and the whole of Psalm 138. Some had heard her parents on *The Pat Kenny Show*. 'I believe when people commit a crime, three people know immediately – God, your guardian angel and Satan. Therefore I've no doubt you're 100 per cent innocent.' A fifteen-year-old from County Cavan said: 'I'm not really very religious but I'll say a prayer for you.'

Peter Beale wrote that he had seen Olivia Newton-John on TV-am saying that the power of positive thinking had helped her to come to terms with breast cancer: 'This is something you must put into practice for your survival over there, Caroline.' Her mother told her to 'keep your chin up'. Sister-in-law Caroline wrote with updates on *Coronation Street* and *EastEnders* and newsflashes on Princess Diana's new hair-styles. Friends wrote with gossip and news of new boyfriends – 'very fit, tall, dark and a firm bum' – and exhortations to keep her spirits up. Mandy Goff wrote to say they had watched the interview on GMTV and she and two workmates ended up in tears.

Maureen Faraway, Paul's mother, wrote that Peter Beale was being 'quite unpleasant' to Paul. She said that Paul had tried to contact Paul Vladimir many times without success, and could not understand why Vladimir did not return his calls. She offered to send books and magazines, and expressed her concern that Caroline was getting good legal advice.

But the letters that Caroline most wanted to receive were from Paul. On 8 October he wrote: 'I want to stay in touch as much as possible, it is the only real way to understand the problems surrounding this terrible event.' He was staying at his brother Dominic's both for the company and to escape the attention of the press. 'My dad has been great. He has used all his legal skills to get the best help for you possible. I can't begin to understand the horror of your situation. It makes me feel very sad.'

On 17 October, came another letter in which Paul reassured Caroline of his support. He had had a difficult meeting with her father, but she was his prime concern. 'You must have endured such terrible mental torment for such a long time. I feel sad that you could not confide in anybody, even me.' He had realized, he said, that they had drifted apart over the last year, and that the relationship had not been working well, but hadn't known what to do about it. 'If only you had said . . .'

Almost a week later, on 23 October, he wrote: 'Please believe that you have my support.' Again he encouraged her to keep her spirits up. 'When you get very depressed please try and think of the huge support you have over here. I am confident you will find an inner strength to get through this so keep fighting on . . . Please hang on in there.'

On 4 November came another letter, after they had spoken on the phone: 'I was so pleased to hear you sound so level headed and sane, everybody is very proud of the way you have held yourself together.' Araminta had told him of her visit: 'It sounds so terrible, it hardly leaves my mind.' He told her that their cat Toby had been to the vet to have his teeth cleared because his gums were infected . . . 'You would be proud of how tidy the house is.'

Chapter Eleven

While Caroline was making friends among the inmates, she was also having to prepare herself for the trial. Paul Vladimir, her attorney, came to visit: 'She was in a state of collapse when I first saw her on Riker's Island. She was adamant that she was not guilty.' He tried unsuccessfully to get her bail and was disappointed that it was refused. 'She couldn't go any place as she had no passport and no money and she wasn't going to be violent. The nun [Sister Marion] was going to put her up some place. There was a great deal of pressure from the English press and all types of indications that they would go the bail, which is not meant to happen. It was the usual rat race. I had an affection for her and for her parents. It was a horror for them and for her all I could do was hug her and say I'm going to fight for you. Her story was incredible and very difficult to believe.'

Vladimir had defended Joel Rifkin, a serial killer accused of twenty-seven murders. He saw Caroline's case as one in which a plea bargain should be sought: 'There is too much to risk at a trial, all trials. I was looking for a period of probation.'

Caroline remembers their meetings. 'Sister Marion said he was a good man. I thought he was OK, he held my hand. Then he told me that the DA wanted to put me in jail for twenty-five years. I was hysterical and had a panic attack. I went into a trance and he kept saying, "Come back to me, come back to me," because he couldn't reach me. He was telling me that somewhere along the line "you and I and Marjory" have to come to an agreement.'

Meanwhile, in London, Peter Beale had started to keep a diary in the notebook he had used to record the trees he had planted. The accounts of Caroline's travails are in stark contrast to the homely notes at the other end of the book detailing the date the purple beech and the juniper were potted and how much the Japanese bush clover cost. In his entry for 25 October, he recorded: 'We spoke to Sister Marion. She said Caroline was OK, had even smiled today. She said she had never known, in all her years in the prison, anyone get as much support and letters as Caroline.'

Later he noted: 'Paul V[ladimir] says the medical view is that a third party was involved ... [This was never substantiated and was abandoned as a theory early on.] She seems to be bearing up, God bless her. We never stop thinking about her. Paul V says he thinks about her at home and he says he could quite easily fall in love with her. He says he does not usually let work interfere with business but she is getting to him.' A few days later, on 9 November, Peter wrote: 'She said Paul V had seen her and was telling her about the worst scenario. Why?'

On 19 November, he wrote: 'I have done nothing for Caroline today. I am in need of some inspiration. This is just so wrong what they are doing. Saw a programme about [Princess] Diana on TV. She seems very concerned about women's situations. Could she help us?'

Every well-known person who might assist was contacted. His diary recorded that someone knew a friend of John Major or that someone had suggested he should try to persuade Alastair Cooke to feature the story on *Letter from America* on Radio Four. He was told to get in touch with the wife of the Mayor of New York or Barbara Bush, wife of ex-president George Bush, or Hillary Clinton. Someone suggested writing to Lady Tebbit, who had told Sue Lawley on *Desert Island*

Discs that she had suffered from severe post-natal depression. A photographer from *TV Quick* urged them to read *Some Other Rainbow*, the book by Beirut hostage John McCarthy and his then girlfriend, Jill Morrell, because it is 'a good insight into getting in the news'. A few weeks later, Peter Beale was working his way through it: 'I am making a serious effort to get into the book in the hope of getting some ideas for our efforts to support Caroline. It seems to me that they started at something of an advantage to us – both journalists, both working for a large news agency – they had lots of support from fellow-travellers, too.' The same photographer told them of a story he covered about a girl in Norfolk being taken to hospital for appendicitis and giving birth to a baby when no one knew she was pregnant; his telephone number was duly logged.

On 28 December Peter wrote: 'Caroline's phone call was very upsetting. She wants to get out of that place. It is as though they are deliberately trying to drive her insane. The cruelty is beyond reason – what can we do?' He concludes his diary of the day with one of the quotations that were to sprinkle his pages: 'To sin by silence when we should protest makes cowards out of men.' In February, he added: 'There is little hope for humanity if the hearts of men and women cannot be touched by a call to something greater than themselves.'

The efforts to secure Caroline's defence continued. The Beales found that their quarterly phone bill had rocketed from fifty-seven pounds to more than three hundred.

Jackie Cerdan, who had become Caroline's link between the jail and the Consulate, visited her and found her still 'crying, sobbing, hardly able to get a word out'. Cerdan would visit her every week or two throughout her time in Riker's Island. The Consulate spells out what they can and cannot do for prisoners – they cannot get better treatment for foreign inmates than the local prisoners or pay fines – but the visits were more frequent than most British prisoners would receive because Caroline was seen as a particularly vulnerable case.

In October the Beales, who had never been to America before, had been able through the assistance of the media to make the journey and learn the ritual of the prison visit as they prepared to see their daughter for the first time since her arrest.

The visit would start at the stop for Bus Q101 from the one of the unlovelier parts of Queens, where the railtrack hovers like a deranged roller-coaster over a dozen fast-food joints and decrepit little stores. The passengers for the twenty-minute journey are almost all blacks or Hispanic, clutching little packets of permitted treats and essentials for the inmates. After arrival and form-filling, the visitor's hand is stamped with an indelible dye and all outer clothes are left in a locker. Then it's through the metal checker, take off the shoes and click the heels together to show that there are no hidden drugs, roll the socks down for same reason, and then wait in the overheated visiting room for the inmates to be called to take their places on the fixed plastic seats. They will have been alerted when the visitor arrived at the main gate.

Waiting for the bus to the jail, the Beales were told they had to have the exact $1.25 fare and did not have any change. 'We were the only two white people there and we didn't know what to do and suddenly all these dollar bills were coming over our shoulders, it almost moved us to tears. Another bloke said, 'How you going to get back?' and he gave us the money for the return fare. Most of these people were so battered and broken and didn't have a lot of money. They were decent people and they were treated like cattle.' They were tickled by the attitude of some of the visitors: one large woman told a prison officer who was giving her a hard time that he obviously wasn't getting enough sex. They were struck, too, by the enormous behinds of the prison officers.

After a visit, the inmate is made to strip and squat so that she can be searched back and front to see if she is concealing any drugs or contraband. Some of the women find the whole process so humiliating that they prefer not to go through with a visit. Some visitors make the same decision.

For Caroline, the first visit of her parents was a cause both for relief and of apprehension. She had spoken to them on the phone but was still uncertain about their reaction to what had happened. At first the Beales were amazed at the indifference of the prison officers, who sat blowing bubble gum and lounging around. 'Then, they brought Caroline out and she collapsed in my arms,' says Daphne. 'She said, "I've done nothing wrong. Why won't they believe me?" She couldn't understand it. She was shaking and so thin, so thin.'

'We told Caroline not to worry,' says Peter Beale. 'I said to make as many friends as she could, eat the right food, drink plenty of liquid and look for some people who were worse off than she was and try and look after them to take her mind off her own situation.'

After the visit, they saw Paul Vladimir. 'All the time we thought we were going to be attacked in the street because of what we'd read so when we went to places away from Manhattan we would be standing with our backs to the wall. I think Vladimir said, "I'm sixty-eight, I've had a lot of cases and I've won some and lost some." I asked him which he had done the most of. He seemed like a gentleman.'

During the visit the phone kept ringing in Vladimir's office: it was British tabloid newspapers wanting information and offering money. Vladimir hung up on them, which upset the Beales who felt they needed the support of the media.

They were told that the baby had been alive for ten to fifteen minutes so they asked for another autopsy and were told that this would cost more money. They felt near to collapse.

'We had a terrible fear we could lose everything we'd

striven for,' says Peter Beale. 'I said, "We cannot spend all our money on Caroline because if we've got no money we'll be so preoccupied with survival we won't be able to give ourselves to her support." We thought that it could go on for ever and she may get life and we will have to make trips over there when the media don't feel we're newsworthy any more. Or maybe she would be released and be insane.'

They found a little Caribbean restaurant near their hotel that charged $6.25 for a three-course meal: 'Everyone in there was black,' says Daphne. 'We said, "Is it all right for us to be here?" because we were the only white people there and they said, "Come in, come in."'

Caroline's friends also started to visit. Araminta Thorne was the first, travelling to the prison in the consular limo with Michael Carter. 'The most stressful time was waiting to see if Caroline would see me. When it came through that she wanted to see me I was so elated. It meant I could give her some kind of lifeline. It also meant that she was not in a totally negative abyss . . . When we held hands, her nails were digging into my hand. It didn't look like Caroline because she hadn't mascara or any make-up and I think it was the first time I had seen her without it. She was very thin with her hair tied behind her and very pale and washed out – just bones in a grey sack.' Caroline mainly wanted news of Paul, who had sent a letter with Araminta. 'It was reassuring that she was still herself. She had been pregnant and I hadn't known so suddenly you didn't know what you knew about anything. To discover that she was still the same person was very reassuring.'

In February 1995 Mandy Goff and Clare Webb visited for the first time and found it, in Mandy's words, 'horrendous. Her physical appearance was appalling. Her face was pale and had a waxy look to it like someone who had just died. She was desperately thin. She was wearing a gross, grey bodysuit and you could see her collarbones and shoulderbones sticking out. She shook virtually the whole two hours we were there.

She told us that Paul's mother had written to her and said, "Don't call my son, don't have any contact with my son." It was one body blow after another. To see someone you love in that situation, you just want to wrap them up and take them home. It was really difficult to say goodbye.' (Paul had contracted glandular fever and his mother was concerned about his health, he explained later. She feared that the strain of constant contact with Caroline would exacerbate his illness.)

Peter and Daphne had returned for a second visit in January, and Peter recalled in his diary: 'Caroline seems much more controlled. She seems to be getting on with people. Some poor black girl was in the next cubicle and she was told by her lawyer that she is going to get three years for selling "coke" whilst on parole. She was crying and rocking in her seat. Caroline waved to her and she smiled. Caroline suggested that we should go . . . perhaps she wanted to go and see this girl. We are very proud of her.'

Chapter Twelve

Following through the advice he had received, Peter Beale had contacted Professor Channi Kumar at the Maudsley Hospital in south London, one of Europe's most respected psychiatric institutions. Kumar recalled that a former colleague of his was living and working in New York who might just be able to help. He rang her one October morning.

Meg Spinelli answered his call. A bright, extrovert, attractive woman in her forties, snappily dressed, she knew and admired Kumar for his work at the Maudsley. 'Channi said she needed a psychiatric evaluation and would I be willing to go to Riker's Island. He wanted to know what Riker's Island was like and, although I'd never been there, there was never good news about it, it was always an awful place. I was ambivalent – no, that's not true. I have very strong feelings about post-partum and how women are treated but it wasn't your average house call to go out to a jail!'

Dr Spinelli is from an Italian–Irish family in Brooklyn. Her father was a bartender and she had married young, a policeman in the NYPD, and now had two grown-up sons, one, like his father, a policeman, the other a firefighter, which made her the mother of one of New York's Finest and one of New York's Bravest. Her marriage had ended some years previously and she had recently married a film editor called Bob Reitano who at the time was working on a film called *The Juror*, starring Demi Moore and Alec Baldwin, a bloody psychodrama about Mafia attempts to coerce a jury.

She had been an obstetrics nurse for fifteen years, had applied to medical school at Cornell at the age of thirty-six and was agreeably surprised to be admitted. She had been particularly interested in psychiatric disorders surrounding the reproductive cycle. She was now assistant clinical professor of psychiatry at Columbia University Medical College of Physicians and Surgeons and director of the Maternal Mental Health Programme. Three or four days a week she does private practice in her office on the Upper West Side in Manhattan. In her third year of study she had gone to England and had met Dr Kumar, who had become a mentor and role model. She had not been aware of Caroline's case at the time but agreed to visit her with Jackie Cerdan.

'Caroline was in a very fragile state. It was the first week in December and it was very bleak and cold, like a ghost town in there.' They spent two or three hours together while Meg Spinelli started her evaluation. 'I found her very easy to talk to. Her dad had told her I was coming and she could tell me everything. She knew I was an ally. She was very open. She didn't have the classic post-partum depression. There was this question that she was suffering from post-traumatic stress disorder. I was absolutely sure that she was psychotic.

'I would say to her things like, "Were you having any hallucinations, seeing things you wouldn't normally see?" Right towards the end she mentioned that a couple of days after Alison's funeral she realized her baby was dead and that really struck me, being parallel to Alison's death, that she would come to this conclusion. I was almost worried – why aren't I hearing anything that's a little more abnormal, why aren't I seeing any classic psychotic symptoms?

'She was very obsessional, she kept coming back to Paul and the family and would she ever see Paul again. It was very hard to break through that. That was why I had to go back. You couldn't just barge in on her and say, "What's going on in your brain?" She was very compliant. This is when she came out about all that stuff about O'Donnell [the detective who first questioned her]. She would say I can see this man, I can see his ring, his clothes.'

Caroline told her that on one occasion in prison she had been shaking and her cell-mate Mary had put a coarse brown blanket over her and suddenly O'Donnell's face had been superimposed on Mary's. She had screamed because she had been sure that O'Donnell was trying to strangle her. In the hallucination, he would tell her that she was not going home and that everything was her fault.

'So I'm listening to this,' says Meg Spinelli, over an iced coffee in her Manhattan consulting rooms, 'and I said, "Does he talk to you?" and she said, "Yes, he says Paul's not going to come back." I said, "Are these flashbacks or halluci-nations?" I probed around a lot.

'She would look up from her book, she would look anywhere and O'Donnell would be there. There was also this auditory component and you usually don't have that with flashbacks. It was also mood congruent, nasty things he was saying which were congruent with her depressed mood. This guy was really frightening her and saying things that were outside her head. She was delusional when she was pregnant so she was psychotic back then.' Caroline also told her that she had spent two weeks not talking to anyone and a couple of weeks barely eating. 'I came away sure that she was psychiatrically ill.'

Dr Spinelli contacted Paul Vladimir, who was now Caro-line's attorney. 'He said, "Well, this is what the autopsy says, air in the lungs." I said that whether it did or not she's got real psychiatric problems. Basically what he was saying was she should take a plea bargain for twelve years, I think, and listen to him or she would be there for twenty-five years or life. That was his advice. I could see he wasn't budging at all.'

Paul Vladimir for his part was not happy about dealing with Meg Spinelli. They did not, to put it mildly, see eye to eye. 'Spinelli had a different agenda,' he said. It was clear that they were not going to work together as a team. Meg Spinelli decided that she would find another lawyer for Caroline.

She got in touch with the National Organization for Women's legal defence fund, who gave her a list of names of attorneys who did *pro bono* [free] work. At the top of the list were two names who had successfully defended women in cases where their gender was particularly relevant. One of them was Michael Dowd.

'I asked a Supreme Court judge I know about him and she said, "Great guy." I asked a journalist friend and they said he was a saint. He seemed to have a good reputation for that kind of work. I met him and we hit it off from day one. There was also kind of a cute link. Sister Marion when she first heard me on the phone said, "Oh, you're Italian – it's good luck." And she went on to tell me about her Italian family. My response was, "Sister, I had nuns my entire life, grammar school, high school, nursing school, college and my feelings are not great," and she's so wonderful, she said, "Who did you have?" I said, "The Mercy nuns," and she said, "Ahhh", and I said, "You won my heart." She was really sweet. So I pulled on Mike the Catholic school thing and said, "You have to do this because there are nuns behind this."'

Having decided that Michael Dowd was the right attorney for Caroline, she told Peter Beale to speak to him and told him he would have to make the decision about changing lawyers. Caroline says, 'My dad said, "How do you feel about changing attorneys?" Vladimir had said that Meg was an impressionable young doctor who was too emotionally involved. She said she liked the young bit but the impressionable was a bit insulting. Dad told me about Michael Dowd who Meg wanted us to go with and said phone him up and talk to him and see how you get on with him.' She duly did so.

Meg was also using her media contacts to alert the television documentary programme *20/20* about the issue.

This caused a further rift with Paul Vladimir, who felt that media coverage would be counter-productive. Meg Spinelli disagreed. 'I felt right from the beginning that this was an atrocity that people should know about.'

She started to formulate her conclusions about Caroline and her actions. 'It was a psychotic act to try and bring the child back. If someone does that, that's crazy. Eventually there seemed to be some identification with Alison. I saw that she identified her baby with Alison, she lost Alison, she lost the baby. This is what we call a psychotic identification. It was almost as if the next day, carrying her round in a duffle bag over her shoulder, she was carrying a coffin.'

She contacted another expert in the field, Dr Susan Hickman from San Diego, whose name Peter Beale had already been given. She, too, came to Riker's Island and saw Caroline, who found her reassuring: 'She looked like my mum.' Caroline had to answer many of the same questions she had already been asked by Detective O'Donnell, Marjory Fisher, Paul Vladimir and Meg. She would have to answer them many more times.

Dr Hickman asked her about the name she had chosen for the baby: Olivia Ann. Could this be, asked Dr Hickman, that she was trying to say, 'Oh, Live, Alison'?

Although Meg Spinelli had little experience of court work she was also preparing herself for the fact that she might have to give evidence and present it in a way that a lay jury could understand. What she would need to explain to them was that alterations in the hormones affect the brain chemistry. She would also be drawing on her experience of denial of pregnancy.

She had treated two women who had denied their pregnancies and pressed them as to how they had reached that state: 'I said, "Come on – you're pregnant and you're big and out to here, how do you go through the day?" One laughed, although it wasn't such a funny thing, and she said, "Well, you kind of don't think about it." It's nothing they decide to do but at the back of their mind it just becomes part of them. It's their mechanism of protection and it probably comes from much earlier when they needed protection from something else. In these women it is as if one part is disassociated and rejects the knowledge of the pregnancy. It's not only denial, it's lacking the knowledge of pregnancy. You kind of don't think about it. It just becomes part of them and that's their protection.'

She believed that this would explain the amnesia that affected Caroline over what happened that night in the bathroom at the Off SoHo Suites Hotel. 'She lost a lot of time. The way she described the delivery makes it sound as though it went on for only minutes but it must have been hours.'

Meg Spinelli also had to confront the fact that the psychiatrist, who had first examined Caroline to determine whether she was capable of being interviewed at Queens General Hospital, had decided that she was not suffering from a psychosis.

'I said, "Well, how did you know? Did you do any formal testing?" and she said, "No." I said, "What about the fact that she carried her dead baby through the airport? Don't you think that's kind of psychotic?" and she said, "Yes." It's too bad the lawyers and the DAs don't have a bit of psychotherapy under their belts!

'The thing is these women have amnesia through many of these events throughout this delivery so they don't even have their own defence. I think sometimes they're not sure whether they're guilty or not – even though it's clear they're not guilty. I think Caroline always knew in her heart she didn't do anything wrong but when you have a vulnerable ego and superego it's hard to stand up against something like that.'

Chapter Thirteen

He was, Caroline told her mother, like a teddy bear. 'He' was Michael Dowd, the man who was to be her attorney, the trusty cornerman who would prepare her for her big fight, patch up her bruises and tell her to keep her guard up. In fact, he looked more like a broth of a boy than a teddy bear, the kind of sturdy character who would have stepped off the boat from Galway or Cork at the turn of the century, with a big, open, cherubic face, sky blue eyes, broad shoulders and the sort of amiability that seemed just on the edge of ordering another round of stout for everyone in the bar or demanding another verse of 'Danny Boy'.

Michael Dowd's grandfather had indeed landed in 1905 from Cavan, on the border between the north and the south of Ireland. His father had been a 'letter-carrier' – a postman – his mother from a well-to-do Carolina newspaper family called Grist. He had been born in Astoria, the original home of the film business whose chief claim to fame today is that it is home to more Greeks than any city outside Athens. He is still a Queens boy with a house on Corbett Road in Bayside named after James J. Corbett, the turn-of-the-century heavyweight champion of the world who had lived in the corner house. The house opposite had once belonged to W. C. Fields.

Dowd had a classic New York Roman Catholic education, graduating from Xavier High School where his powerful build – six foot two inches and 218 pounds – helped him to be a football star, thus attracting many scholarship offers. He spent three months at Naval Academy before he realized it had been a bad mistake and went instead to Fordham University, where he enrolled in a course for political science – 'the haven for those who knew not where they were going'. From there he went to St John's University, then in Brooklyn now in Queens, to study law.

To pay his way through college he worked as a clerk in a law office owned by his uncle and specialized in maritime law. By the end of the first year in law school he was married and had his first daughter the following year – she is now thirty-two and the mother of two children. He argued with his uncle and walked out of the firm but fortuitously met up with a friend from law school, who was starting a practice in Queens. The work was mainly small criminal cases, involving illegal bookmaking or drunk driving, but he was enchanted by it. He read every book about trial lawyers and then the books by the lawyers themselves. Francis Wellman's *The Art of Cross Examination*, which was last updated in the thirties, became his bible. 'Parts of that book I have probably read thirty-five times. It is timeless.'

Then on 3 July 1972 – he remembers the exact moment a quarter of a century later – as he was falling asleep at home to the film *Wake Island* on television he got a call from a partner's client who had been arrested for alleged sale of cocaine. It was a sign of the times that the prosecution accepted that it was a harmless, although illegal, drug. There were overtones of politics and corruption in the charges, and Dowd relished it. It was his first big case and he worked all the hours available to prepare properly for it, partly out of sheer terror. The other attorneys in the case exuded experience and self-confidence but once Dowd got to his feet for the jury selection process he knew he had found what he wanted to do for the rest of his life: 'All of a sudden I found myself in a place that you know is right, you're doing the right thing for a living.' His client was acquitted of the drugs sale and convicted of a lesser offence with a maximum sentence of seven years that was reversed on appeal. Dowd had found his mission.

He was also, like many young Irish-American lawyers in New York, interested in politics and ran unsuccessfully for the assembly in 1972. By the end of the seventies he was even more involved in the political machine and worked for the Democrat Mario Cuomo, once a potential presidential candidate, who was then running in the mayoral primaries against Ed Koch. It was a mucky campaign, and Koch wrongly suspected Dowd of hiring a private eye to investigate his private life; a smear campaign played on Koch's sexuality with the unofficial slogan: 'Vote for Cuomo, not the homo.' Although Dowd was not involved in this, he was part of the Cuomo team and Koch would remember his name. It was a chastening experience: 'I was stunned by the ugliness of the process.'

Meanwhile he had made a friend who had been involved in civil-rights work in places like Wounded Knee with Native Americans. Through this he came to represent a woman called Anne-Marie Boon who had killed her husband with a machete after he had attacked their child. As Dowd questioned her, it became clear that she had long been violently abused by her husband and he contacted Julie Blackman, an expert in the field of domestic violence. It was one of the first cases in the United States to use the 'battered woman syndrome' as a defence – as happened in the United Kingdom in the 1990s with the cases of Kiranjit Ahluwalia and Sara Thornton. Dowd's success in it was widely hailed by campaigners for women's rights.

His Irish roots led him into another of the controversial legal battlegrounds of the time: the cases involving alleged members of the IRA and their supporters in America. In 1981 he represented five alleged gun-runners and there were to be other cases involving extradition proceedings. He came to know lawyers in the United Kingdom involved in similar work,

like Gareth Peirce who had been the solicitor for members of
the Guildford Four and the Birmingham Six. Later he came to
England and saw Michael Mansfield, QC, the barrister whom
he perhaps most closely resembles in the United Kingdom, in
action in the successful appeal of the Birmingham Six.

His work was becoming well known in the Irish com-
munity. In 1982 he successfully represented Patrick Mullin, a
Brooklyn man charged with plotting to smuggle arms to the
IRA. In 1984, he acted for Joe Cahill, the then leader of Sinn
Fein, in a deportation case.

Then in September 1988 came a case that led him indirectly
to Caroline Beale on Riker's Island. Ann Green, a nurse
suffering from post-partum depression, was alleged to have
killed two of her newborn children over a two-year period.
The first child had been seen as the victim of a cot death, the
second had lived for a while. Four and a half years later, she
brought a third child to hospital and the child survived. Ann
Green and her husband were threatening to sue the hospital
and hired an expert to act on their behalf but he came to the
conclusion that she had caused the deaths. She was confronted
with the charge, allegedly made some admissions and was
admitted to hospital where she was charged with murder and
attempted murder. When Dowd saw her, she told him how
she had seen 'another pair of hands' place a towel over her
baby's face. Dowd was now in a new field of defence.

'The learning curve was like Everest for me. We went to
trial charged with murder and attempted murder and we
demolished the prosecution experts and the jury found her not
responsible.' This was the first case of its kind. Ann Green was
acquitted but sent for therapy, which she continued for six
years. Her husband died and she remarried.

It was a high moment in his career. In 1986, he had
remarried, a woman called Irene – 'a great romance, still going'
– and their daughter Lauren arrived as the Green case concluded. He had other high-profile cases that attracted the New

York media to this attorney who apparently had the golden touch in what looked like unwinnable cases. In 1989, he defended LouAnn Fratt, aged fifty-six, who stabbed her husband to death after he had raped her at their $2 million Upper East Side flat. Again the New York media were impressed. So was the defendant: on her release she hugged him. Her case became the subject of a book *To Honor and Obey*. He also successfully won an appeal for Sarah Smith, who shot her husband after years of being battered.

He loved the work: 'It was all about liberty, justice, right and wrong. It would be true to say that I got much more than I ever gave in representing battered women and the Irish because I met some extraordinary people who were fighting for what they believed in and you had to be moved by it.'

By now Dowd was a partner in Manton, Pennisi, Dowd and Swarz of Queens Boulevard. He and Pennisi also owned 82 per cent of a firm called Computrace, which Dowd had seen as a way of making a little money and having something ready for his eventual retirement. It made its money from collecting unpaid fines for the city's Parking Violations Bureau. But, as with many public-sector contracts at the time in the city, a little sweetener was required. As Dowd tells it, in 1982 he was told by a city official he knew as a friend that if he didn't play ball and pay up he would lose the business and his law practice might be destroyed. He duly paid up for eighteen months, a total of around $25,000, until the 'bagman' died of cancer. At the funeral in 1983, at which Dowd wept, he was approached by Donald 'The Fatman' Manes, the high profile and ambitious Queens borough president who told him that there was a new bagman that he would have to keep paying. Dowd was shocked. He had hoped that the pressure would have died with the buried man. He paid up reluctantly, handing over the money wrapped in a newspaper, for the next eighteen months but finally decided he would pay no more.

In December 1985, at a meeting in a diner Dowd was told

by the bagman: 'I'm personally disappointed in you.' Dowd told him: 'Just do what you gotta do.' He decided he would blow the whistle and started to consult friends and lawyers about the best way to do it. Meanwhile an investigation had already begun into kickbacks and commissions and the veteran journalist and author of *The Gang Who Couldn't Shoot Straight*, Jimmy Breslin, was on to the story. When he saw the list of names of those who had supposedly been asked to come up with bribes he recognized the name of Dowd as an old buddy from Queens. According to *City for Sale*, an examination of New York corruption, by Jack Newfield and Wayne Barrett, the two men met in a journalists' hangout in Manhattan and Breslin advised him on how best to deal with it.

Events were taking yet uglier twists. Manes made a botched suicide attempt and Dowd started to fear for his life and that of his daughter, suspecting that, as a key witness, the criminal fraternity might have good reason to deal with him. Manes was in a fraught state. One evening he was on the phone to his psychiatrist when the latter's doorbell rang. He asked Manes to hold on for a second. Manes grabbed a kitchen knife and stabbed himself fatally through the heart. New York, which loves a scandal more than any city in the world, was agog.

Dowd co-operated with the authorities and was never charged with any offence. He was well aware of the risks he had run by whistle-blowing and what it might mean in the future: 'I know the Palace guard will get me even if you kill the king,' he told the prosecutors at the time. 'It was like opening the door and not knowing if you were going to get the lady or the tiger,' he told the *New York Daily News*.

With the case over, a happy new marriage and a chance to continue with his work as an attorney, his life seemed back on an even keel. It was not to be.

He found out that he was being investigated by the disciplinary arm of the appellate court on the charge that he had failed to report corrupt conduct on the part of another lawyer, Donald Manes, the man who had put the squeeze on him in the first place. This seemed the cruellest blow, because Dowd had come forward with information before the prosecutors had any suspicion of his involvement and he had been the victim of Manes rather than the other man's collaborator. But there were unforgiving elements within the New York legal establishment. In August 1990 he received a call telling him that he was suspended for five years. 'I was dumbfounded.'

Mario Cuomo, by now the governor, told him that his experience was too valuable to lose. He was asked to work for the state and teach other lawyers how to run cases involving domestic violence and similar defences. In 1991 he became director of special projects in the New York state office for the prevention of domestic violence at a salary of $66,000 a year.

He learned who his firends were. The television programme *Sixty Minutes* blasted the suspension. Jimmy Breslin published an article in which he said that the only thing the judges didn't send with the suspension order was a dead fish. Another commentator, Murray Kempton, wrote supportively but Dowd was now out of the game he loved. 'I was gone and I never thought I was going to come back.' Then, after three years, he made an application to return, which was granted in March 1994. He was back.

Once he had taken on such a high-profile case as Caroline's his past came under public scrutiny. But his work in cases involving battered women was still well known. In 1994, the *New York Times* described him as 'a John Wayne throwback, the big guy out to defend defenceless women'.

He had remained politically and socially active, helping to start the Wig and Pen club in Manhattan and taking part in a demonstration against Hertz, the car-rental company in 1989, because they had retained the services of a (then slightly lesser known) football player called O. J. Simpson after a battering conviction. He was also openly attacking the CIA for giving

SAM missiles to the Afghanis in an interview with *Newsday* in 1990.

On the wall of his office at 425 Park Avenue is an artist's impression of the Karen Straw case. It shows Dowd doing what he does best, addressing the jury, cajoling them into giving the decision he seeks. Karen Straw was a twenty-nine-year-old who stabbed her crack-smoking, violent husband Clifton to death with a kitchen knife in a Jamaica welfare hotel and was tried and acquitted in 1987. Reports of the case note how the grateful Mrs Straw personally thanked Dowd for her freedom. With a less committed lawyer, as she knew well, ten years later she would still have been looking out through cell bars somewhere in upstate New York.

'The old notion is: don't blur the line between lawyer and client but I think the legal profession in the States overdoes it because I think some lawyers are so clinically cautious just trying to save themselves emotionally whereas I believe you're a better lawyer if you relate to your client at some level,' says Dowd, sitting on the fire-escape steps at the back of the building, the only place he can have a cigarette without going down to the street. 'If you don't have a passion for your case, why the hell should the jury care about what you say?'

Meg Spinelli had called him and told him he had to get involved on Caroline's case. 'It was kind of – this is your kind of case, you'll like it. If I was to describe Meg Spinelli one of the ways would be to say that it's clear she never got fifty miles from New York City. Some people would see that as derogatory but I don't mean it as such. I think the world of her.'

Dowd agreed to meet this strange English girl who had found herself caught up in the American criminal-justice system. Riker's is not his favourite place – 'one of the most godawful places in the world' – because it is a time-consuming way to spend a day and often difficult to concentrate on what a client is saying because of the screaming going on all the time in the background. Privacy is marginal.

He faced a dilemma, however, as Caroline was already represented by someone he knew: 'Paul Vladimir is a nice man who, up until the last day, would greet Caroline when he saw her in court so one should never think this was a man who didn't care what happened.'

The most remarkable thing he found about Caroline when he first saw her at Riker's was that 'this emaciated, drawn, pasty-coloured person in a pastel jump suit was shaking so badly that I felt I could not interrogate her.

'It was very hard at first to tell whether I was with someone with all their faculties,' he says, stubbing out the first of many Benson and Hedges menthol butts into a paper cup. 'I take my time so it was several months before I asked Caroline about the particulars of what happened that night. I worked on the borders about Alison. It's rude, if nothing else, to just burst into someone else's life regardless of whether you're a lawyer and I don't think you're likely to get much.

'What struck me was how young she looked, how young she acted, how vulnerable and naïve. I don't think I could have seen someone more bewildered than if she had arrived from Mars.'

Caroline remembers her first sight of her new attorney when he arrived at Riker's with Jackie: 'It sounds pathetic now but I remember telling Mother he looked like a giant teddy bear, the sort of person you could just hug. He looked so friendly with this nice boyish face. One of the first things he said to me was, "If you had been an epileptic and you'd fallen over and your arm had got broken, would you blame yourself?" and I said of course not. And he said, "Why do you think everyone blames you for all of this?" He said, "We're going to get you out of this," and I believed him from the moment I met him.'

Michael Dowd realized early on that it was essential that he get her bail so that he could properly prepare the case. He also feared for her sanity the longer she stayed inside. 'The idea that she's going to get good mental health care in Riker's Island is like suggesting that she's going to get good elective surgery in Bosnia or Iran. Forget it. I had to figure a way to get her out and the name of the game was we had to get the money for bail.'

Many of Dowd's friends are in the media – one close friend is Peter Maas, the author of the book on Serpico, the corruption-busting New York policeman, that was turned into a film by Sidney Lumet, starring Al Pacino – and he is, by any standards, a media-sharp lawyer. Like Meg Spinelli, he knew that the media had the financial resources to fund the experts he would need to present a proper case. He decided to approach journalists whom he believed would do an honourable job or who needed a break: 'I'm very sensitive to people who might need a break because they've taken a knock,' he says.

He had not reckoned on the British media. His first shock was that a woman from a British daily newspaper arrived at Riker's Island claiming to have brought presents to Caroline from her parents in England. In the event, Caroline decided that she did not want to see her but it gave Michael Dowd a clue that he was not going to be dealing just with the entertaining newshounds with whom he would share a bite at Elaine's, a fashionable Manhattan restaurant, or a drink after court. His initial strategy was to get the British press involved first, to get bail and the money for bail. 'The aim was to reach the American press nearer the trial when it might be important to create a climate to acquit.'

He knew from the start that he would be taking on Marjory Fisher and he knew her to be a tough operator. He started to work out his strategy for the trial. 'Here there are no rules. There is a somewhat naïve belief that you can always get a fair jury. You have to be somewhat stupid not to take your opportunities. Studies show that sixty-five per cent of people coming in are predisposed to convict, twenty-five per cent to acquit and ten per cent are undecided. If you get the opportunity to level the playing field, you take it. Essentially you have the prosecution and the police saying we have arrested this person who's killed a baby. O'Donnell had made some pretty distorted comments about the case, which were damaging. You have to do something to get back to even, which usually you never do.'

Dowd says that he would agree with Marjory Fisher on about 96–97 per cent of legal issues, which was an odd level of agreement to have with the average DA, he reckoned. He had noted her performance in a number of domestic violence cases and trials where the accused was a woman who had been subjected to violence. He had been impressed. 'This is not a reckless, irresponsible woman, but she let it become too personal. She said to me, "I'm a Jew from Ohio and here I am completely out of place." I thought she was going to be very tough as an adversary. I thought this was going to be no picnic, she was smart, I did a lot of research on her. I do a lot of research on the prosecutors – if I find they've got a bad knee I'm going to give it to them on the bad knee. She had a reputation for being tough but fair. Juries liked her.'

Dowd also believed that one of the reasons that Fisher felt driven to pursue the case against Caroline was a belief that the law should treat everyone equally. 'I think she thought, Here's this nice-looking white woman from England who gets Dowd the heavy hitter, and the five black women ahead of her don't have a dime, have lousy lawyers, get badly represented and end up in jail. Why should this woman walk away from it?'

This is a variation of the theme of the Great White Defendant whom Tom Wolfe immortalized in *The Bonfire of the Vanities*. Wolfe's thesis was that DAs who spent most of their time packing blacks and Hispanics off to jail were more than grateful when they were finally able to prosecute a reasonably privileged white person.

'From the beginning Marjory Fisher believed that Caroline

Beale was guilty, that she was morally and legally responsible for the death of that baby. She believed it from the beginning and she believes it now. Marjory Fisher is an interesting person. She agonized about the righteousness of her case throughout and she was secure in her decision and wasn't questioning whether she was right or wrong.'

There were other issues between them. Fisher reminded Dowd that he had been disparaging about her handling of another case, something he says he cannot remember. More friction developed between the two as the case went on.

'Marjory over-identified herself with the case. She couldn't accept that Caroline couldn't measure up to her standards and was not accepting of the idea that she could be excused from this act. I kidded her – "You and Camille Paglia would have made a great team, going round the country talking about female accountability." She was a true believer. She believed Caroline was a killer.'

As he contemplated the trial, Dowd looked at a variety of angles. He considered asking to have Marjory Fisher struck out of the case on the grounds that she could have been a witness because she had taken statements from Caroline immediately after her arrest. 'When it comes down to the nitty-gritty, if I could get rid of Fisher, that's good. I don't need a really good opponent, I like 'em when they're not good.'

The more he examined the case it became apparent to Dowd that right from the beginning the detectives and the District Attorneys had not believed Caroline's account because the autopsy had suggested that there had been oxygen in the baby's lungs. More damagingly, an initial pathology report that Paul Vladimir had had carried out for the defence appeared to agree with the findings of the prosecution. The case against Caroline with which he was confronted would be based on the autopsy's findings, Caroline's own statements to O'Donnell, who would be chief prosecution witness, and

Fisher. Already there was pressure from within the DA's office to settle the case, reach a plea-bargain agreement and consign Caroline at least to a period of incarceration. But the more Dowd studied the paperwork and the interviews, the more certain he became that here was a case he could win.

'I became completely convinced that Caroline Beale did nothing to cause the death of her baby. The most compelling part of the case – and you didn't have to be a rocket scientist or a doctor to understand it – was that this woman was carrying the baby on to a plane under a coat. Juries are ordinary people. She's doing something that by any standard is nuts! Bringing that baby on to the plane going through a metal detector. You can build back for the jury twenty-four hours to get them to understand that whatever happened in the hotel she was not responsible by reason of mental disease or defect. In layman's terms, she was insane at the time.'

Dowd likes the big dramas: the only two videos he has ever been given are *Citizen Kane* and *Dr Zhivago*, both stories with mighty themes and a certain timeless quality. He felt that another drama was unfolding and he did not want it to be a tragedy. He intensified his efforts to have Caroline granted bail even to the extent of offering to have her to stay with him and Irene, a highly unusual move for a lawyer to make. 'People survive jail but I didn't think she would. She was a woman-child. This was a kid who wouldn't hurt anyone consciously. I've been doing this twenty-five years and some pretty miserable human beings have walked through my door. You can almost smell it, sense it, what capacity of violence they have in them. But there's a cliff you have to climb to demonstrate that to a jury. This was a woman who couldn't hurt a fly.'

He began to prepare his strategy: he would find the best pathologists in the world who would be asked to assess whether it was possible for a baby that was still-born to have oxygen in the lungs. He would seek out the finest psychiatrists who had studied the behaviour of women who concealed their pregnancies or who behaved as Caroline had done afterwards. He would mount his media campaign to create a climate in which she could be tried sympathetically and he would adopt a high-profile approach to the case to let the DA's office know that he was not about to accept a plea bargain and see his client dispatched to the joyless cells of Bedford Hills Correctional Facility.

He was more than ready, he felt, for another high-profile trial. He already had more than two hundred jury trials under his belt and other attorneys were coming to court to watch him work. He thrived on it. 'I like a packed house,' he says, although he admits to having blown vital putts on the golf course in pro-am matches because people have been watching him play.

But already early on in Caroline's case there were complications. It had been suggested by Marjory Fisher that Paul should take a DNA test to prove whether or not he had been the baby's father. For Fisher and Detective O'Donnell, evidence that the baby was not Paul's would point towards a possible motive for murder: that Caroline had killed the child because Paul would have known she was not pregnant by him. Dowd was certain that the child had been Paul's and was deeply unhappy that there should be any suggestion otherwise. He made it clear to the Faraways that if they proceeded with the request, Dowd would personally let the British tabloid press know and leave them to do their damage.

'Caroline was in tears at the idea that the child was not his. But she was willing to have the test done to clear it up. That was her instantaneous reaction.' In the event, Paul declined to take the DNA test and the DA's office eventually dropped their attempts to persuade him to do so. Caroline herself recalls her reaction to the request for a DNA test. 'I was quite happy for that to happen although I was angry about it. I didn't have any problems with it. When I spoke to Paul on the phone, he said he didn't know anything about it.'

But as Dowd prepared the defence, he knew that there were already risks for Caroline. He would have preferred a Manhattan to a Queens jury because the former are reckoned to be more sophisticated and he knew he would be presenting a complex defence. He also had to liaise with the British Consulate, who were increasingly aware of the great interest being expressed in the case and how it was handled in the United Kingdom. 'The British government and Consul played it by the book. They never expressed an opinion about what should be the outcome of the case. If they had tried to, the judge would have jumped all over them.'

All the while Dowd was engaged in the time-consuming business of trying to get bail for an increasingly despondent and pessimistic Caroline. He had to temper his own optimism that she would soon be allowed out of jail with the reality that the DA's office was playing a tough game and was reluctant to let a foreigner out on bail on a serious offence. He had many telephone discussions with Peter Beale as they tried to achieve a package that would reassure the American authorities that she would not try to skip bail. The Beales' home in Chingford was valued at £90,000 which more than covered the required bail of £48,000. The British Consul was more than happy to give assurances that she would not be issued with a passport, and Michael Carter, before his transfer, then Michael Dwyer and Jackie Cerdan put their energy into finding her a place to stay on the outside. The court was unhappy at the idea of Caroline staying with her attorney – the idea seemed to blur the line between the client–lawyer relationship – although both Michael and Irene Dowd had said they were more than ready to have her until the trial.

Then, in May, the bail was agreed. Caroline emerged from the court building with Michael Dowd and the new British consul Michael Dwyer acting as her bulky minders. She managed to express, haltingly, her gratitude before being whisked off in Michael Dowd's car.

When the news came through, her cellmates were delighted: 'They rejoiced,' said Sister Marion. 'There was none of – "You got out because you're white, because you're middle class" – which they could easily have said. They were so happy. When I look at them and how they survive, I admire them.'

Sherain Bryant remembered the moment, too: 'We were all delighted for her. We celebrated.' A new chapter in Caroline's life was about to begin.

Chapter Fourteen

In March, when Caroline had spent nearly six months in prison, Meg Spinelli had given her a diary in which she inscribed: 'May this journal be filled with happy thoughts and memories . . . as only you deserve.' Caroline immediately started to write in it and continued to do so until her release. Her early hopes of a swift return to the outside world had faded and she now realized it might be many months or even years before she could hope to go home. She had made friends in prison, established a routine for herself and was mainly concentrating her hopes on getting bail. She was always anxious for news from Paul, but was buoyed up by visits from friends.

Saturday 18 March
We now have two new room-mates, Barbara and Deena. Deena talks to herself continually, a bit annoying in the middle of the night. She washes her clothes, then puts them in the locker wet and the water drips all over the floor. Mail came early today for a change. I got three letters so it's over 600 by now. Professor Brockington [Professor of Psychiatry at Birmingham University, and the author of *Motherhood and Mental Health*] came today, quite heavy-going but he really is such a dear and so easy to talk to. Spoke to Irene. She told me Mike [Dowd] is trying to arrange for me to go and stay with them until all this is sorted out, a kind of house arrest. I would have to work for him for my room and board but it would be worth it.

Sunday 19 March
Velma [one of her friends and cell-mates] did 30 sit-ups, I did 100. Phoned Meg early. She thinks living with Mike would be a wonderful idea . . . Velma and I get 241 (one cigarette in exchange for two later) from Becky. Sherry came to visit me. Sold a book of matches for a spoon of coffee and shared it. Velma's kids got here late and missed the visit.

Monday 20 March
Woke up at 5 a.m. to Shebass shouting over the microphone. 'Building 9 on the door for meal'. Crazy Deena was wandering around talking to herself. Mondays are really hard as people don't have any sweets or fags and there is no means of getting any. Nearly finished *Firelight and Woodsmoke,* a brilliant book. Spoke to Mum and Dad on the phone, as always really good to speak to them. It seems as though they are close even though they are far away. Mum has finished Meg's sweater. She is going to give it to Clare to bring over. I'm really looking forward to seeing her and Mandy. I hope they don't get lost trying to find the place. Everyone keeps telling me how awful it is to find.

Tuesday 21 March
I've just realized I have no money in my account. The first time we have shopped early for ages. I waited an hour for an escort to go the short distance to Sister Marion's office. She is hoping something will happen in court next Monday. So am I. We have another new room-mate Chris. She looks a bit like Jerry Lee Lewis. She's an alcoholic who at one point drank four pints of wine a day. She walks round in just a huge pair of underwear. This evening rushing to find Velma I hit myself on the head with the door, a huge lump has now come up. No mail today but plenty of fun. Chris is making us laugh, flirting light-heartedly with CO Byman. He's cool!

Wednesday 22 March
It's 8 in the morning and Clare, Mandy and Brian [Mandy's husband, a classic-car restorer]ob are all coming. I can't wait . . . Well, Clare and Mandy came. Brian had to wait outside with the cameras [visitors who arrive with cameras or tape recorders are not allowed in]. In a way I was relieved to be able to talk to them alone but I felt sorry for Brian stuck out in the cold for four hours, he must have been frozen. The visit lasted two and a half hours. I think we were all close to tears but it was a good visit. Sister Marion came to meet them. Clare could not believe she was a nun. And with an American accent. It just does not seem to fit. Clare said Sue Tinkler had married a guy whose surname is Allen but she does not want his name as Sue Allen sounds like an actress, Mandy says more like an alcoholic. [Sue Ellen was the heavy-drinking character in *Dallas*.]

Thursday 23 March
Mandy and Clare and at last Brian came. What a good time. When Clare saw how hairy my legs were she asked why we could not have razors. Typical Clare but I do love her. Malloy [the CO in the visit room] went through the package so they did not have to wait to see me. He let me have quite a lot of the stuff. The T-shirts even have my name on the sleeve. They called Venisa at about 6 this morning. She spent the whole day at the wrong hospital. A cock-up by the doc. What a complete waste of time and effort. She was really mad as well as tired by the time she got back. I was happy all night. New clothes, shampoo, deodorant. I feel like a new person.

Friday 24 March
Well, Mandy, Brian and Clare should be back home by now. I miss them already. I've written a small verse for them:

Friendship
When we measure our prosperity
We should take care to note
It's the friends you have
That matter
And the material things that don't.
We spend our whole lives
Acquiring our wealth
But these things mean nothing
Compared to life itself.
And though we are so far apart
Divided by the sea
There never were any truer friends
Than what you are to me.

This afternoon Crazy Doris tried to strangle Christy with a shoelace. She has a big burn mark around her neck but is okay.

Saturday 25 March
Phoned Meg early and managed to catch her before she left. Told her how much I missed Clare and Mandy already and how anxious I am about going to court on Monday. It's the stress as much as anything as well as it being so tiring that it knocks you out for a couple of days. I have told Velma if I leave on Monday to give my stuff to Sister Marion but to keep the things she wants including any clothes. Stuff like shampoo and stuff which you take for granted on the outside you really have to hold on to or it walks out of your locker before you can turn your head. Most people in here are okay, us in 43–48 [the dormitory] don't steal from each other.

Sunday 26 March
Began the day at 8 a.m. going to recreation. It was a bright and sunny morning. Venisa and I shot the ball through the hoop a few times. We were out for half an hour when Chris had a

seizure. When Venisa told the rec officer she said: 'And what am I supposed to do about it?' Then I went to church. It was quite a noisy affair with a gospel group. Went to see the doctor and had the normal 'I'm all right' conversation with him. Phoned Mike. He told me that the DA was not agreeable to me staying with him. Every time I feel that something might happen I get kicked in the balls again. Phoned Meg and Sister Marion, they were nearly as upset as I was. Mike says he has not given up.

Monday 27 March
Well, the day of court is here again. Up at 4.30 with that awful burning sensation in my eyes. Then to the receiving room to wait for 8 o clock when the bus comes. The worst bit is getting chained up. It always makes me begin to cry. Today there were 10 girls in court. The holding pen looks like it should hold about five at the most so there really is nowhere to sit. Mike came in at 11 to see me. He told me that Paul had phoned the DA and asked for a DNA test. [In fact, it was the other way round: the DA, Marjory Fisher, had wanted Paul to take a DNA test to prove that the baby was his. In the event, he declined.] He asked if it made me angry but angry is not the right word. It felt like being punched in the stomach and gasping for air it really hurt so very much. I just cannot believe that Paul would do that.

Tuesday 28 March
Getting back here yesterday was awful. We waited till 6.50 to get the bus back here to Riker's at 7.50 to the normal welcome of being stripped being told to take your pants down to your ankles and bounce up and down three times while the COs go through all your clothes. During the wait to get back to the housing area one of the girls tried to hang herself by tying a shoestring round her neck and jumping from the bars. The captain went charging in and handcuffed her. He was taking her to the clinic when from behind she put her arms over the top of his head and tried to strangle him. The COs had a field day in the wire meat pen. They really laid into her.

Duncan Campbell

Wednesday 29 March
I phoned Mum and Dad quite early. It was really good to speak
to them. They told me to phone at 11 a.m. on Friday as the
BBC people want to film them talking to me. Very strange. The
doctor came again today and we went through the now familiar
routine. I spoke to Sister Marion and told her what Mike had
said about Paul. She could not believe it. But I really can't
believe it. I really don't think Paul would do anything like that.
Talking about Paul, when I spoke to Sister Marion she said a
man with an English accent phoned her house when she was at
work. He didn't say who was calling nor leave a message. I have
a feeling it was Paul.

Thursday 30 March
Got called to Mental Health to see Miss J. She really makes me
feel very uneasy. While waiting to see her Sister Marion came
in. I went through to the chapel and Sister Jane was also there.
She said that Paul had phoned and would phone Sister Marion
at 2.00 and she would come and let me know what he had to
say. In the meantime Jackie came to visit. She had to wait one
and a half hours to see me. Had a row over what kind of soap
she was able to bring me. Anyway, after persuasion from Jackie
they eventually let me have it along with some paperbacks. As
always, so good to hear someone speak with an English accent.
True to her word, Sister Marion spoke to Paul. He is going to
phone at 2 tomorrow.

Friday 31 March
I've written a poem to Paul today and sent it just in a plain
aerogram letter. It is how I am hurting not being with him.

> *I needed you to love me*
> *I needed you to care*
> *But when I needed you most of all*
> *I found that you weren't there.*

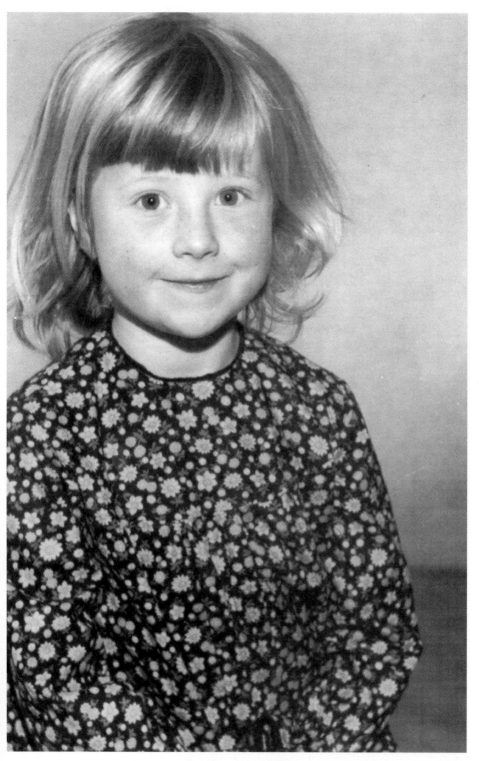

Caroline as a child

Above: Caroline with her
mother, Daphne

Left: Caroline's parents,
Peter and Daphne Beale.
(*Jez Coulson/Insight*)

Above: Caroline with Paul Faraway

Below: Caroline in Riker's Island. (*Ellen Binder*)

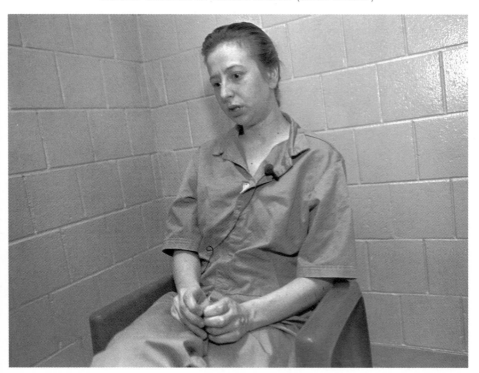

Above: Marjory Fisher

Below: Michael Dowd

Above: Meg Spinelli

Below: Professor Ian Brockington

Above: Father Tony, Caroline and Margaret Brower

Below: (Left to right) Caroline with Sister Marion, Meg Spinelli, Irene Dowd and Lauren Dowd (front)

Caroline with Michael Dowd (left), leaving court after pleading guilty to manslaughter. (*Associated Press*)

Judge Robert J. Hanophy. (*Associated Press*)

A Stranger and Afraid

I told you everything
And everything was true
But now I know my world alone's
Not good enough for you.

So if you really love me
You really have to say
It's going to take an awful lot
To ease the pain away.

Riker's Island, March '95

Saturday 1 April
Well, I spoke to him yesterday. He says he knows nothing about
a DNA test but he still does not say what I need to hear that he
loves me as much as I love him. I know he has been through a
lot but God knows so have I. If only he knew the half of what I
have been through and how hurt I have been. I needed him so
much. I haven't seen him for six months and I miss him like
crazy. Why won't he even come and see me? Think how I feel
when everyone else comes over and supports me but not the
person I love most in the world. God knows I gave him all the
love I had in my heart and it just seems he doesn't care.

Sunday 2 April
I have read a whole book today. The first time I have achieved
this. For lunch it was roast beef and yams. Velma ate the yams.
We managed at long last to get 241 from Becky. What a farce.
She always gets double what everyone else has and is always so
reluctant to give anything up. Mike has gone to the DA asking
him to reconsider the proposal. Let's hope he has some
influence in that department because I really don't know how
much more of this I can take. It would be just so good to be
back home to do things that we used to take for granted and see
the people who I love and care so very much about.

Monday 3 April
Today the clocks went forward so we are only five hours behind the UK. I went to Sister Marion's at 10. We had a good talk. I asked her if she thought this nightmare would ever end. She says it will soon. Once again I hope she is right. I spend the whole morning working as her assistant making phone calls for her. Well, it certainly made the morning go quickly. Came back here and phoned Mum and Dad way past the usual time. Missed Department of Correction lunch but had a lovely lunch with Sister Marion. Fresh bread and apples with herbal tea. It was lovely and peaceful. Dinner in the housing area was meat patties and pudding. The string beans were cold as usual but at least the patties were okay.

Tuesday 4 April
Today is Venisa's birthday. I have still to finish the card. At breakfast Velma managed to get a fag from Ebony, the girl who serves the food. But at least we can go shopping today. Cindy, the new girl, went to court so we all got woken up early. Got called to see Sister Marion. Araminta phoned at 2. It was so good to speak to her. I don't know how I can ever thank her enough for her support. I had a good long talk to Sister Marion and told her exactly how I was feeling. She really is so easy to talk to. She is going to phone Michael tonight to try and find out first hand what is happening and call me in the morning. I really don't know if I am strong enough to cope.

Wednesday 5 April
I have never really spoken to Cathy before. Having a long talk with her the other day in Sister Marion's office I guess she is going through the same small changes I experienced when I first came to this place. The loneliness, the fear, the loss of self dignity, the hunger (and that really does exist). The worst thing of all is going to bed hungry and drinking water to fill yourself up. This place is hell on earth. I think if a judge or DA was to

spend a month here they would certainly be more hesitant about incarcerating people in this place. There must be some other way of doing things. Well, I guess America is not all that it purports to be. It really is a land of the haves and the have-nots.

Thursday 6 April
The foundation of true strength is a gentle loving nonresistant attitude . . .' *Daily Word*, April '95

Phoned Mum and Dad, Caroline and Steve. Am trying not to get over-anxious about phoning Michael. It's very hard not to clutch at straws the whole time. Velma and Venisa went back to court yesterday so it was very peaceful. Flores is on duty which always makes the place seem a bit more cheerful. He is one of the only officers who have an ounce of human feeling. Chrissy got a letter from home which really cheered her up. Evidently she left home at eleven and travelled round the country with truck drivers until she ended up in New York living on the streets or in shelters stealing from stores and earning money through prostitution, a really bad existence. I'm gonna have to start using two pages a day!

Friday 7 April
'One must be poor to know the luxury of giving.' *George Eliot*

I spoke to Michael last night. He said that the DA has agreed to the no money part of the package but they are still not happy about me staying with him. But he says that he is hopeful that they will change their minds. Well, at worst it's a 50/50 shot. Velma has gone back to court today. It's always really quiet when she's not here. I managed to evade Miss J. Sister Marion is going to start her crusade against Jack Ryan [from the District Attorney's office]. I hope he is open to her power of persuasion. The little birds are back at the window. They are similar to sparrows in size but with bright red heads. It must mean spring is here. They are looking for stuff to build their nests. Spoke to Sister Marion. Things looking good.

Saturday 8 April
'Nothing in life is to be feared. It is only to be understood.'
Marie Curie

Venisa's shampoo has gone missing. Charlotte and Denise took Cindy's in retaliation and changed it into a different bottle. Phoned Jackie and told her about Sister Marion and Meg phoning round their friends to find me somewhere to live. She said things are looking very promising on that front. Michael is still Plan One. We had those awful sausages for lunch and cold potatoes and cold plums with two slices of bread. Velma found out that Cindy stole my shampoo and sold it for one cigarette to one of the girls next door. The Mystery of the Disappearing Shampoo has been solved. Jackie is going to get me a pair of jeans. I'm really looking forward to having something to wear.

Sunday 9 April
'If writing did not exist, what terrible depressions we would suffer.' *Sei Shangan*

Got up early. Talked to Venisa about her early childhood in Jamaica. She was thinking too much! Had a shower and tried to go back to sleep. No luck. Had lunch at 11. Turkey and rice. Tried to eat as much as I could but I have no appetite. I guess I'm apprehensive about what will happen next week [when she was to apply for bail]. Last night I dreamed that the Boon Squad [riot squad] were walking up and down Station Road beating people up with their sticks. I thought a lot about Paul today and how much I am missing him. What I would do if he was to leave my life period. I can't even look at photos any more, they just make me feel fearful and alone. And make me remember all I have lost.

Monday 10 April
'The logic of the heart is absurd.'

It's 3 and lock-in. There are none of the regular officers here
today. The officer in the bubble was screaming, 'Ladies, lock
your arses in.' Venisa and Velma are playing Zap [a card game].
The others are asleep. I earned two fags from Denise making a
card. Saved one for Velma. Went to see Sister Marion this
morning. She is confident something will happen later today or
tomorrow. Wouldn't that be great. Maybe I should phone Paul.
I don't really know what to do. If I do will I just end up getting
upset? I don't know if it's worth it. Then again, I feel that I
really want to. Mike and Nick [Catliff] from BBC [the *Inside
Story* team] are coming in the morning. These things are always
stressful but it could be worth it in the end! Will Bynam manage
the impossible and get Velma a fag?

Tuesday 11 April
'The source of justice is not vengeance but charity.' *Bridget of
Sweden*

Called for visit at 10.30. Once again lots of lights and cameras
and stress even though they are really nice people. Daniel
[Jeffreys, of the *Independent*] asked me if I ever think about
Olivia. Of course I do. Not a day goes past when I don't think
about her and what she, Paul and I would be doing as a family.
Now I just feel I have lost everything and it just gets too much
to cope with. Now Michael tells me that Marjory Fisher says
that Paul has a lawyer in the States. [His father had arranged for
an English lawyer now practising in the US to represent him if
this became necessary over DNA tests.] I really can't believe
that is true. What possible reason would there be for that? He
would have told me if he was going to do that.
  [Stuck to the diary entry for that day is a poem entitled
'The Gift of Friendship' and dedicated to Caroline, Venisa

and Velma from Chrissy, who was due to leave jail the following
day:

> Friendship is a priceless gift,
> That cannot be bought or sold
> But its value is far greater than a mountain made of gold . . .
> So when you ask God for a gift,
> Be thankful if he sends,
> Not diamonds, pearls or riches,
> But the love of a real true friend.
> Amen.]

Wednesday 12 April
> *I need your love, I need your touch*
> *But just to see your face would mean so much.*

Phoned Mum and Dad. Spoke for only two minutes before time
ran out. Jackie came this morning. Brought me some clothes,
new shampoo and two suits which Jenny lent to me for court. I
went to the commissary but the money had not cleared so I
have to go back in the morning. I hope Becky can wait that long
or else I will wake up with two black eyes as I owe her two
packs of ciggies. Mary Alice lent me two Bear Claws which I'm
going to give back tomorrow. Please let something happen soon.
I want to be home so very much. Even out of here would be a
blessing. But when?

Thursday 13 April
'Any mind that is capable of real sorrow is capable of good.'

Had breakfast with Chrissy this morning as she is leaving today.
Velma put her hair in paper rollers made from a brown bag and
I gave her some clothes. She still did not receive the money
order her Mum had promised to send her. I really expect that
she will be back here before too long. I learned to play Zap

today and even won. It must be beginner's luck. One of the officers in the bubble looks like he is having a hair transplant. Cathy said it was called the Helsinki Treatment and she has seen it on the TV. No news yet from anyone about getting out of here. I really am beginning to doubt it will ever happen. Mike says he is hoping to get me home by my 31st which means another whole two months of this wretched existence.

Friday 14 April
Today is Good Friday. I phoned Mike and spoke to Irene. She said Mike spoke to Paul for quite a while yesterday. I am glad that they have spoken at long last. Sister Marion has not been at home all day and the consul is closed so I could not phone home. We played Zap for most of the day. Velma won. We are on the monthly search so I have hidden most of my things under the locker. Gaskin [a CO] would not check for the mail today but he gave Velma three bananas, God knows why. A Spanish girl moved in for a few hours then moved out after us being so nice as well. I'm going to phone Meg tonight. After today only three more days till Tuesday. Please let something happen.

Saturday 15 April
> *Better by far you should forget and smile*
> *Than you should remember and be sad.*

We played Zap and 500 [another card game] all night as the new girl in our room snores so loudly it wakes you up from the deepest sleep. Phoned Sister Marion. She said she was going to phone Mike with details of her sister's living arrangements. I don't think Sister Marion is going to be right about something happening on Monday. I only wish she were right and I was out of here. I want to go home so much I'm tired physically as well as mentally. Our other room-mate is a bull dagger/aggressor or the male half of a lesbian couple. Velma says she's not worried as the girl sleeps next to me.

Sunday 16 April
'If you get through the twilight, you'll live through the night.'

The monthly search for contraband happened during lock-in.
Although all our stuff was hidden we really got away lightly as
they only did the downstairs housing area. The aggressor is only
in this housing area to get out of going to the bing [punishment
area]. She told them Elvis was telling her to OD on Tylenols.
Phoned Mike and asked him if there was any chance of me
getting out of here on Tuesday. He said it's possible but not to
get my hopes up. I hope Sister Marion's miracle happens.

Monday 17 April
Once again I have been up for most of the night, partly the
snoring and partly Tina waking up and screaming. Also the stress
of yet another uncertainty in court on Tuesday. If only I had
some idea of what, if anything, is going to happen. The thought
of yet another day in that bullpen [the holding cell for prisoners
appearing in court] makes me feel physically sick. I spoke to
Irene. She said Fisher has not made any decision about the tapes
yet [the tape-recorded interviews conducted by Fisher in
hospital, the day after Caroline's arrest]. She agrees I am no
threat to society and that I won't leave the country. Sister
Marion's sister is the ace card if they don't agree to me being
with him [Mike and Irene]. He is working really hard today. MF
is phoning back at 10 tonight. I really hope it's good news. I'm
gonna try and phone Meg. Fingers X.

Tuesday 18 April
Up at 4.30 to go to court and another disappointing day. Mum
and Dad are putting their house up for bail. Mike says we are
closer than we have ever been. MF has to check with her boss
and if he agrees then I have to go stay at a hospital. Officer Scatt
lent me a fag. The DA has found a psychiatrist [Dr Naomi
Goldstein, who would interview and assess Caroline on behalf of

the prosecution]. Mike said it could be six days. MF said Mike
was full of shit. Mike said she was too ambitious for her own
good and that she was persecuting not prosecuting me. [This
exchange, since denied by both parties, appeared in the press at
this time.] I'm writing in the bullpen of the court. There are
seven of us in a tiny, tiny room. God, I hope we are on the first
bus back or we will be here till seven.

Yes, Mike, Mum and Dad and Sister Marion and Meg have
done it. The DA has agreed to bail. With the help of Mum and
Dad I can choose where I want to go. I'm going to go to Mike's
and Irene's.

I met a guy in the bullpen. Very strange. He sent the officer
over with a box of cigs and a note. Then he sent over another
box. The girls in the court were really pleased as they had not
smoked all day. The first bus left the court by 2.30. They could
not take the women. By the time we got back to Rose M. Singer
centre it was 6.00, then had to wait three hours for an escort
and to be searched.

Wednesday 19 April
I went to see Sister Marion. Gave her some books to hold and
phoned Mum and Dad. I told them about the DA agreeing to
me staying with Mike and Irene. I don't think they wanted to
get too excited unless it turned out not to be true. This made
me doubt myself a bit so I had to phone Irene and double-check
and I was right. They first have to get the papers together and
let the DA have them. Then I can go. I had a row this morning
over would you believe it fags. Crazy but true, very sad, isn't it?
But Charlotte sorted it out. Velma was upset today. I made a
promise that I would write to her once a week and I'm going to
do that. I know that letters are one of the key aspects to survival
in this place.

Thursday 20 April
Phoned Mum and Dad early. Gary in London had phoned them
to say that Mike Dwyer [now the British Consul] had to go to
court to tell them he won't give me a visa. I can't wait to get out
of this hell hole. Velvet [a prisoner who was briefly housed with
Caroline] is going back to GP [general population]. She was
only here to beat her ticket [avoid punishment by pretending to
be crazy] and now the 72 hours has passed maybe we will get
some sleep tonight. Velma is feeling a bit low at the moment. I
guess as the time gets nearer for her to go upstate all the length
of time begins to sink in. I doubt in England she would ever be
in this situation and she would be treated as a heroine rather
than a criminal. She thinks I'm looking forward to air, walking
and not hearing the sound of jangling keys.

Friday 21 April
> *What right does some man have to be*
> *In control of another man's destiny.*

Today I wanted to try and describe the inside of this housing
area in case in the future it begins to fade from my memory.
The walls are painted an insipid shade of green and the halls in a
dirty yellow. Downstairs in the day area an array of plastic
furniture occupies most of the space with a small TV at one end
which daily churns out soap operas from 9 a.m. till 11 p.m.
Surrounding this area are the single cells. Upstairs are the basic
six beds and one toilet with a sheet tied up for privacy. Today
nothing much has happened. I lost both my phone calls trying to
get hold of Mum and Dad so I now won't be able to talk to
them until Monday. And I also wanted so much to speak to Paul
and let him know the good news. Hopefully he will phone Mike
in the week. No mail today and none yesterday so I don't know
if there is any and they can't be bothered to get it or what.
Venisa got a visit from her baby and his social worker so she was
just over the moon when they called her. I do hope that the visit

goes well for her. Velma woke up in a bad mood but has been playing cards all morning. I managed quite a lot of sleep as Tina was not dancing round the room all night with the Walkman on. It really freaks me out when she does this slow motion dance and then laughs to herself. Velvet has gone back to GP and two new girls have arrived. One is a really strange-looking Spanish girl, the other has been asleep since she arrived in the early hours. I really hope Flores is working tonight as it really is gonna be a long evening. This is the second day with no hot water. Yesterday I just dived under the shower. It was freezing. What's worse – dirt or cold – I really don't know.

Saturday 22 April
Spent the first part of today with Velma in Cathy's room. The new girl in the dorm is dope-sick. She messed the toilet and was sick all over the floor. It stinks in here. It's only 7 in the morning and already Velma is on a cleaning binge. Mike told me yesterday that they don't want me staying with him but I'm going to be staying with a woman Sister Jane knows who lives close by him. So I guess I will be with Irene during the day and at night with this lady. I really hope I get some mail today. I wish Paul would write. Tina got me a cig which I clipped [stubbed out] till after lunchtime. Crazy, isn't it, one between three people. B is the escort and he makes people wait. I guess he sees it as part of his job to be as nasty and rude as possible. I hope we get some mail today. Velma has not heard from Patrick (who is in an English jail) in a month. Velma's upset because the dope-sick girl has soiled underwear and vomit in the bed and it's making the room stink as she does not clear it up. Velma's going to throw it away. She's paranoid about catching something. It's the second time she has disinfected the floor today. I love you Mum and Dad and Paul.

> *Sister Marion you came to me,*
> *You gave me hope and strength*

When all around was adversity
You were the one person I could count on
When I was completely alone
When I felt everyone was gone
You gave me the strength to see
That many people love and care about me.
So how can I thank you
Where will I start
If only words could express
The love for you that's in my heart.

Velma's kids came to visit. Miracle has had her hair put into braids.

Sunday 23 April
Got up early and went to church with Velma, Venisa and Sherry. Phoned Sister Marion. Found out Choc [Araminta, who got her nickname because a friend had shortened her name to Mint, thus Mint Choc Chip] is going to phone at 2 on Monday. Looking forward to speaking to her. In a way I am scared to come away from this place because in an awful way it has become familiar. I spoke to Irene a while ago. She says I will be spending a lot of time with her and I can stay over whenever I want to. The other lady lives only five minutes away which is really good. Davis and Williams worked today so I'm hoping Flores will work tonight. Velma and I played Zap. She won every game. One of the crazy girls threw all the furniture upside down then tore down the shower curtain. We've improvised with an old sheet which only just about does the job. It's a bit embarrassing really as the COs in the bubble can see directly in! For some reason Sundays feel so much worse than the rest of the week. Hopefully this may be the last one in this place. Wouldn't that be wonderful and it could really happen. Mike did say five or six days and by that it works out to be Thursday of next week. Please let this be right.

Just tried to phone Meg but she's not there again. Flores got attacked by Claudia who hit him round the head with a Walkman and he now has a gash down the side of his face. I could understand if it was Gaskin or one of the others but he's about the best we have in this place.

Monday 24 April
Had to go and see Miss J. It really is awful having to go down there and talk to her and then wait hours for an escort to go back. Choc rang dead on 2, it was really good talking to her and hearing the news from home. Also I was able to talk to Sister Marion for a while. Another new Spanish girl came to the dorm tonight. Tina spent the whole night running water and laughing to herself. It really is freaky. Venisa says they run water when they really start to bug out.

Tuesday 25 April
I've no money to shop today. This morning Tara collected all the fags. She collects these and apple seeds and threatens to send them to starving people in Africa. It does not seem anything is going to happen today. Maybe in the morning. Today Williams, Davis and Gaskin have on their best CO uniforms and everyone is frantically cleaning due no doubt to the visit of the Commissioner in the imminent future. A bit like Herbert Lamming visiting LR [London Region] really!

1.10 they went to the shop taken there by a really arrogant individual who knows people will do just about anything he wants in return for being taken to buy fags and cakes. He uses this power to its full advantage. I had not had anything sweet for nearly two weeks. Hopefully Denise will pay me today for the cards I'm making her. Ryan is even being nice at the moment, yesterday he took my pencils to sharpen. The test of course is if he will bring them back today. Oh, forgot to mention Cindy. She's a new room-mate. At last we have a decent room again. She can also braid hair which is a real blessing as mine is getting beyond a joke. I dread going to the beauty parlour after the way they cut it last time. Irene says she is coming Thursday or Friday with this woman Julie [Wheelwright, a freelance journalist who was writing an article for the *Guardian* Weekend] who Dad told me about. Crack is evidently a good high but has fucked-up consequences. This girl robbed a preacher's house in the Bronx. When she gets out she's going to give a serious donation to the church.

Wednesday 26 April
Velma has been in jail nine months today. What a thing to celebrate. I have been to see Sister Marion for nearly three hours today and it was as if a miracle happened because earlier today I said to Velma how much I wanted to speak to her. [Sister Marion was in the prison three days a week and often had to see other prisoners.] I spoke to Sister Jane about her friend Margaret. Venisa said it would be a good idea to sell dildos in the commissary for sexually frustrated women. Don't know that the commissary man would agree to that. Some chance! I made up my mind to have my hair cut short as soon as I get out of here. At the moment it feels like Mike's weeks and days are dragging on and on. Phoned Meg and spoke to her for half an hour. Told her how angry I was at the way they had treated me, how angry I am with the doctors here and the therapist who have offered no form of help to me at all. And how sorry I feel for people who get lost in this barbaric system.

Thursday 27 April
Today for some unknown reason which is rumoured to be a bomb threat we have been locked in for two hours since 10.30 this morning with nothing to eat since five this morning. Venisa has got cinnamon rolls. The plan is to get it from Darlene as 241 and then replace Venisa's. We have sent a note via the SPA [Suicide Prevention Aide] and are hoping for a positive reply. Had to eat in the dorm. We must have been locked up for most

of the day. It was not a bomb scare, they were searching the
whole jail for drugs. Phoned Sister Marion. She is going to call
me for Catholic service on Saturday. Irene is coming in the
morning with this woman, Julie. I hate having to talk to these
people. I just wish Paul would contact me. I miss him so much.
I'm sure he blames me for all of this. I wish he would talk to me
about how he feels. I wish he would talk to someone.

Friday 28 April
Well, they came to interview me today. I really hope it was for
the last time. It was the first interview which went okay. Irene
was there as well, it was really nice to see her, she is a real dear.
[Irene Dowd attended many of the interviews Caroline did with
journalists.] She says I'm gonna get out of here soon. Only one
shower is working again and the water is freezing cold. It was a
case of just jumping straight in and out. The CO from
downstairs says they're gonna collect my books from the front
desk but I don't hold out much expectation. Seeing is believing
as you never can take these people at their word. I'm so hungry
at the moment, nothing has turned up yet. I got mail today and
a letter from the guy I met in court and a poem he wrote for
me! A bit of a worry really.

[She kept the letter. It read: 'Caroline, I like you for a friend
(smile). I am not like other men you may have had in your
country (not a freak for panties). My intentions are to please not
tease you as long as you're in this country . . . Send me a
picture. I promise no one will see it and you will never have to
worry about it getting stolen because my name rings bells in
here, meaning that guys in here would never even think about
violating me.' It included the poem he had written for her:

> *I ask God in heaven to send her to me*
> *One who will hold me and set my heart free*
> *I sit here in patience with bars all around*
> *I've infinite patience and won't make a sound.'*]

Saturday 29 April
Went to Catholic service taken by Sister Marion. It was really
nice. Came back and read one of Julie's books. Went to Sister
Marion's office and stayed for a couple of hours. It was really
reassuring having a normal conversation in a quiet atmosphere.

Sunday 30 April
Today was one of those awful Sundays. Tina kept me up for
most of the night. A fight on the line at lunch-time resulted in
Williams locking the whole of the house down. I'm getting a bit
pessimistic about anything happening next week. Sister Marion
seems to think it will, I really hope this time she is right. I know
Mike has to get it right but it's so very hard, each day seems
endless and I miss everyone so much.

Monday 1 May
Went to Sister Marion's this morning. Had a good talk with her.
Phoned Mum and Dad. Christine who left just a couple of
weeks ago is now back after stealing a wallet off a woman
attending a hospital. She says she missed us. She now has to do
six months in this place. I'm so hungry and they did not save me
any lunch. Well, spring is now coming to an end. But there is
still no end to this turmoil. When will it all end? When will I
ever be home? Sister Marion came down after lock-in to tell me
Paul had phoned and that he was concerned and that he would
phone at 1.45 tomorrow. I'm really looking forward to speaking
to him.

Tuesday 2 May
I did manage to go back to sleep after breakfast. I've been
making Mother's Day cards, quite a profitable business as there
is no chance to buy anything like that here at the moment. I'm
waiting to be called to Sister Marion's to speak to Paul while
everyone else is waiting to go to commissary. What a really sad
place this is: the COs with their almost sadistic approach to the

girls in here, the feelings of horror, the loss of dignity. Brenda – grandma – left this morning to go upstate. She was a really quiet woman, about 50 I suppose, she really did not look the part of the criminal at all. I had to make a card for Charlotte as I owe her cigarettes and she was going to beat me up. They just called for the commissary. I hope I get some things to eat from someone. I am just so hungry. Maybe this time next week this will all be a thing of the past. And all that is available on the outside will seem like it was always available and all this will seem like a memory.

Wednesday 3 May
The pen ran out today. No chance of another until Chrissy steals one from one of the officers. The intolerable noise of fighting and shouting continues. Went to see Sister Marion and we tried to get hold of Meg but she was not available. So phoned Mum and Dad. Had a long talk which was nice. Also phoned Caroline and Steve, it was good to be able to speak to them. Jackie is coming to visit in the morning and things look like they are moving at last.

Thursday 4 May
This morning they woke us up at 2.45 a.m., the reason being that they have taken Velma upstate in the bus. I'm really feeling very sad about it. She was the last of the original people in this room and now she's gone. She left me a legacy of a battered old T-shirt and a book that says Jesus Loves You. At least Jackie is coming to see me and it will sort out the problem with Charlotte and the cigarettes I owe her. Either that or she's gonna beat me up. Michael said they wanted to photograph some of the artwork [the drawings she had done in prison] in the *Guardian*. Well, it will give Paul's mum a laugh anyway as she never thought through playing Pictionary that I was particularly good at anything I tried to draw. Maybe all the practice has paid off!

Friday 5 May
It's so hot in here today that it's almost unbearable. Spoke to Mum and Dad. They said that all the papers would be with Mike by Tuesday so it would be some time next week that I will be out of here. I miss Velma and she's only been gone a day. Hopefully Flores will be working tonight. Roll on this time next week! I got a really nice card from my cousin who I have not seen for years and a nice one from Jackie as well. That cheered me up a great deal. Mike, please get me out of here and home. I miss everyone so much. It's so hard to keep being brave but you have to for all the people who support you through these long and lonely days.

Saturday 6 May
Another weekend. It's at the weekend I miss Paul the most, even the arduous trip to Sainsbury's seems more pleasant than another day here. I tried to phone Meg but for some reason the number was not accepted.

Monday 8 May
Went to see Sister Marion and phone Mum and Dad. While I was there an English [prison] warden visited the housing area. I hope she realized what a disgrace this place is in a land that purports to be fair and just. Apart from the normal humdrum, nothing much else happened. And I'm not gonna phone Michael with the call I have left. Instead I'm gonna try and get hold of the elusive Dr S [Meg Spinelli].

Tuesday 16 May
Today quite a lot has been going on. [It had finally been agreed that she would be released.] Choc phoned, also spoke to Mum and Dad. I received some photos from Sandra which was nice though they made me quite sad. Yesterday the ordeal of going to court was made worse by the fact that transport was delayed until 11 o'clock, then they took myself and another in a small

van. They waited until they were outside the jail until they
pulled over on the side of the road to chain me up. This was
after we had spent from 5 a.m. asleep on the floor of the
bullpen. Mike says I have to make a statement to the press
tomorrow about being glad to get out etc. He says we can't
avoid it and it will stop them hounding us. I am really nervous,
never being one to like the spotlight. I'm still tired after getting
back so late yesterday.

Chapter Fifteen

A neat flower-bed of red and white Busy Lizzies, a small pine by the front step, a couple of cats called Nutmeg and Juliet, a basketball hoop above the entrance to the garage, squirrels in the back yard, a neatly trimmed lawn. You might almost expect Norman Rockwell to emerge from behind his palette and say, 'Will this do?' The house at Number 45–47 171st Street in Flushing, Queens, could have been lifted off the cover of the *Saturday Evening Post* for its reassuring all-American calm and 1950s serenity. It was less than a fifteen-minute drive from Riker's Island yet a million miles away from the six-woman cells and the baleful cries in the night.

At one end of the street is the well-tended cemetery where one of Flushing's most celebrated former residents, Louis 'Satchmo' Armstrong, is buried, at the other a Jewish charitable institution. The front gardens are neatly tended and it is the kind of place where neighbours help each other shift the snow in New York's harsher winters. Queens, named after Queen Catherine of Braganza, the wife of Charles II, does not have the street credibility of other parts of New York, like Greenwich Village or Brooklyn, but it is the city's largest borough and the only one where the average black wage is higher than the average white. The neighbourhood was mainly white, originally Irish–Italian–Polish, heavily Christian – both 'churched and unchurched' – now becoming increasingly Asian, Korean and Chinese, with few black or Hispanic faces. The immediate neighbours were schoolteachers, nurses, a fireman. The houses, built in the 1920s, sold now for around $250,000.

It was here that a somewhat apprehensive Caroline arrived to stay after being granted bail. She did not know then whether she would be there for days or months or how her hosts would react to a woman charged with killing her baby. Her first impression was of the stern family portraits of the Gruners and Hoenighausens, the Germanic forebears of the Browers, whose unbending expressions lined the stair walls. There were books of French cooking and Irish short stories next to *Household Blessings and Prayers*, Chinese checkers and dominoes and a dozen toys awaiting the visit of Brower grandchildren. She spotted a cuckoo clock.

All she knew was that she was being taken in by someone from a prayer group, something that gave her a slight sense of foreboding, as someone who had little faith in the organized Church, despite her recent encounter with Sister Marion and Jane Leggett. Would she be expected to pray, to affect an interest in religion that did not exist, in order to justify the hospitality she was receiving?

Margaret Brower met her at the door, a widow of fifty-four – her husband, a laboratory supervisor in a now defunct hospital, had died five years earlier – with brown hair swept back over an open face. From a German–American family, she had married Bill Brower at eighteen and raised seven children, all now working except for the youngest two who were at college. Her house was well known in the neighbourhood for having an open-door policy for waifs and strays, teenage boys who had fallen out with their parents and had been sleeping in the back of their Buicks, unmarried mothers from disapproving families, four stranded French-exchange students who had ended up staying a month.

Margaret had brought up her family before taking a degree in liberal arts at Queens Borough Community College and starting a master's degree in archaeology. She had then

143

seen an advertisement for an airline company at La Guardia airport that offered part-time work and full flight benefits – $5 trips for her and her family – for a relatively small number of hours. She started work and travelling, even flying on a whim to Florida to meet her brother for lunch. Eighteen months later her husband had died. After eight years in the travel business, she realized that she was more interested in where people were going and why than in selling them tickets. She gave up her job and became a social worker with Catholic charities for the homebound elderly, providing meals on wheels and transport to doctors on behalf of the Department for the Ageing.

Her children were scattered now: Marybeth, the eldest at thirty-six, lives with her husband, Darryl, in Safety Harbor, Florida; Robert worked in construction in Long Island and was married to Angel; Theresa, married to a childhood sweetheart, was a nurse; William also worked in construction and lived nearby with his police officer wife, Ro; John was married to Rosa, who worked as an analyst for a financial company; Barbara was then twenty, a psychology student just about to join a Jesuit volunteer corps in Phoenix, Arizona; Paul, the youngest at nineteen, was at college in Rochester, studying communications and philosophy.

Barbara, an idealistic young woman who was about to head south to work with teenagers at risk was enthusiastic about the new arrival, anxious to help someone in trouble. Paul was less than pleased, feeling that his mother had no right to ask yet more people into his home. Some of Margaret's other sons were wary, concerned that she was now giving a home for an indefinite period to someone from jail – 'What are we going to do with Mom, now she's taking in people from Riker's Island?' asked Theresa, who was the most sceptical about the new arrival. Did this mean that Mom was about to embark on a new phase of her life, giving house-space to felons with hard-luck stories? Margaret told them gradually what was happening but all of them, perhaps inevitably with such a large family, felt that they were the last to know.

Of all the children, Barbara was most positive: 'I thought it was wonderful. My mom kind of explained and I knew that Caroline was being accused of killing her baby. My mom didn't judge her, she knew that she needed to be in a safe house. I didn't know about the case but I did my own research. She kept very much to herself at first and would go up into her room when there were a lot of us around. You could tell that stuff was going on in her head. She was kind of nervous. I wasn't nervous about my mom having her to stay because I trust my mother's judgement and she was always taking people in.'

Barbara noticed how Caroline changed gradually during her stay and how her sense of humour came out: 'My mom can be very particular about putting things back in the right place and Caroline would make a point of putting all the knives and forks back in the wrong place. Some of my brothers and sisters had a very different attitude.

'When I first learned about it I thought – Ohmygosh! – but I watched a woman who was struggling and who was trying to sort out her words and feelings and she became a friend. I have a great faith in God and I watched a miracle happen. She taught me a lot. To see someone come back from what she had gone through and stand on her own two feet was a lesson. I never brought up what happened on the night. A friend of mine had shown me on the Internet and I felt her presence was like a social injustice in our country.' Barbara's boyfriend was the manager of a cinema in nearby Port Washington and she and Caroline would watch films together. For her birthday, they went to the Jekyll and Hyde theme pub in the East Village. 'I would take her out with my friends and, as far as they were concerned, she was just someone staying with my mother. There was no need to tell everyone about it, my mom's always taking people in so only my best friend and my boyfriend knew. She is just a human being and yet everyone was so quick to judge her without knowing what had really happened, just the fact that she had been arrested and been in prison was enough.'

But Theresa says, 'I thought – what next? We thought at first that she should have been sent back to England so that she didn't cost America all the money it cost to house her.' Of all Margaret's children she was, perhaps, the most direct with Caroline and would quiz her about prison when the others felt that they did not want to probe into what was obviously such a raw subject.

William says, 'This is an after-school horror story. We couldn't believe it and I wasn't keen at first.' But he would sit with Caroline in the back yard as the squirrels scuttled across under the weary gaze of the cats – a previous cat would eat them leaving only the bones – and talk about everything but the case.

Paul and Caroline would argue and she would face him down, which Margaret thought was healthy for both sides. Paul objected not to the fact that a prisoner was coming to stay but that anyone was coming to stay in his home, which he felt had been invaded too often by strangers in the past. 'He would never eat anything I cooked, just to be a pig,' says Caroline.

John described having people to stay in the house as a hobby of his mother's. 'We were protective of her and concerned about Caroline. I thought, She's lost it this time. It was a horror movie. It was shocking and I didn't tell people. I didn't ask Caroline about what had happened at all and I didn't really know the details until the 20/20. My brothers and sisters would say things like "What's up with the criminal?" Caroline hated the [legal justice] system but that's true of anyone who's in the system and I understood that. When they showed the local station and her on the train on television, I thought any journalist could have tracked her down here and I was surprised they didn't.' Margaret's grandchildren soon got used to Caroline. Theresa's son Jes would say: 'How long are you going to be here – five years? Ten years?'

Much of this passed Caroline by, so relieved was she that she was out of jail. She had recorded her first day's freedom in her diary:

What a relief to have a bath and shave my arms and legs yesterday. Mike had told me there were going to be press people outside the court but what a lot there were with loads of cameras and lights. I felt so weak coming out, I felt I was going to collapse. Mike had both sides of me. Meg phoned and we are going to Manhattan to see her in the morning. Irene and I are going to take a walk around the park. The sun is out, the day is beautiful and warm. What a contrast to a couple of months ago when life seemed so desolate and not worth carrying on. I must remember to write to the girls in the jail as I did make a promise to them and I really do want to stick to it. How good the first cup of real coffee tasted yesterday. To be able to breathe in the air and to be able to walk without an escort or the restrictions of a CMC set-up: handcuffs, body chain and ankle shackles.

Although we have a long way to go, life this morning improved 100 per cent from even the day before yesterday and it almost now feels as if Riker's Island is just a painful memory for me. But in perspective for thousands of other women, the nightmare continues on a daily basis and if it were not for Sister Marion and Jane would be far, far worse. I wonder if Paul is good and what he is thinking. Maybe he will phone but it's in his hands and I will not push him as his mother has made it clear that she does not want me to! But it would be so good if he still loved me and wanted me.

A week later she recorded a visit to Meg Spinelli. 'I have been going to see Meg twice a week, she really is a great help to me. When I come out of her office, it is almost like a huge weight has been lifted off my shoulders and the burden seems that much lighter. She is just so easy to talk to. The fact that she believes in me is a great help as she makes me feel much more positive about myself as well as this situation.'

The prayer group to which Margaret Brower belonged, and which was the route that had brought Caroline to 171st Street, consisted of eight people who met every two weeks at eight p.m. in one of their homes. They would read the scriptures together, discuss a chosen text, 'share' their feelings, pray and socialize briefly over cakes and sometimes not entirely reverent jokes before breaking up at around eleven. They are from the tradition of active, maverick Catholics and would talk of the splits within the Church and of the approaching presidential elections, of the new, harsher welfare laws, of the problems faced by Mexican immigrants. Anything could be discussed but nothing said was meant to go outside the room. There was a priest, Father Anthony Ercolano, an ex-priest married to a former widow, a divorced woman with two children, a married man in his sixties. One of the members of the group was Jane Leggett. She had asked Margaret if she had a room. Margaret said yes, without asking why or for whom.

When Caroline arrived, Margaret gave her a room with its own lock at the top of the house up a narrow staircase so that she could retreat from the rambling Brower hordes when they came to visit. There was a rocking chair, a teddy bear and copies of Cardinal Spelling's *The Foundling* and Lucille Borden's *Silver Trumpets Calling*. There was also a television and Margaret noticed how excited Caroline seemed when she could watch a British programme and how she livened up when she heard an English accent on *Monty Python* or *Dame Edna Everage, Blackadder,* or *Only Fools and Horses* tapes sent to her by sympathetic television crews. A contribution to Margaret's costs was made by the St George's Society of New York, a charitable organization founded on St George's Day, 1770, at Bolton's (now Fraunces) Tavern in New York. Since pre-revolutionary times, it has helped people from the United Kingdom and the British Commonwealth or their descendants.

Margaret found that she had acquired a thirty-one-year-old daughter. She soon discovered that Caroline had no desire to talk about her case – 'I learned more about it from watching 20/20' – and that Caroline equally had no desire to read any reports or watch any television bulletins on the case. 'She didn't want to hear the story from anyone, not from herself either. She would stay away from the television.'

A pattern began: a morning cigarette on the back porch of the no-smoking house, which she would have barefoot regardless of whether there was snow on the ground, a cup of strong coffee rather than the decaffeinated variety that Margaret Brower favoured, the daily call from her anxious parents, the twice-weekly downtown visit on the Long Island Rail Road past the Shea Stadium to see Meg Spinelli, visits to Michael Dowd in Park Avenue. There was a local life, too: pizzas at the Gable Inn just round the corner from Sleepy's The Mattress Professionals, expeditions to the twenty-four-hour A and P to seek out a more outlandish mayonnaise, visits from relatives, friends and the media, playing softball, being part of a large American family. If the neighbours recognized the haunted figure they had seen on the early-evening news they did not let on; this was a 'back porch' rather than a 'front porch' type of street where privacy was respected.

Caroline was adamant that she did not want to return to Riker's Island: 'She had said, "I'm never going back," and we were very concerned that she was suicidal.' She had started to hoard the anti-depressant pills she was given and told Margaret that she had picked the spot where she would kill herself rather than go back to prison.

'You take in a stranger, but they're not a stranger long,' said Margaret Brower. 'She was very fragile, like a broken doll that had just been glued together but not very securely. I wanted to protect her but I knew I couldn't touch it.' On some occasions, such as when the prosecution psychiatrist Naomi Goldstein's report had not been completed when she had anticipated that it would be, Caroline became hysterical and would curl up in a foetal position on the sofa, sucking her thumb. They would call Meg Spinelli 'who had a magical ability to put her back together in a few minutes', as Margaret Brower put it.

The court appearances, of which there were to be more than twenty before Caroline finally came to trial, became a regular feature that Caroline would attend, supported by her 'team' – christened 'the Carolinettes' by one of the reporters covering the case.

'Marjory Fisher embodied the harm that was continuing to happen to her,' said Margaret Brower. 'Clearly she was doing her job and I never thought that this woman had a vendetta against her but if you were the person that's not how you feel, especially if it's something that would not have happened in your own country. A lot of her frustration and anger and pain could be focused at Marjory – "Why is this woman doing this to me?"'

One of the other members of the prayer group who took a particular interest in Caroline's case was Father Anthony Ercolano or, as he soon became known to Caroline, Tony the Priest or T the P. Father Tony was in the finest traditions of the New York priest of legend and a hundred Hollywood movies: a good-looking, idealistic fifty-year-old with a fine irreverent wit, an enjoyment of life and a taste for Johnnie Walker Red Label whisky. For the last eight years he had been the chaplain at Christ the King school in Middle Village in Queens County, ministering to its 1700 mostly Catholic students. He led the daily religious services, organized retreat programmes, a subject on which he was writing a book, and was available for their problems 'or happy moments they want to share'. It involved dealing with everything, from breaking up the occasional fight to consoling students who had lost a close relative and asked him how there could be a God if He could let a brother or sister die, and counselling pregnant girls. 'I don't offer a lot of advice. I lay out the options before them.' He had seen how students bowed down with their own problems had responded when asked to work in the community with lonely old people and asked Caroline if she would be prepared to visit an elderly woman in Auburndale who needed help. She agreed.

Brought up in Flushing and Bayside, Father Tony had trained for two years at Crosier seminary in Onamia, Minnesota, in the Mid-West then at Cathedral College, Douglastown in New York City for his bachelor's degree in philosophy. He was ordained at the age of twenty-six on 26 May 1973 – he is specific about the date – for the diocese of Brooklyn and Queens.

From Italian–Polish–Irish roots – 'with that kind of ethnic background I could probably run for Pope' – he lives in the Church of the American Martyrs in a small, neat apartment with a pile of Ken Folletts among his books on the scriptures.

'She was clearly depressed, she seemed to be very frightened,' he says, of his first encounter with Caroline. 'The fear was most obvious at first. We had one of the weirdest relationships. We would constantly be badgering each other, joking with each other. I think I was probably the humorous release, the comic relief.'

He realized that, with Caroline's now regular court appearances – to find out if the psychiatric reports had been completed – in front of the judge, Robert Hanophy, that he might have a key role to play. 'I felt my presence, particularly dressed as a priest, would lend a credibility to Caroline's case. I knew the judge had been elected on a Republican–Conservative–Right to Life ticket and I wanted to remove any misconception that this was a right-to-life issue. In court I sat with my arm around her shoulder because she was trembling so much. The fear was that any time the judge would say, "Right, back into jail." Marjory Fisher seemed very business-like, she had a job to do and she was going to do it. I can't see how someone could do that job so efficiently but maybe if you've been surrounded by crime you have to develop that kind of a side. There was a coldness there. I detected no sympathy. Maybe she felt it but couldn't exhibit it because of her role.'

They would head off to Bear Mountain, an hour and a half's drive upstate, for picnics and pedalos. They had to take care not to cross the state boundary and thus break Caroline's bail agreement, which required that she stay in New York State and that she did not drive a car. Father Tony set about campaigning in other ways. He wrote to 'Bill and Hillary', to the New York members of the House of Representatives and the Senate, to the Justice Department.

He did not probe Caroline too closely on what had happened. 'We tried to make her time here as normal as possible. We skirted the issue a lot. Caroline brought me to the hotel room and told me about it afterwards but we never really discussed what happened during that critical time.' He had done his own research on the case. His mother was, as he described her, a 'news junkie' and was familiar with it. 'I started downloading articles about the case; *Newsday* and the *Daily News* and AP but it was not a story that seemed to be of much interest to the American public.

'I'm a product of the sixties so I come with a bias against authoritarian structures, which sounds funny for a priest to be saying. I don't think what had happened to Caroline changed my perception of things, I think it gave me more evidence to be very critical and very careful when it comes to dealing with these structures. There was a tremendous amount of harm done in Caroline's case.'

As the story gradually unfolded he listened and reached his own conclusions on it as he watched her slowly starting to trust people on the outside. 'If your mind is telling you that the child is dead, that child could come out screaming and yelling and kicking and it doesn't make a damned bit of difference. For all practical purposes that child is dead, that's what your mind is telling you. I've seen her interacting with children and babies – she's a tender person. My brother Stan, a computer consultant, is very conservative about law and order issues and he loved Caroline. There was never any sense when she was with children that they were in any danger because a "predator" was here.'

Another member of the prayer group, Kathleen Connell, a schoolteacher born in Brooklyn who has lived in Flushing for the last twenty years, soon met Caroline. A feisty New Yorker with short hair, big glasses and wearing a grey T-shirt 'In Memory of Our Brother' for a New York policeman who had been shot dead on duty, with the words, 'May God have mercy on his soul' on the back, Kathy had also decided early on that Caroline's case needed public awareness.

An avid Internet user, she wrote an account of the case and put it on the Internet as a 'Prayer Request'. She recounted Caroline's story and informed Internet readers: 'I don't know what she did, I only know she's not a murderer.' There was a regular and heavy response. 'If I had put it out on the orthodox Catholic list, I would have got lunatics. Instead I got flaming liberals. I wanted some more fuzzies for her. I wanted people to be aware of what was happening. Sometimes it seems as though people in this country are in denial about what's happening in their criminal-justice system. They would just rather not be bothered about it.'

Back came the responses on the Internet, from Buffalo and Ontario, from Jerusalem and the Isle of Wight. 'I am a college seminarian for Milwaukee, WI,' said one. 'I study at Marquette

University and live in community with seven other young men who are discerning their vocation ... Please tell Caroline that she has my prayers and the prayers of the entire college seminary program in Milwaukee.'

Many others offered their prayers, too, someone quoted the Tao of Pooh.

Kathy's own experience had made her deeply cynical about the system: she had been on a jury that had acquitted a man of an attack on a homosexual only to find out after the case that evidence which would have convicted him had been withheld for technical reasons. She had also watched a jury uncertain whether to convict a clearly guilty drug dealer so she did not have enormous faith that Caroline would get a fair trial.

Kathy kept respondents up with the news. In one missive she wrote: 'Only God knows the details of what happened at the birth. What I do know is that Caroline is not a murderer, not a "baby-killer" which is what she was called constantly for eight months while in the mental health ward at Riker's Island.' She would slide the responses under the door for Caroline to see. Father Tony would scan mail and messages in case they were unpleasant ones but they were almost all friendly and supportive. Caroline, for her part, would sometimes read them, sometimes not, taking them up to her room and keeping them with the mountain of cards that had arrived while she was in prison.

She became a friend, too, of the other members of the prayer group: she got to know Jane Leggett better, and Pat Doherty, a nurse, whom she amazed with her tales of Riker's. Pat was sympathetic: through her hospital work she knew how difficult it was to tell whether a newborn baby was alive or dead – sometimes even experienced doctors were unsure.

So Caroline, who had grown up in a house where there was little religion, found herself in the midst of a crowd of practising Christians, albeit from the liberal wing of the Catholic Church. 'They did try to get me to go to church on several occasions: "If you want to come, come, but if you don't, feel guilty for the rest of the day." I did go a few times when Father Tony was performing but I'm very sceptical about religion. I think it's something that people turn to when they have nothing else. I like to think that being a Christian isn't about going to church and praying, it's about doing decent things.'

While Margaret provided Caroline's official residence, Michael and Irene Dowd's house nearby became her second home. Irene Dowd had been born in Brooklyn into a Russian–German family but had been living in Queens since the age of three. Her knowledge of English people prior to meeting Caroline had been gleaned from an English war-bride friend of her mother's. She had worked as a teacher for ten years and as a book-keeper at the Sly Fox restaurant on Northern Boulevard for twenty. She had been married to an Irishman, with a daughter now in her late twenties, and had sworn she would never date another one. Then she met Michael Dowd: 'I not only dated him, I married him.'

She had first got to know Caroline in the early months of the case. 'When the Consulate was closed, she had nobody to talk to so she would call here and we would start chatting and I talked to her for quite a while before we met. We would talk about everything.'

Irene became Caroline's unofficial media minder and would accompany the journalists who went to interview her in prison. She met her first on Riker's Island with Daniel Jeffreys of the *Independent*. 'She was very upset and was working very hard at trying to keep herself together. When she first came out you could see the difference almost immediately.'

In her first week of freedom, Irene took her shopping in

the Bayside shopping centre. 'She couldn't deal with other people talking to her so we went to Barnes and Noble [the bookshop] where no one bothers you. Then she came with me to pick up Lauren at school.' Lauren is the Dowds' daughter, a composed and articulate child who seems completely at ease with adults without in any way being brattishly precocious. 'Lauren said, "I've been looking forward to meeting you," and Caroline looked at her and said, "Oh, my God, the child's so formal, what am I going to do with her?" Before she arrived, Lauren and I had had a talk and I said, "Look, she doesn't want to discuss things that happened, they make her upset," and she said OK. It was really astounding because that's not Lauren. Lauren asks questions about everything but she understood that it might make her feel uncomfortable so she never asked.

'Caroline was very frightened for a while but she wasn't shaking so much except when she got upset. She wouldn't go out on her own at first. The first time I really felt that she had relaxed was when she said she liked to run and she put on a pair of sneakers and shorts. We were walking down to Crocheron Park and she just started to run. We were on the bottom of the hill and you could see her on the top, running across the skyline and you could see the hair and it was the first time I saw her let loose and she wasn't afraid of getting home any more.' Caroline recalled the run and telling her father about it. She was tickled that he expressed concern about the idea of her running alone in a suburban New York park when she had just emerged from one of the country's roughest jails.

She would go to the North Hempstead Country Club where Irene would play nine holes of golf and Caroline would swim with Lauren in the pool. It became a regular part of her routine. The pool attendant had asked Irene if she wanted nanny rates and she said yes, so Caroline became the 'English nanny'. It was a sociable place and Caroline would talk to the real nannies and the manager, whose father had been stationed in England during the war and who liked to talk about England.

Irene had never before been so involved with any of her husband's clients. 'It's not something you do! You're trying to make sure that when Michael has to make a decision he can do it objectively. It's very difficult to have a client here all the time because you're making a decision based on your emotions.

'She always missed home. She would get depressed and the only person who could really get her out of it was Lauren because Lauren loves her. I could sit here and talk to her and she would give me a wall, but Lauren was six and she couldn't stop her. She'd say, "All right, we'll go and have an adventure." They would go to the animal store or the park – she had unconditional love from Lauren so she never felt she had to be anybody but herself and Lauren adored her.

'She learned how to make coffee' – Caroline also learned to mimic Irene's Brooklyn pronunciation of 'cawwwfee' and 'becawwws' – 'and would make me a cup of coffee all the time. Then all of a sudden I just couldn't sleep any more. And I couldn't think what was going on – was it the menopause, I just can't sleep. And then I watch her make a cup of coffee and she's putting in twice as much as she needs. She was slowly poisoning me with coffee!'

There was awkwardness sometimes at parties. 'It could be difficult for her because when you meet a stranger at a barbecue what do you say? "What are you doing in this country? What do you do?" "Oh, I'm out on bail." At the club it became a little awkward until they decided that she was my nanny and she went for it.'

So Caroline, who had been sharing a room with crack dealers and arsonists and murderers and living on cold hot dogs and Koolaid, going to sleep to the sound of screaming and weeping, and waking to the sarcastic orders of the correctional officers, suddenly found herself falling asleep to the sound of cicadas and an occasional local terrier, dipping her feet into the country-club pool and having a beer and a burger with young lawyers at parties under the starry skies in Queens. It was a new world, different from Riker's Island and from her life back in Chingford and Leytonstone. The people were larger than life, louder, warmer and wackier, and she found herself involved in expeditions and baby-sitting and picnics and nights out at a Mexican restaurant where mariachi bands played and cocktails came with parasols and fruit salads. At times it was hard to remember that she was still facing the possibility of a prison sentence that would stretch into the next millennium. But in the meantime a different life had opened up before her and she was happy to learn from it.

When her brother, Stephen, visited with Caroline Two and son Josh, they found her in good spirits. 'She was very adamant that she was not going back to prison,' says Caroline. 'We saw the Statue of Liberty and Caroline went "Huh!" at it. When we went to the zoo there was an eagle chained to a piece of wood in a cage. It was meant to be the national bird, the bird of freedom – we took a photo of it.'

Once when her parents were visiting, they and Caroline were in Penn Station, where the trains from Flushing arrive. Caroline had gone to buy tickets with twenty dollars her father had given her and they saw her embrace a black woman. She turned out to have been on Riker's Island with Caroline and was now begging in the station. Peter Beale was secretly proud that Caroline came back needing another twenty dollars for the train fare.

Back in England, the Friends of Caroline Beale had been launched at the Bond Street offices of Alec Reed, the founder of Reed Employment, who had read about the case and had expressed both moral and financial support for Caroline. More than thirty of Caroline's friends, relatives and colleagues had set about canvassing support and raising money for her defence.

But throughout this time, Margaret Brower was concerned that Caroline was still sometimes close to despair and that suicide was a strong possibility. She became reluctant to leave her alone for long periods in the house when she was out at work and would pop back at lunch-time or ask Father Tony to drop in and see that all was well. She noticed again that Caroline was hoarding her tablets. She shared her concern at a prayer meeting one evening in October. The group sat in silent prayer for Caroline.

Chapter Sixteen

Caroline's case was now moving towards its climax. It was part chess match, part game of poker with her future as the stake. Michael Dowd was approaching the trial on the assumption that it would take place before a jury, and Marjory Fisher, who had believed that – like 85 per cent of all the cases that passed through the Queens DA's office – it would be dealt with by plea bargain, was now coming to the same conclusion.

Caroline greeted the trial delays with growing impatience. Although the police investigation had concluded within days of her arrest, the prosecution were anxious to have their own psychiatric assessment as a counter to the reports being prepared for the defence by Meg Spinelli, Susan Hickman and Ian Brockington. Caroline was required to attend sessions with Dr Naomi Goldstein, Professor of Clinical Psychiatry at the New York University Medical School, whom she met at the DA's office on Queens Boulevard. Dr Goldstein was around sixty and Caroline's first impression was that she was small, blonde and 'wore a lot of gold'. Caroline was unhappy to discover that Marjory Fisher would also be attending the sessions. Michael Dowd would be there, too, although he did not sit in on Caroline's interviews with the defence psychiatrists.

In her diary for 21 June 1995, Caroline noted:

Today we had to go and see Goldstein at the DA's office. MF was there, that was the worst bit. Seeing her brings everything back although she was civil to me and I was polite to her. Seeing her is just like reliving a nightmare. At least Araminta will be arriving tonight, the one thing that got me through the worst part of the day. Tony the Priest – T the P – took me to Grand Central Station and we picked up Choc from there. How good it was to see her, the first person from England in what seems like ages. It took away a bit of the pain today but it all has to be continued in the morning.

The following day she added:

I guess today was not a great success story with Goldstein and Fisher. I just could not handle it. The emotional stress got to be too much and I was physically sick. I could not even form words. Mike got really worried, called Meg and stopped the interview. It was a relief in one way but now it just means that we have to go back again.

The first meeting took place the day after her thirty-first birthday and she saw Dr Goldstein around five times. At their first meeting, the psychiatrist asked about how she had grown up and if her father had been an alcoholic or had beaten her up. 'The worst thing was that Fisher was in the room and both were taking notes.' It was a long session punctuated with coffee and water breaks. 'She would say, "I know this is painful for you but it's painful for me too," and I would think, God, not that painful. If Fisher hadn't been there it would have been easier but all the time I could see her out of the corner of my eye. I think if I feel bitter about that woman it's going to eat me up but I do feel bitter about her although I don't want to.'

During the second visit, as she recorded in her diary, Caroline became hysterical and started to vomit. She became unable to speak so Michael Dowd had to call Meg Spinelli for tranquillizers to settle her. The prosecution said that they would 'take as long as it takes' to conduct the assessment and that if Caroline was unable to continue with a session then a further one would be scheduled until such time as Dr Goldstein had what she needed. Michael Dowd disagreed with this strategy and argued that if the prosecution had been serious about carrying out a psychiatric assessment they should have done it while Caroline was in Riker's Island rather than wait and delay the trial. He sought a ruling from the judge to place a time limit on the assessments so that the trial could be scheduled. Caroline recalled the tension between the two sides that resulted from this, with Marjory Fisher pacing up and down outside the court while Michael Dowd muttered, 'Calm down, Marjory, calm down.'

Caroline became used to seeing Ms Fisher. 'She usually wore this navy blue dress just above the knee. She would always say, "Hi, Caroline, take care," and all this crap.'

In October 1995, Peter Beale noted in his diary a phone call from Caroline who had just been to see Dr Goldstein: 'She says Naomi Goldstein had said, "I wish you all the luck in the world." Marjory Fisher said to Caroline, "I expect you hate all Americans." Caroline replied, "I love my Americans and I do not hate you because I do not know you but I hate what you have done to me."'

Peter Beale was still puzzled by what had happened. 'I say to myself, what have I done to bring this about? If we had been separated, if we had been alcoholics, if we had been child abusers, physically or sexually, you could have said this is your nemesis. But we have done all that we could possibly do which doesn't preclude the fact that we've done something wrong but we did what we thought was right. We've done most things in moderation – maybe that's a fault. When this happens to you you become much more vulnerable. I read one article about the ordinariness of this family ... I said we're ordinary people.'

A Stranger and Afraid

To complete her assessment, Dr Goldstein decided that she would need to speak to as many people connected with Caroline as she could, and one of her first calls was to the Beales. Peter noted in his journal: 'She seems very pleasant. I feel she likes Caroline. She says she gets the feeling Caroline is liked by everyone. "A fine and likeable person she is." In her final conversation with us, she mentioned the words racial and political in the context of Caroline's situation. She said there is a lot of crime in New York and that there is another white girl on trial for killing her baby. She said the baby died by unnatural means. I said, "Is that not a difficult thing to prove?" She said, "That is another issue . . ." We were on the phone for one hour and she said the New York office of the prosecutor will pay.' Paul Faraway, whom Dr Goldstein also contacted, told her that Caroline's father 'treated her like a little girl' and as if she was a child.

While Dr Goldstein was carrying out her research, the DA's office in Queens was also having to decide how to process this increasingly controversial case. Although the British Consul was playing a low-profile role in the case, reports in the British press, which were filtering back to the USA, were almost universally hostile and critical of the American justice system. Should Caroline be allowed to slip away on a minor charge such as failure to report a death?

That was the decision that they were having to wrestle with at the DA's office. Any would-be cop-film scriptwriter would only have to sit down for a few moments in the DA's reception area to come up with half a dozen storylines: a young tousled DA is listening to an elderly woman recounting how much blood a police officer had said was coming from a wound and explaining that this was hearsay and inadmissible and she had better not try to repeat it in court. The elderly woman was puzzled by the concept – 'But that's what he said!'

Another young DA is carrying out an existentialist conversation with a young man in a shiny baseball jacket: 'You have to go back to the clerk and tell them that you're not who you are.'

'But I am who I am!'

'Yes, I know you are, but you're not who they think you are.'

The defiant smell of cigar smoke drifts out of Gregory L. Lasak's office on the third floor of the DA's office on Queens Boulevard. The pictures on his wall and the books in his cabinet give a snapshot of a street-wise DA who has handled 1500 homicides in his career and has every intention of handling 1500 more. On one wall is a picture of him addressing the court in the 1986 Black Liberation Army trial of two men charged with the murder of a policeman. Reports of the case show that Lasak told the court that the men had 'pumped bullets into a police car like it was a shooting gallery'; a second picture shows him examining a witness in the so-called 'stungun trial', a police corruption case based around the 106th Precinct; and a third, which will bring us in a circle that links back to Caroline Beale, is an artist's impression of him interviewing in hospital the corrupt politician Donald Manes who had so damaged Michael Dowd's career. Photos show Lasak with New York's first black mayor David Dinkins, with one of the stars of NYPD Blue, Dennis Franks. A box under a table in the office is marked 'trial transcripts' and another 'death penalty' – which was reintroduced in New York State in 1995. There's a softball trophy won by a Queens court side called the Violent Felons and a sign that says, 'Remember We Work for God.'

Greg Lasak, as one of the prime movers in the DA's department, has much to remember about the Caroline Beale case and his manner is as spruce and self-confident as his crisply ironed white shirt. There is a combative twinkle in the eye of someone who is used to jousting with defence attorneys and journalists and he has a reputation among crime reporters for being one of the more approachable, open-minded DAs.

'It was not an unusual case in terms of a newborn child being the victim but it was an unusual case in the manner in which the homicide was uncovered,' he says, after asking if it is all right for him to continue smoking his cigar. 'Caroline Beale was found coming through the airport with a dead baby in her bag. That was highly unusual.'

It had been Lasak who had dispatched Marjory Fisher and Lori Ann Fee to take a statement from Caroline as soon as he was notified of what had happened. He consulted with them after their return and they decided on a murder in the second-degree charge because the first medical report indicated that the baby had taken a breath.

Regarding the rationale behind a plea bargain, Lasak says, 'Every case is looked upon individually . . . In general, the defence attorney comes to us with mitigating factors which he or she feels put their client in a position to merit certain charges.' There had been a number of discussions, he said, and Caroline had been treated in the same way as an American citizen and within the same time-span.

He had, he said, felt under no pressure from the British Consul or anyone else to settle the case with a plea bargain that would allow Caroline to return home immediately. 'I don't feel any pressure from anyone.' On the delay in bringing Caroline's case to trial, he said it was 'in our best interests to try a case as soon as possible because of memories fading. In most cases it is not helpful for the prosecution to delay.'

The British Consulate had been wary all along of appearing to be intrusive: Michael Dwyer stressed that he had no role in interfering in the legal process and was merely monitoring it and reporting back to London so that the Foreign Office could liaise with the Beales. He had met the DAs and the defence attorneys and had tried to discover what the likely outcome might be so that he could prepare the Beales for it. In March 1995, when Caroline was still in prison, Dwyer had attended a meeting at the DA's office with Marjory Fisher, Richard

Brown (the Queens DA), and Mary de Bourbon, the public-affairs liaison officer who was handling the press inquiries on the case. 'It was not to plead her case but to establish the facts and to discuss what might be – crystal-ball gazing.' By then it had become clear that the jury would be asked to choose between two alternative charges of murder. The system for sentencing was complex: one charge carried a maximum of twenty-five years to life and a minimum of fifteen years and the other a maximum of eight and a third years to twenty-five years and a minimum of two years to six years.

Daniel Jeffreys, the journalist who had followed the case most closely and who had established a working relationship with Marjory Fisher, said that as the trial drew close, machinations appeared to be taking place. 'We got the impression that there was pressure from the top to accept a deal. Only two weeks before the trial Marjory was saying very adamantly that Caroline was not going home without serving time. When we asked her about what was happening, her answer every time was that Caroline was going to jail. But a trial is very expensive and there is a financial calculation so there were two reasons to settle: it was going to cost a lot of money and it would have been a high-profile case.'

Jeffreys was also hearing from within the DA's office a variation on the theme of Tom Wolfe's Great White Defendant theory: 'We couldn't go too easy on her. She was white and middle class. We get baby-killing cases all the time but the perpetrators are usually black or Hispanic and we give them a really hard time. It would not have been politically acceptable to let Caroline walk without some kind of guilty plea.' He also felt that both Dowd and Fisher were anxious to reach some kind of accommodation: 'In court they were almost nauseatingly friendly towards each other.' Another journalist said that just before the case, Marjory Fisher had assured them it was going to trial and saying that she was looking forward to it.

But Marjory Fisher herself said, 'We had been talking all

along to try and reach an agreement, really the conversation never stopped.'

She reacted to suggestions being made in the British press that she was showing a lack of compassion by refusing to give ground: 'A system that takes into account the life of the child is a very compassionate one. Sometimes I got the impression that people were more concerned about the defendant than about the victim and I was just representing the victim in this case as I do in other cases. I try to treat every case individually. She hid it, she concealed it. To me that merited a murder charge.'

She had also been stymied in her pursuit of a possible motive by showing that the baby might not have been Paul's, which she believed was possible. Initially, she had been confident that Paul would co-operate and provide a DNA sample but it eventually transpired that he would refuse to do so for reasons that, to this day, he is unwilling to discuss.

Fisher says now: 'We can't do the tests without the dad's blood. Paul said it had been ten months since they had sex. Usually there is some motivation that goes along with offing your baby and that would have been [some motivation]. They usually tell their husbands. It would have been something to explain what had happened. It would have undermined her defence. We tried and we failed.'

Dowd says he was never worried about the possibility of Paul giving a sample which indicated that he was not the father since he was satisfied in his mind that he was. But at the back of Dowd's mind were two worries: the possibility that a predominantly Catholic jury – because of the area's large Irish and Hispanic population – might be hostile to anyone accused of anything to do with babies; and how well Caroline would be able to stand up to the rigours of what would have been probably a three-week trial. As Jeffreys had observed in her court appearances: 'It was horrible to watch Caroline in court: she would shiver, she would shake, she had a wild look. She would be incoherent, she would start a conversation and then break it off.'

As the trial neared, the Beales' concern heightened. They had been scheduling their visits to Caroline between those she was now receiving regularly from friends. They, like Caroline, had been pinning their hopes on Dr Goldstein's report, that in response to it the charge would be dropped and Caroline would return home. However, they were told in January 1996 by Michael Dowd that Marjory Fisher was now seeking a sentence of between two and four and a half years. When the news was broken to Caroline that she would still be facing a charge, she phoned home: 'Caroline is very upset but they are looking after her . . . Oh, God what are we to do?' wrote Peter Beale in his diary.

On 13 February the deal had changed slightly. Peter Beale wrote: 'Mike Dowd phoned and said that Caroline has been offered one and a half to four and a half years for manslaughter, which means as she has done eight months she will only have to serve four months. Mike says she knows this and she wants to fight. Does she understand the consequences?' He underlined the last five words.

However, Peter Beale recognized what was driving the prosecution: 'I think Marjory Fisher in the light of what she had before her was compelled to call for a prosecution but if she could have seen the extenuating and mitigating circumstances it might have been different. Anyone who had killed a baby would put as much mileage between themselves and the baby as possible and the carrying the baby with her was bonding. If someone is traumatized like that they revert back to their basic instincts.'

As the trial approached, the negotiations took on a sharper edge: Judge Robert Hanophy made it clear that he wanted the lawyers to keep talking and present him with a deal that they had agreed.

On the Thursday before the trial, Dowd saw Fisher at a

symposium. There was no indication that any deal was imminent. 'She had got to the point of saying, "Take a plea on manslaughter two and let the judge decide what the sentence should be." I said, "No." The maximum they were proposing would have been eighteen months but I didn't think that would have been fair or right for her to go back to jail. So I was under the impression that all bets were off and we were setting a date to go to court. So we were going to set a hearing. Then on the Friday morning Marjory went into chambers and asked if I would be willing to see Dick Brown [the DA]. It was clear to me at that stage that there was going to be a deal. I didn't tell anybody. I went over and met with Fisher, Dick Brown and Greg Lasak at the DA's office on Queens Boulevard. What we agreed to was essentially probation if the judge concurred. I was surprised but not stunned to hear that Brown had read all the papers. He is known as a prodigious worker and he had read all the files on the case in detail. He was very careful to indicate his strong support for Marjory Fisher – I had no sense that this was her choice. He wanted to make sure I wouldn't take unfair advantage of him in the press and blast his office. I agreed because it would have been the height of disingenuousness to do that. He has a reputation as an honourable man and I had every respect for him and Greg Lasak.'

Caroline had had to make a painful decision. 'Michael said to me – did I want to go to trial? He said if there's a chance that they will say to you, "If you will take this plea, you can go home tomorrow," hypothetically speaking, would you take it? I said, "Well, I'm not going back to jail for one day." So he asked, "What if they say, 'If you take this plea, you go to jail for three years then you go home, would you take it?'" and I said no. Then he said, "What if they say take a plea and you can go home?" By that time I was so frightened, they grind you down into a state where they say if you plead guilty to this and you can go home, then you'll do it. No matter what your heart tells you you just do it. Then on the Friday night before we were due in court, he said, "If you plead guilty to manslaughter you can go home on Thursday."'

Peter Beale was still keeping his diary. On 1 March, three days before the trial was due to start, he wrote: 'The judge seemed like a cheery, round sort of man, the best so far I would guess. Marjory Fisher clip-clops in, takes her coat off and goes smiling to Mike. Daniel Jeffreys said, "An icy wind swept through the court." Mike has been talking to the judge in his casual relaxed way, he is taller than those around him, he seems to have a presence of his own ... Before we left [court] Mike had pulled us to one side to say he had been asked to speak with Richard Brown, the DA boss man. Mike says he thinks it is looking good for Caroline to be sent home – not to tell anyone ... Speaking to Tony he said that he had phoned Marjory Fisher's assistant, Scott someone, and he spoke of doing the work of God. Tony said the work of God is mercy.'

The deal that was now being offered was this: that Caroline would have to enter court and admit to manslaughter. After eighteen months of protesting her innocence she would have publicly to admit her guilt.

Chapter Seventeen

What became of crucial importance as the date for the trial approached were, inevitably, the medical reports, reports that as it eventually transpired were never to be tested in court. These were of two types: the pathological reports suggesting how the baby had died and the psychiatric reports indicating the state of Caroline's mind before and at the time of the death.

The initial autopsy had been carried out by Dr Kari Reiber, the City Medical Examiner, on 23 September, the day Caroline was arrested, at the Queens County mortuary in the presence of two other doctors, Veress and Charles. Dr Reiber's examination found that the baby was 'a normally developed, term newborn baby girl weighing 3,560 grammes [seven and a half pounds] and measuring 20 inches from head to toe'.

The examination also found: 'There are faint petechiae [small dots which can denote bruising] on the bulbar and subpalpebral conjunctival surfaces ... There are no intraoral petechiae ... There are no facial or scalp injuries. There are no neck injuries.' Of the neck organs and cervical spine the report found: 'There are no petechiae in the mucosa of the upper esophagus.' Of the respiratory system, the report found: 'The lungs are uniformly expanded, pale reddish brown ... with no blood or fluid exuding from the cut surfaces.'

Dr Reiber had also asked Dr Melvin H. Becker, a doctor from Manhasset, to review the radiographs of the baby. He responded on 26 September: 'The chest films show the lungs

171

to be aerated and the heart normal. There is air in the stomach. These findings indicate that the baby had taken at least a few breaths.'

Dr Reiber's final summary, which was sent to the District Attorney's office, was blunt:

Diagnosis: 1. Suffocation with a/ petechiae of
conjunctivae and esophagus.
2. Normally developed, term newborn baby girl
(3,560 gm).
3. Aerated lungs.
Cause of Death: suffocation.
Manner of Death: homicide.

This conclusion, which Dr Reiber completed on 29 November 1994, was a dagger blow to Caroline's defence. Given the importance that lawyers, whether prosecution or defence, attach to medical evidence, which is much less rarely challenged than other forms of evidence such as identification, it seemed to indicate that there was little doubt that the baby had been killed, in stark contrast to Caroline's version of events.

Paul Vladimir, Caroline's first attorney, had already sought an alternative medical diagnosis of the baby's death and this doctor had come to the same conclusion as the official examiner that breaths had been taken. On the purely medical front at that stage it appeared that Caroline had no defence: the child had been a victim of homicide. In early television interviews, Marjory Fisher suggested that the baby had been alive for 'fifteen minutes' and this figure was often quoted subsequently both by the prosecution and the media.

But it was not as simple as it had appeared at first. Peter Beale had come home one day to King's Head Hill during the weeks after Caroline's arrest and had found a message on the answerphone from a friendly-sounding man who introduced himself as Professor Ian Brockington from the Department of Psychiatry at the University of Birmingham. He said that he thought he might be able to help. He had read the article about Caroline in the *Independent*.

The upshot was that the Professor flew to New York and visited Caroline in jail on 16 and 18 March 1995. Brockington reached a conclusion about Caroline's mental state but, equally important from the defence point of view, he decided to find out on what basis the conclusion of suffocation and homicide was based. His own belief was that the pathologists had to justify their diagnosis of suffocation 'in the absence of the classic signs of asphyxial death'.

His colleague at the Birmingham Maternity Hospital, Dr Ian Rushton, a fellow of the Royal College of Pathologists, assessed the pathology findings and expressed his grave doubts about the original conclusion. He found that there 'are no characteristics of the haemorrhages described that allow them to be identified as being due to suffocation rather than to labour and delivery. There is no corroborative evidence that the baby was suffocated.'

He added: 'It is possible to construct a scenario in which a distraught, unattended mother delivers a moribund baby that makes a few gasps after delivery that are not observed and then succumbs ... The failure of any challenge to the initial pathological opinion as to cause of death may be considered a major failing in this case since it is likely that a specialist perinatal pathologist would have cast sufficient doubt on the alleged asphyxiation-by-suffocation theory to justify early release from prison.' He believed that this meant that there was, at the very least, a reasonable doubt that should have led to the abandonment of the prosecution.

Professor Brockington sent the documentation to two of the acknowledged experts in pathology in Europe: Professor

Brinkmann of Munster University in Germany and Professor Bouska at the Charles University in Prague.

In July, Professor Brinkmann responded thus:

A suffocation has been diagnosed after post-mortem. This is difficult to accept mainly for the following reasons: from a general point of view the pathology of asphyxiation can be the result of two major reasons: 'external' asphyxiation, i.e. suffocation; 'internal' asphyxiation, either resulting from internal disease or from certain types of intoxication or as a reaction to metabolic disorders (e.g. hypoglycemia) or reactive to acute anemia (hemorrhage).

The pathology of asphyxiation is more or less the same although gradual differences can exist. Therefore, the diagnosis 'asphyxiation' is in the forensic practice a word without meaning. Only if one can with certainty attribute the pathology to either external or internal, one can specify ... It is possible that suffocation pathology results from restrictive mechanisms like hindrance of breath excursions of the lungs.

Professor Brinkmann went on to criticize the original diagnosis from New York:

All 'internal' mechanisms ... must be excluded with certainty ... The diagnosis of suffocation is not valid at all. Since the medical background and the pathology are the same internationally and since in the actual report there is no new sign or definition of asphyxiation, this diagnosis will of course not be acceptable by a court.

He attacked the assumption that the presence of petechiae was a reliable pointer towards asphyxiation:

It has been shown in the literature that conjunctival petechiae are specific neither for asphyxiation nor for suffocation. Especially in the actual case it must be borne in mind that the baby died obviously shortly after delivery. There exist of course multiple mechanisms during birth that can cause petechiae especially in the conjunctivae and also in the upper oesophagus . . .

The gross description of the lungs is not sufficient, it is neither suspicious for asphyxiation (there is no description of acute emphysema), there is no description of petechiae, neither macroscopically nor microscopically. Also, the microscopical findings have nothing to do with lung morphology in cases of asphyxiation . . .

It must also be considered that suffocation could have taken place accidentally after having placed the baby in a plastic bag. Even if the plastic bag has been left open to prevent the baby from this mechanism, a side position of the baby with the mouth in contact to the plastic could have affected this mechanism . . .

The pattern and findings and the documentation in the actual case does not fulfil minimum requirements to establish homicidal suffocation as final diagnosis. This strategy is scientifically not acceptable.

Professor Bouska responded from Prague: 'There is no doubt that the child breathed when born . . . The cause of death is by my opinion asphyxia which took place shortly after the delivery. What was the cause of the asphyxia cannot be said exactly without other information.' He posited some theories: that either the baby had been deliberately suffocated or the child could have suffocated accidentally when lying in a prone position or could have suffered from hypothermia.

Professor Brockington also sent Dr Reiber's report to John Emery, Emeritus Professor of Paediatric Pathology at the

University of Sheffield and a man who had more than forty years' experience as a paediatric pathologist, concerned with all types of infanticide, neonaticide and crib deaths.

In December 1995, with the trial approaching, Professor Emery sent back his report: 'The only abnormal features described in the child are: some petechiae in the conjunctivae, a single, small haemorrhage in the bulbar conjunctivae ... an unspecified number of petechiae in the mucosa of the upper oesophagus and what are described as the usual reflection petechiae in the sub-scalpular soft tissue and along the sagittal suture in the mid-line.'

More tellingly as far as the defence was concerned, Professor Emery went on:

The extreme paucity of petechiae and lack of description of brain swelling suggest that the death of this child was rapid, that death was more likely to have occurred in-utero than after labour, or that labour was extremely rapid. The presence of gas in the lungs and stomach indicates that the child had either breathed after birth or had been stillborn and manipulated in some way after birth ... The aeration of the lung is compatible with a few normal breaths but also with a normal stillborn child who has had some attempts at artificial respiration or has been manipulated in some way. The tissues of the lung show no evidence of any post-natal struggle to breathe or of any air trapping or of any foreign material ... The presence of gas in the lungs and stomach is the usual finding of a stillborn child in whom some attempts at resuscitation have taken place ...

The petechiae in the deeper layers of the scalp and in the conjunctivae and upper oesophagus are not uncommon in normal labours and in no way indicate that any attempt has been made at suffocating this child ...

To me the appearances of the tissues and structure in

this child are more compatible with death associated with apnoea [no attempt to breathe] than with any form of respiratory tract obstruction or suffocation.

In his conclusions, Professor Emery spelled out his views, which were to give the defence a clear belief that they could now successfully fight the case:

> I see no evidence that the child has been molested either before or after birth and no evidence that there has been any deliberate attempt to harm the child in any way.
>
> The child shows little evidence of any struggle to breathe and that death, if of respiratory origin, was of an apnoeic [failure of respiratory drive] rather than asphyxial type ... The only feature that is compatible with the child being born alive is the presence of air in the lungs. This air could have been introduced by natural breathing for less than a minute or by artificial means. This could have occurred by manipulating the child (flexing and extending it). It seems that the child was carried around in a bag that was occasionally dropped. I think that it would not be unreasonable to say that air could not have been sucked into the lungs during this time.

The professor went on to list his possible scenarios of what had happened, which are worth listing in full:

> 1/ A mature formally formed female child had a placental catastrophe and the baby died. This was followed by a rapid labour, the baby being born dead. Air was introduced to the lungs artificially later.
>
> 2/ The mother went into precipitate delivery. The baby was born shocked and attempted to breathe but

breathing was not established and the baby died
essentially from primary apnoea.

3/ As (2), but the baby was born precipitately into a
bath of water. An attempt at breathing took place but
some water came into contact with the pharynx and
epiglottis producing reflex apnoea and immediate death.

Of these three scenarios, Professor Emery was most
inclined towards the first – a natural death and one that he
said could be described as an 'intrauterine crib death'. Effectively, Professor Emery would have given evidence that natural
causes were the most likely explanation for the death of the
baby and there was very far from being any conclusive
evidence that pointed to homicide.

But Michael Dowd was anxious that his experts should
not be exclusively European, lest a Queens jury react on
nationalistic lines. He contacted Enid Gilbert-Barness, Professor of Pathology and Laboratory Medicine at the University of
South Florida and Professor Emeritus at the University of
Wisconsin. She, too, examined the initial reports and came to
her own conclusion. Like Professor Emery she felt that 'death
most likely occurred in utero after a precipitous onset of
labour'.

Professor Gilbert-Barness believed that the presence of air
in the lungs suggested that some 'manipulation' had taken
place after birth. She added:

I see no evidence of child abuse or any suggestion that
this infant was suffocated . . . It is my impression that the
appearance of the lungs is more consistent with stillbirth
than a liveborn infant in whom extrauterine breathing
had occurred.

In summary, I believe that this baby most likely died
during delivery or immediately thereafter following a

catastrophic event, possibly excessive twisting of the cord or abruption which resulted in a precipitous labor and rapid demise of the infant . . . The features in this case do not provide any conclusive evidence of suffocation.

This conclusion meant that Dowd now had three highly qualified professors and one senior doctor with vast experience in paediatric pathology in three different countries prepared to give evidence on Caroline's behalf. All three would have told a jury that there was no evidence that Caroline had suffocated the baby. (It was decided not to call Professor Bouska, said the defence, because he was not entirely comfortable in English.) The Beales were told of the findings, which came as an enormous relief to them, but that they were not to release details of them at this stage in case the delicate negotiations going on between Dowd and the DA's office were undermined. What had also become clear was that there was no foundation for the much-quoted '15 minutes' of life.

But if Dowd now had what he believed to be an unbeatable team of pathologists, he also needed psychiatric evidence in case the jury did not accept the defence pathologists' version of events: if they believed, as did the DA's medical expert, Dr Reiber, that the baby had been suffocated, Dowd would have to argue that Caroline had been either unaware of her actions or suffering from temporary insanity. He believed that he had assembled an equally prestigious team of psychiatrists all of whom had had access to Caroline while she was still in prison and all of whom had studied the statements taken from her and other potential witnesses.

Susan Hickman, of the Postpartum Mood Disorders Clinic, had been to see Caroline at Riker's and by February 1995 had drawn up her initial report. She noted of her first encounter that Caroline's hands were cold and sweaty but that she made good eye contact. 'She was rubbing her arms, picking her

179

elbows and holding herself with a slight rocking motion . . . Caroline's thinking is tangential, she must constantly be brought back to the topic.'

She noted that Caroline had told her that after Alison had died she would sometimes see her out of the corner of her eye. Although 'seeing' a dead friend or relative is common enough, Caroline had also told her, as she had told Meg Spinelli, that she had 'seen' Detective O'Donnell, sometimes with his face imposed on the body of a prison guard.

Dr Hickman believed that when Caroline felt that the baby was dead – at the time when Alison was dying – she was suffering from a dissociative state related to the hormonal upheavals of pregnancy and the stress of Alison's impending death. The fact that she gained barely any weight would have added to her belief that the child was dead, Dr Hickman felt.

Caroline had recounted the events to Dr Hickman in the same detail as she had to the police and the DAs after her arrest, saying that the baby was not moving and that she had panicked and got a bag from the hall to put the baby in. She was unable to explain why she had not told anyone: 'Caroline reports that these incidents all seem as though they were happening in a dream where everything is in shades of grey.'

The doctor came to the conclusion that Caroline had been suffering from a 'major depression, severe with psychotic features . . . with postpartum onset'. She went on to define postpartum depression as a

> mood disorder which impairs her cognitive functioning and results in extreme anxiety and severe mood disorder of the nature Caroline exhibited during the pregnancy . . . She was unable to take into account the consequences of her actions . . . lost contact with reality and believed her infant had died during pregnancy and was born dead.
>
> She believed she was worthless and that her infant's death was somehow her fault although she could not

think of anything she had done which might have contributed to it.

Dr Hickman believed that Caroline had suffered amnesia for periods of time during the delivery and afterwards that were the result of the psychotic episode: 'She was incapable of knowing or understanding an act as right or wrong.' Her recommendation, made more than a year before Caroline stood trial, was that Caroline should be held 'not criminally responsible'. She believed that reoccurrence was extremely unlikely and there was no need for further incarceration to protect the public.

Professor Channi Kumar, who had come so speedily to Caroline's aid at the request of Peter Beale, had also completed his report on the basis of two interviews carried out on Riker's Island in February and March 1995 and on a study of the documents.

Professor Kumar noted that Caroline's depression was characterized by persistent tearfulness and feelings of hopelessness. She recalled the whole period of her pregnancy as being in a daze, on 'automatic pilot' and she told him that on one occasion she had nearly been run over because she had not noticed the traffic. She explained to Professor Kumar that she had felt unable to tell Paul that the baby was dead inside her as he would have had to cope with two deaths, the baby's and Alison's. She was convinced that the baby was dead from the third month of pregnancy and this was corroborated in her mind by the lack of movement from the child.

Professor Kumar felt that her mental and physical state at that time was evidence of a major depressive disorder, which had the additional characteristics of a prolonged and pathological grief reaction to Alison's illness and death. Like the other psychiatrists, Professor Kumar believed that there might be some form of amnesia about the birth because Caroline's memory of the events seemed patchy and she had not described any of the tiny events that mothers typically recall after a normal delivery. 'After placing the baby in the bag, which is analogous to returning the baby to a kind of womb, she reverted to a detached state of dissociative equilibrium.'

Again, like the other psychiatrists who examined Caroline in jail, Professor Kumar decided that she was telling the truth. He added that she now also felt guilty because Paul's grandmother had just died, at the age of eighty-three, and Caroline believed that the stress of what had happened to her and the media intrusion could have contributed to the old lady's death. Professor Kumar concluded that the balance of Caroline's mind had been not only disturbed at the relevant time but that her acts or omissions could be regarded as a direct consequence of her mental disease. She had suffered from and continued to suffer from a major psychiatric illness. It was therefore inappropriate to charge her with a criminal act, he wrote, when she should be treated for a mental disease. He undertook to supervise that treatment at the Maudsley Hospital in London.

One of Caroline's visitors in prison had, of course, been Professor Ian Brockington, a tall, thin bespectacled man with an engaging academic demeanour and an infectious enthusiasm for his subject. He and Professor Kumar had been at the Maudsley together in the early 1970s; they had remained friends and had co-authored two books. Photos of the two young doctors together sit alongside family snapshots on Brockington's cluttered wall at Queen Elizabeth Psychiatric Hospital in Birmingham. Over fish and chips in the hospital canteen, he recalled reading about Caroline's predicament in the press. He had just finished his book *Motherhood and Mental Health*, and thought he could be of assistance. He contacted both Peter Beale and Michael Dowd. He was not impressed with the initial pathology report: 'I felt that there was no evidence that the infant had been molested in any way.' With Dowd's agreement he contacted the most respected pathologists in Europe.

'I feel that they [the prosecution] realized that they were in grave danger of being humiliated by foreign experts and so they struck a bargain. I was not very happy about that because she came away with a conviction for felony and I feel that if she had gone to court it is very unlikely that that would have been the verdict, although you can never tell in a jury trial. I feel she had been so demoralized that she was in no position to stand up to a trial. They had slung her into jail, they hadn't recognized mental illness. If you put a mentally ill person in that kind of environment and you terrify her with belligerent statements about what is going to happen to her, then you will disable her as a witness.'

Part of his work is with the pioneering residential mother-and-baby unit at the hospital, which deals with young mothers suffering from severe depression or an inability to bond with their babies. It was with this experience that he was able to assess Caroline. His first impression was that she seemed at least ten years younger than her thirty-one years: 'She had a spontaneous, warm-hearted manner, with charming facial expression and gestures. Her charm was not in her sophistication but in her extreme lack of it. She appeared sincere and completely open and strikingly free from malice. Of her treatment by the New York police she said, "What is the point of being bitter? There are a lot of people who are a lot worse off. Some of the people in here have no one to help them."'

Professor Brockington said that he was well aware that the truthfulness of the subject when he was preparing a court report on them could be a problem and that he was used to people lying to him. 'I had no doubt that Caroline gave me a true account of her experience as she remembered it.' She was completely consistent in her account to him. It was very difficult, he said, to maintain an untruthful account over a long period and what she told him tallied exactly with what she had told the police and the DA nearly six months earlier. 'Consistency is in favour of truth, especially if a person is very open and fluent. There was nothing about Caroline that favoured lying or confusion.'

He also recorded her feelings of guilt which she expressed to him thus: 'If it was my fault the baby died – if I could have saved it – then I deserve to be in here ... That's why Paul doesn't love me, he thinks it is my fault that the baby died.'

In his report, Professor Brockington recorded her response to a question about the loss of the baby: 'It feels like part of me is missing. I don't even know where Olivia is. When I think about what we would all be doing, I hurt so much. I was crying all the time for the baby, for me, Paul and Olivia.' He noted that, considering that she was in labour for four hours, her account was short on detail. She told him: 'I can remember vividly bits of it, but others I can't remember. It is like looking at an old black-and-white photograph.'

He wrote that he believed it was possible that the baby 'in an enfeebled state, breathed or gasped in the bag. Being in a poor condition, she either stopped breathing again or ran short of air or found her airways blocked by the polythene of the bag. Death could have been accidental.'

He felt that there were two possible psychiatric explanations for the baby's death: her mother's delusional depression or transitory confusion. He believed that the dominant influence on Caroline was her belief that the baby was dead, which had led her into an inactive role. The fact that she had carried the baby with her throughout the day and was planning to take her home was something beyond his experience in the hundreds of cases he had studied, although he had encountered cases where the mother was found sitting in a bemused state with the dead baby beside her. 'It is completely incompatible with the theory that she killed the baby in cold blood in order to conceal the pregnancy. No one in their right mind would put themselves in such a dangerous situation. It is the clearest indication that she was mentally ill. It also shows that she had a strong attachment to the baby, which is incompatible with neonaticide.'

His conclusion was that it was impossible to establish that there had been an intentional killing, that her depression and the belief that the baby was already dead fully explained her failure to attend to the baby's needs after the birth. 'In my opinion, she is innocent of any crime. I do not see how, in all the circumstances of this case, including the pathology, her behaviour and her obvious signs of mental illness, *actus reus* and *mens rea* [a deliberate intention] could be proven.'

Of the five psychiatrists who had interviewed Caroline since her arrest, Meg Spinelli was the one who had seen her most frequently, initially in prison and then twice a week, while Caroline awaited trial. They had also spoken regularly on the telephone both while Caroline was in jail and when she felt in despair during the period before the trial. Dr Spinelli would also have given evidence based on her final report. She had pointed out that Caroline's brain neurochemistry would have been altered and the hormone levels dropped, disrupting what was already a vulnerable central nervous system. She concluded:

> Caroline's psychotic denial and acute psychotic state render her unresponsible for the events by virtue of the biological and the psychopathological processes sur-rounding the birth ... The bizarre act of hiding her dead baby under her shirt is psychotic and not consistent with murderous intent ... Caroline was in an acute state of psychosis, out of contact with reality and incapable of discerning right from wrong. She was unable to appreciate the wrongfulness of the alleged act because of her fixed delusional system around her belief that her baby was already dead ... In my judgement, she lacked capacity to form intent by virtue of a defect in her ability to reason

and should therefore be found innocent of charges under
the insanity defence.

Caroline had, of course, also been interviewed on five
separate occasions for a total of more than ten hours by Dr
Naomi Goldstein. Since Dr Goldstein was carrying out her
inquiry on behalf of the prosecution, and Marjory Fisher with
another DA, Scott Kessler, had attended the sessions, it was
clear that her final report, delivered on 22 January 1996,
would carry most weight in the DA's office. It is a thorough
and detailed report. Dr Goldstein had also investigated Caroline's background and story through her relatives and friends
before reaching her conclusions. She had spoken to Caroline's
parents and to Paul and Dominic Faraway and had listened to
the taped statements Caroline had made immediately after her
arrest.

In her report, Dr Goldstein noted that Caroline told of
her hallucination that Detective O'Donnell had appeared in her
cell: 'In her vision she thought she saw him crouching over
her and she thought he was going to strangle her. She heard
his voice saying something like, "We've done it for you now
... Paul, Dom and Sam are on the airplane and you're never
going to see them again."' She had also told Dr Goldstein that
the BBC broadcast had left her feeling 'ridiculed and made fun
of' (although Caroline never saw the programme and was later
full of praise for the team). She noted that Caroline had not
wanted to speak to her parents initially but that Sister Marion
had helped her to make contact with them.

Dr Goldstein was clearly aware that Caroline was far from
happy at having to submit to the examination: 'Ms Fisher's
presence was particularly disturbing to Ms Beale as Ms Fisher
had first interrogated her in the hospital and the hospital scene
being nightmarish, first advised her that the baby had been
born alive. Ms Beale was deeply resentful of the evaluation
itself and let me know that other doctors, particularly Dr

Spinelli, had been much more supportive.' Of Caroline's demeanour, she said: 'She was angry and wept at times but also had a sense of humour.' She also surmised that

> There are some hints that Ms Beale was not quite as interested in Alison as has now been suggested, that she did not attend to her friend as much as might have been expected toward the end. She claims she was unable to cope with terminal illness. She has expressed enormous guilt toward Alison on a variety of grounds, for example, wishing that she could have died instead of Alison, for being pregnant and having a healthy body while Alison was losing all of her functions as well as her hopes, for being falsely supportive of Alison when she knew she was going to die.

Her diagnosis was that Caroline suffered from an adjustment disorder with depression and anxiety, a probable major depression and a probable post-traumatic stress disorder. She believed that Caroline was clinically depressed during the relevant time prior to the birth.

> I am sure this neonaticide involves multiple, complex psychological determinants . . . It has been suggested that Ms Beale identified the dead baby with her friend, Alison Taylor, psychologically, but while this is a possibility I think any understanding based on the data obtained thus far must take into consideration first Ms Beale's own profound sense of abandonment and her psychological neediness and dependency and, second, the unusual degree of guilt she has expressed towards her deceased friend . . . Alison became the object of intense, unacceptable feelings which may have displaced from other figures such as her mother and Paul. It is possible that Ms Beale identified the baby with herself, unwanted, rejected, abandoned and

feeling dead, that is depressed and possibly suicidal. She did not name this baby initially but then gave the baby her own (and her mother's) middle name. At the same time, Ms Beale may have identified herself with the 'aggressor', that is, she rejected the baby as she felt she had been by the important people in her life.

Perhaps Ms Beale's deep need was to be the only child and the arrival of another baby, even her own, threatened all her important relationships.

Dr Goldstein also suggested that the arrival of Caroline's niece at the time of Alison's death could have exacerbated her fears of abandonment:

I wonder if, considering her own troubled pregnancy and depression and over-sensitivity, Ms Beale was re-experiencing some deep, unresolved fears of abandonment triggered by her mother's illness at the time of her brother's actual birth many years before.

She speculated that

given her neediness and her identification with the baby, it may be psychologically understandable that she would take the baby home to England where it could have been reborn in fantasy (even dead), welcomed with much sympathetic attention and a different legal climate and mourned but not abandoned, although we do not know what Ms Beale intended to do, if she actually knew herself ... I think it would be very difficult to penetrate Ms Beale's denial of responsibility for the baby's death for intrinsic psychological reasons, as well as for extrinsic reasons related to her defence. She has been told she was not responsible.

Her final conclusion was that, although Caroline was suffering from a significant depression at the time of the delivery,

> there was no evidence of a major mental disease or defect as a result of which Ms Beale would have lacked substantial capacity to appreciate the nature and consequences of her alleged conduct or that it was wrong.

She accepted that Caroline's judgement was impaired and

> memory for what happened may be consciously or unconsciously selective. It has been argued that Ms Beale's memory for the relevant time was cloudy but she is sure the baby was dead and that she did not kill it. Her behaviour was consistently purposeful ... Her agitation serves as a smoke screen, a child-like defence as it is so difficult to reach her, at the same time as it reflects underlying conflicts. It helps to maintain the positions of denial and innocence.
>
> Whether the baby was very still, whether she identified the baby with her deceased friend, whether she identified herself with the baby, which I think is more likely, whether she wished unconsciously or consciously that she were not pregnant and the baby and girlfriend were dead, these are all possibilities ... In spite of Ms Beale's profound feelings of unreality, there was no evidence of psychosis in my opinion, that is, a mental disease, to support an insanity defence at the time of the delivery or the next day.

That, then, would have been the battleground: a prosecution pathologist adamant that the baby had died by suffocation and was the victim of homicide, opposed by defence pathologists who would have argued that such a diagnosis was flawed and inaccurate and that there was no substantive evidence that the child had been born alive or that Caroline's actions had been responsible for the death. A prosecution psychiatrist who would have argued that Caroline was aware, to a vital extent, of what she was doing and was not suffering at the crucial time from a psychosis which would allow her to use a defence of insanity, opposed by defence psychiatrists who would have argued that Caroline was clearly not of sound mind at the time of the baby's death and was thus innocent of any crime.

Professor Brockington described Dr Goldstein's report as perfectly competent but felt that it was flawed because it accepted the original pathologist's report, which he and the other defence experts did not.

In any event, that was the evidence that led Marjory Fisher to believe that, while the original murder charge was untenable, a manslaughter charge could have been substantiated to the satisfaction of a Queens jury; and that was the evidence that Michael Dowd believed could have led – coupled with Caroline's own testimony in the witness box – to an acquittal on a manslaughter charge.

Chapter Eighteen

When Caroline had first seen Judge Robert Hanophy during her earliest appearance in court to seek bail, he had reminded her of David Nixon, the television magician: a cheerful, bald, avuncular man with an easy, friendly manner.

Certainly the man in the emerald green blazer sitting in Court Room Number 44 looked more like the genial president of a Mid-West golf club than one of the state's most learned judges. He had been a Supreme Court judge for ten years having been originally appointed by Mario Cuomo (for whom Michael Dowd had once campaigned) to cope with a rise in crime and a consequent increase in the number of defendants.

From an Irish–American family, he had been born in Flushing in 1934 and grown up in Corona, studying for his doctorate of law at St Johns. He had worked as an attorney in mainly civil cases and had become a civil-claims judge before his elevation. A prominent member of the local Roman Catholic Church, a Knight of the Holy Sepulchre, which is a Catholic benevolent society, his two sons had been educated at Christ the King, the school where Father Tony Ercolano works.

It was later suggested that Hanophy might have had his own political reasons for the way in which he handled Caroline's case but in fact he was not running for election as a judge, neither had he been elected on a specific ticket, although he did have his own political hinterland: he had been a candidate for the Conservative Party, the small party that stands to the right of the Republicans, but had run only modest campaigns – he had spent only $7000 to $10,000 in one bid for office but most of the time spent nothing at all. He had, in fact, once run against Donald Manes for the Queens borough president's job in 1981 but was quoted at the time as saying, 'I even wonder if it's worthwhile having the office.' In 1971, he was chairman of the Flushing Conservative Club, and in 1977 he ran on a Conservative–Liberal–Republican ticket against the Democrats for the civil court judge's job in Queens, but even his detractors would not say that he let his political affiliations influence his decisions.

Hanophy was known as a tough sentencer. He told Joel Rifkin, the serial killer who had murdered more than two dozen women and whom Paul Vladimir defended, as he added a life sentence to the 175-year term that the man was already serving, 'In case there is such a thing as reincarnation, I want you to spend your second life in prison.' Another convicted defendant was told that the probation officer who would be handling his eventual release had not yet been born. The previous September he had jailed a doctor for twenty-five years to life for allowing a woman to bleed to death after a botched abortion. In 1989, he had sentenced a man to twenty-five years to life for drugs offences and attacked him for getting his wife pregnant during the period before his trial. 'That was not an act of love, that was a dastardly thing to do,' he bellowed at Fidel Lara, aged twenty-three. 'That child will grow up in a one-parent household.' But in 1992 he showed leniency to Daisy Hutson who was given five years for killing her crack-addicted daughter, telling her, with reference to the girl's eight-year crack habit, 'You have already eight years of time served.'

'He's very fair, but if you're convicted in front of Justice Hanophy, goodbye – you get the max,' said a court official.

But by the time Caroline walked into the Supreme Court-house in Sutphin Boulevard on 4 March 1996, she knew she

would have to plead guilty to a crime she did not believe she
had committed. She was accompanied by Michael Dowd, her
parents, the British Consuls Michael Dwyer and Jackie Cerdan,
Clare Webb, her old schoolfriend who had just arrived in New
York, Father Tony, Margaret Brower, Irene Dowd, Meg
Spinelli, and dozens of reporters. It is within a judge's gift to
allow the television cameras into court for a trial and Judge
Hanophy had decided that the Beale case should be filmed.
The footage shows Caroline, by now almost unrecognizably
more composed than during her earlier harrowing appearances, still shaking and being steadied by Michael Dowd as
she answers the questions fired at her. She speaks in a barely
audible voice and is clearly distressed by the questions and the
answers she is giving. The hearing went as follows:

HANOPHY: You OK?
BEALE: Yes.
HANOPHY: Mr Dowd [MD], you have an application?
DOWD: Yes, Your Honor. Under the second count of the
            indictment, Your Honor, I'd like to withdraw the
            plea of not guilty and enter a plea of guilty to the
            lesser included.
HANOPHY: That being the lesser included, second count of the
            indictment.
DOWD: . . . manslaughter in the second degree, to enter a
            plea of guilty in full and final satisfaction in the
            indictment pending before this Court.
HANOPHY: All right, Ms Beale, you just heard what Mr Dowd
            said; is that what you want to do?
BEALE: Yes.
HANOPHY: Tommy, swear her in.
Whereupon, the defendant was duly sworn by the clerk of the
court.
HANOPHY: What is your full name and address?
BEALE: Caroline Beale . . . Leytonstone, London E11.

HANOPHY: You feel you've had ample time to consult with your attorney before deciding to plead guilty?

BEALE: Beg your pardon?

HANOPHY: Have you had enough time to talk to Mr Dowd before deciding to plead guilty?

BEALE: Yes.

HANOPHY: Have you discussed all the various aspects of this case with your attorney?

BEALE: Yes.

HANOPHY: Do you wish to change your plea from not guilty to guilty to what we call a lesser included of the second count of the indictment which would be manslaughter in the second degree?

BEALE: Yes.

HANOPHY: Do you understand the charges in the indictment and the meaning of what you are pleading to?

BEALE: Yes, I do.

HANOPHY: Do you understand you have a right to continue to plead not guilty and go to trial?

BEALE: Yes, I do.

HANOPHY: Do you understand that at such a trial, you would have the right to representation by counsel, the right to cross-examine and confront witnesses, you could have witnesses subpoenaed to come and testify in your behalf, to remain silent at the trial if you so choose, or to put the State to its proof so that you would be convicted only if the State established guilt based on legal proof beyond a reasonable doubt?

BEALE: Yes.

HANOPHY: You also know you have a constitutional right to trial by jury, that is, you have a right to have a jury hear and decide your case, and that they must be unanimous in their verdict as to guilt or innocence?

BEALE: Yes.

HANOPHY: Do you understand by pleading guilty, you are giving up these rights, and that a guilty plea is the same as a conviction after trial?

BEALE: Yes.

HANOPHY: Do you understand that you are admitting that you committed the crime to which you are now pleading?

BEALE: Yes, I do.

HANOPHY: Has anyone, I include the Court, the District Attorney, or your lawyer, the police, or anyone else, threatened or coerced you, or in any way influenced you against your own free will in order to get you to plead guilty?

BEALE: No, they haven't.

HANOPHY: Have you entered this plea voluntarily of your own free will?

BEALE: Yes, I am.

HANOPHY: Ms Beale, you understand that the sentence in this case will be a period of time served. I believe you have done eight months in prison. You will be sentenced to five years' probation. That probation will be in your home country of Great Britain. As part of the plea, you will be attending some sort of psychiatric service over in England that will last for approximately a year. And in order to get this plea, you are going to have to waive your right to appeal from the plea which we're doing now, and the sentence which will be on Thursday, I believe. Do you understand that?

BEALE: Yes.

HANOPHY: Have other promises been made to you by anybody? I mean your own attorney, the Assistant District Attorney's office, myself, and the police officers; anybody made you any other promise other than what I just stated to you?

BEALE: No, they didn't.

HANOPHY: Counsellor, any other promises made by you?

DOWD: No, your Honor. Not at all.

HANOPHY: You are pleading guilty to a C felony. Under that plea, you would be eligible to receive up to fifteen years in jail; do you understand that?

BEALE: Yes.

HANOPHY: My promise to you is a period of time served plus probation, understand that?

BEALE: Yes.

HANOPHY: All right, you are pleading guilty because you are, in fact, guilty?

BEALE: Yes.

HANOPHY: I didn't hear you.

DOWD: She said, 'Yes,' sir.

HANOPHY: Mr Kessler, I believe you're going to do the allocution?

KESSLER: Yes.

[The Assistant District Attorney, Scott Kessler, Marjory Fisher's junior, takes over. He fires questions at Caroline in rapid order.]

HANOPHY: This happened in Queens County on September 1994.

KESSLER: Ms Beale, on September 22, 1994, you gave birth to a baby girl; is that correct?

BEALE: Yes.

KESSLER: After giving birth to this baby girl, you never went for any medical help or medical treatment for this baby; is that correct?

BEALE: Yes, sir.

KESSLER: You then placed this baby in a plastic bag. At the time you placed the baby in the plastic bag, you were aware that placing a baby in a plastic bag could lead to a baby's death; is that correct?

BEALE: Yes.

KESSLER: Despite being aware of this, you still placed the baby in a plastic bag resulting in the child's death; is that correct?

BEALE: Yes.

KESSLER: With that, your Honor, the defendant has
           successfully allocuted as to manslaughter in the
           second degree.

HANOPHY: Your recommendation?

KESSLER: I recommend the Court accept the defendant's plea.

HANOPHY: The Court is satisfied that the defendant's plea of
           guilty is entered freely, voluntarily, and with the full
           understanding of the circumstances and
           consequences thereof. The People, having approved
           of the defendant's plea for the reason stated, the
           defendant is permitted to withdraw her previously
           entered plea of not guilty and to enter a plea of
           guilty to manslaughter in the second degree, under
           Section 125.15 of the Penal Law. Which plea is
           hereby accepted in full satisfaction of the indictment
           consisting of three counts. The Court believes that
           the ends of justice will be served by accepting the
           plea of guilty, in that, the discretion given to the
           Court with respect to possible punishment is
           sufficient. Mr Kessler, Ms Fisher.

FISHER: Yes, Your Honor.

FISHER: Your Honor, may I make a statement at this time?

HANOPHY: Yes, you may.

FISHER: Your Honor, this case is among the most tragic
           cases in which I have been involved during my
           thirteen years as a prosecutor. And over these past
           few years as Chief of the Special Victims Bureau in
           the Queens DA's office, I would like to outline some
           of our concerns and interests that we had in
           reaching the agreement that you just delineated.

           A newborn baby is dead. She would have been
           almost eighteen months next month. And a young
           woman, the newborn baby's mother, stands before
           this Court charged with having attempted to take

the child's body wrapped in a plastic bag, and put it under her clothes on to an airplane at JFK airport bound for England. During these past many months, Mr Dowd and I have spent hours discussing the facts surrounding this case and working towards a possible disposition of it. We reviewed the results of the examination of the defendant by respected members of the psychiatric community, retained by both the defense and the prosecution in this case. And last Friday Mr Dowd and I met personally with the District Attorney of this county. He, himself, is a respected former member of the judiciary. As the Court, of course, knows, society's purpose in sentencing includes deterrents, the protection of society, rehabilitation, and retribution.

In addition, the following should be considered in the determination of sentence: the background of the individual, and the crime charged, mitigating circumstances that bear directly upon the manner in which the crime was committed should also be considered.

Your Honor, we looked to all of these factors in determining a resolution here. And we are prepared at this time to accept the disposition that you just described. We believe it to be fair and reasonable. It's a disposition that recognizes the defendant's criminal liability and culpability for the death of her child, under the laws of this state, on the one hand; and her acknowledged need for continued psychiatric intervention to deal with the problems that precipitated her actions, on the other hand. The defendant is a thirty-years-old woman who has no prior criminal history. She spent eight months in jail in this country. During the past ten months, she has spent her time volunteering with the elderly, under the auspices of the St Kevin's Church and living with the church family.

Psychiatrist retained by the People, Dr Naomi Goldstein, nationally recognized forensic psychiatrist, spent over ten hours on five separate occasions examining the defendant, and countless additional hours speaking with her family, with her boyfriend, and his family, with those whom she had contact with while she was incarcerated, and reviewing the defense psychiatric reports. Dr Goldstein concluded in a thorough and comprehensive report that has been provided to this Court that while she is satisfied that the defendant knew and understood the nature and consequences of her actions at the time of her baby's death, that she was nevertheless suffering from a serious pre-existing psychiatric condition, depression that could have affected her judgement at that time. Dr Goldstein concluded that the defendant is in continued need of intensive psychiatric therapy and medication.

The psychiatrist retained by the defense, whose reports are also in the Court's possession, while differing with Dr Goldstein's opinion with respect to the defendant's understanding of the nature and consequences of her actions, are very much in agreement with her, that continued intensive psychiatric intervention is necessary, indeed, for the defendant's rehabilitation. The defendant, as you have just heard, pled guilty to manslaughter in the second degree, acknowledged that she recklessly caused the death of her newborn baby moments after the child's birth. We accept that plea, as we've said earlier. We recommend that the defendant be

placed on probation for a period of five years with
the following conditions: that she be permitted to
return within the next few days to England in the
custody of her parents who are with her in court
today and who have been supportive of her
throughout these proceedings. That immediately
upon her arrival in England, she be admitted to the
Maudsley Hospital in London, preeminent
psychiatric institution in the world, where she'll be
evaluated on an in-patient basis, under the
supervision of Channi Kumar and Dr Gunn, a
leading English forensic psychiatrist. It is my
understanding that Drs Kumar and Gunn and their
staffs will determine and provide a course of
psychiatric treatment and care for the defendant for
a period of at least twelve months or longer . . . if
they so determine. And they will report on a
quarterly basis to both the Court and the District
Attorney's Office as to the progress and the results
of her therapy.

    In addition, your Honor, we would ask that
probationary supervision of the defendant be
transferred to the proper authority in England, Dr
Kumar, with whom I personally spoke by telephone
over this past week. And he in a letter faxed to Mr
Dowd this morning and to me . . . a copy delivered
to the Court . . . has endorsed and agreed to the
conditions that I have outlined, and has assured us
they will be carried out. We believe that justice will
be best served in this difficult and tragic case by the
acceptance of this defendant's plea, and the
imposition of the sentence that has been imposed.
Thank you very much, your Honor.

HANOPHY: Thank you. I would like a copy of Dr Gunn's
report. Mr Dowd, do you wish to say anything?

DOWD: Just to thank the Court for its patience and gentle but firm prodding of us to continue discussions which have continued over a long period of time, involved Judge Brown [DA Richard Brown] as well. But I think we owe the Court a debt of gratitude for your continued interest, patience, and impartiality in this record.

HANOPHY: Ms Beale, I have in front of me a form entitled waiver of right to appeal. Have you signed this form voluntarily and knowingly after being fully apprised of your appellate rights by both myself and Mr Dowd?

BEALE: Yes.

HANOPHY: Let the record reflect that the defendant, counsel, and I have all signed the waiver of right to appeal.

Now, to our guests from the press, I understand that cameras are not allowed in the courts in England. I know, I was there about five years ago, and they stopped me from going in with my Instamatic camera. But they did inform me they would allow me to bring it across the street for a slight fee. I think it was a delicatessen, they would hold on to my camera until I came out. But I welcome you here in New York. Mr Dowd and his client have to get to the Department of Probation today. I know you have a press conference downstairs.

Behave like ladies and gentlemen when you leave here.

Don't knock anybody down and make sure you get to Probation before five o'clock tonight, OK. Thank you.

As Marjory Fisher left the court, Daphne Beale lunged at her. Outside, the Beales, surrounded by cameras and thrusting microphones, said what they had been bursting to say. 'I personally think that this has been a cruel and medieval prosecution that does no credit to a civilized society,' said Peter Beale.

'I pity any American girl who finds herself in this situation because the American laws are medieval and should be changed,' said Daphne. Their remarks were widely reported on both sides of the Atlantic as they flew back to Britain to prepare everything for Caroline's return.

The entry in Peter Beale's diary read:

We arrive at the court in Sister Jane's car but they [the press] start running towards us and then as we crossed the road they were tripping and almost getting run over in their eagerness. We were surrounded outside the court and we had to say OK, guys, let us go, we have to get into court. They were very polite and said thanks. There were more as we went through security, some of them offering money for Caroline's diary ... There were about five TV cameras in the court, a lot of media ... Caroline was called out to the front, she was very unsteady. The judge asked if she wanted to sit and the policeman got her a chair.

The judge started with some light-hearted comments about not being allowed into the Old Bailey with his camera. Marjory Fisher started playing her role and went through the case as she 'saw it' and felt it necessary to talk of the baby and that she would be eighteen months old and running about ... She said Caroline would require five years probation and a period in the Maudsley Hospital, one of the best in the world, she said.

Caroline was then required to plead guilty to second-degree manslaughter [by neglect]. She spoke in a hushed voice and the judge told her to speak up. She said her piece and there was more talk and we all started to leave.

Daphne said that she spoke to MF as she left and said, 'You haven't won.' MF made no comment. We all went out and stood with the press. I said 'a cruel and medieval system that does no credit to a civilized society'. Daphne said, 'I pity any American girl who comes up against this in similar circumstances because it is medieval.' . . . Daphne does really well and cannot stop.

Judge Hanophy was furious. As he saw it he had 'bent over backwards' to allow Caroline to leave the country and ensure that she did not go back to jail, and here he was, as he saw it, being told by her parents that he was cruel and medieval. He made his displeasure known. Michael Dowd was worried. He could suddenly see the possibility that the deal would be revoked and that Caroline might have to stand trial and face a prison term, after all. Caroline still had to return to court to sign the necessary papers before her return to London. It was agreed that she should apologize to the judge on her parents' behalf.

Once again the cameras were in court and Judge Hanophy took the opportunity to make his feelings plain. He told the court that what the Beales had called the American system – 'barbaric' and 'uncivilized' – had 'got under my skin'. He described Peter Beale as a 'bigmouth', likened him to a television character called Ralph Kramden, a New York bus driver who was portrayed by the actor Jackie Gleason in the fifties sitcom *The Honeymooners*, which is still shown on late-night television in America.

'I will say this,' said the judge, looking over towards the television cameras, 'with our laws that mandate the prosecution of people who kill their children, protecting the children rather than excusing the killer is our primary focus in this county. I can't fathom characterizing such a goal as either barbaric or uncivilized. Indeed, I believe any law that grants a blanket exemption from prosecution or punishment for those people who kill their children when their children are under one year of age is a law which is primitive and uncivilized. Baby Doe, when born, became a citizen of the United States of America, entitled to all the protections that go with citizenship, including life, liberty and the pursuit of happiness. I'll say to our friends in Britain: God Bless America.'

He reiterated that Caroline would serve her sentence in Britain, 'that great country that has convicted a great many people on the perjured testimony of the police, allowed them to spend fifteen to seventeen years in prison and did everything to see they remained there even though they knew they did not deserve to'.

Judge Hanophy recalled Caroline's reaction after she had made the apology: he had thought that she was about to embrace him and he felt that this might look slightly inappropriate on television so he took her by both hands. Caroline's recollection is quite different: she said she had no intention of embracing him and was under the impression that he had taken her by the hands in a friendly gesture. He told her: 'I didn't mean to jump on you. It just got under my skin. I wish you the best of luck.'

Michael Dowd was relieved at this outcome: 'Hanophy had just extended himself by pressuring the probation service to produce an early report and he reads the next morning that he's part of a savage system. The next day Randy Fleishman [the judge's clerk] said the judge was thinking of telling her to take her plea back and go to trial. He was so enraged. I said, "Judge, she didn't say anything." He was so angry. He made sure that the cameras got set up in the court so that it would be sure to be seen in England. It was embarrassing.'

But Dowd had had no doubt that Caroline would have been acquitted had she stood trial. Yet he had been uncertain that she would be able to stand up to what would have been a three-week trial. And if she had been convicted – 'I doubt whether Hanophy would have given her the minimum. If she had received fifteen years she would have served every day. I was doing what I had to do. But I honestly believed the baby was born dead and that we could prove that.

'I had $150,000 worth of experts acting for nothing, a

superstar line-up. Brockington, a professor with a bow-tie. Spinelli was pure New York and charming. We are a country that goes gaga if you say Princess Di and the idea of civilization in an American mind is someone with a bowler hat and a walking stick. Kumar was a gem of a human being, an intelligence so shining and brilliant that whatever he touches, light shines. This would have been a spectacle, it would have been great. The prosecution wouldn't have known what hit them. Caroline, I thought, was going to be an excellent witness. We had the compelling fact that she was trying to board the plane with a baby and . . . it would have been an unsolved mystery.' But he still believed that the right decision for Caroline had been made.

The District Attorney, Richard Brown, issued a statement immediately after the hearing in which he said: 'This case is among the most tragic cases I have seen since becoming District Attorney. A newborn baby is dead and her mother was charged with causing her death.' He went on to say that psychiatrists for both sides had agreed that although Caroline 'knew and understood the nature and consequences of her actions at the time of the death of her child, she was nevertheless suffering from a pre-existing psychiatric condition labelled as depression that could have affected her judgement'. He added that while the defence psychiatric team differed from the DA's psychiatrist as to whether Caroline understood what she was doing, both sides believed that she needed intensive psychiatric treatment.

While the second part of his statement was accurate, it was hardly a fair reflection of the opinions of Meg Spinelli and Professors Brockington and Kumar to suggest that they accepted that Caroline knew the 'nature and consequences of her actions at the time of the death'. In fact, their evidence would have specifically challenged this view. Brown concluded by saying, 'We believe that justice has been served in this tragic case by accepting this plea of guilty and the imposition of the sentence of probation with the conditions we have outlined.'

The Beales, meanwhile, were unaware of the dramas still being played out in the courthouse but have no regrets about their remarks. 'We never addressed anything personally to Hanophy,' said Peter Beale. 'It was about the system as a whole.' Although he was in favour of Caroline accepting the plea bargain so that she could come home and receive treatment, he felt that the way she had had to answer the questions, after all she had gone through in prison, was inhumane.

'I wanted her to go to trial so she could clear her name completely,' said Daphne. 'I was sitting with Tony when she was pleading to this and the judge was making her say those things over and over again and I was crying and saying, "This is wrong, so wrong." And Tony was saying, "It's only words," and Irene said the same thing. But it isn't only words. She has this thing against her, this stigma which she will always carry, and if she had gone to trial she would have been believed. I believe perhaps she should have gone but I couldn't tell her. It was wrong what they did to Caroline.'

'My parents were emotional and they were just saying what they felt, and the judge, I thought, behaved like a child,' said Stephen Beale. 'He made my sister apologize – like a little kid.'

DA Greg Lasak's response to the spat was typically droll: 'You don't expect a Polish guy to get involved in this?'

Father Tony recalled the process: 'I was ill, I was sick to my stomach after having to sit in that court room when she had to say that she was guilty to each and every part of the indictment. It was done in a tremendously unfeeling way.'

He was puzzled that Hanophy reacted: 'I would have thought as a judge he would have heard it all already. Why would he have allowed the pain of parents to influence him that strongly? I'm sure he must have heard worse than that from hardened criminals. I can't understand how a bright person like Judge Hanophy would be that affected by the comments of upset parents.'

206

For Meg Spinelli, who had looked after Caroline for more than a year, the decision to plead guilty presented a complex dilemma. 'I don't think I have strong feelings about the final decision. I felt no one else can really make that decision for her. If she went to trial with all of the good autopsy reports, is it likely that she would have gotten off? . . . My feeling is that when people hear the word baby-killer they don't hear anything else. Queens is pretty blue-collar, not real well-educated people who would maybe rise to the occasion . . . In some ways a trial would have been wonderful because what are we doing to women in this country? It's a witch-hunt, for Chrissakes, but Caroline shouldn't have to pay the penalty, go through this trial for womankind. It was a very tricky call. I felt she was quite fit by the time the trial arrived. I felt she could have done it. Look at what she went through before any support came along. There's a resilience there. I think she could have done it. The only problem not doing it is that she had to take that plea for manslaughter, which feels morally wrong.'

Irene Dowd found the whole court procedure disturbing. 'It was frightening but I was very, very happy for her that they finally reached an agreement because a trial is such a horrible gruelling experience. It was very, very hard [for Caroline to accept a plea bargain] but I truly believe it was the best possible outcome because a trial would have devastated her, would have torn her apart.

'We had a very strong case and the findings were wonderful. But the thing is, would she have made it through the trial if she doesn't even want to talk about a newspaper article? To watch yourself being pulled apart, that's not easy and basically the results were the same – she went home.'

Detective O'Donnell had his own theory as to why an agreement was reached: 'I think there was a lot of pressure brought by the English Consulate to bring this sentence. When we were kicking it about unofficially, the sentence that

Caroline got is very much in line with what I thought would be apropos.'

Back in England, Caroline's friends were gradually hearing the news that she was about to return. Araminta Thorne spoke to her on the phone: 'She was quite subdued and I got the gist from her that there'd been a plea bargain. And I'd just been told the thing I'd been waiting for for almost two years had happened and I felt utterly deflated, I felt distraught. I could tell she was quite down. It wasn't just that she was over-wrought, it was what had happened. I tried to mask what I was feeling and say, "Caroline, it happened, you're free." And she said, "Yeah, I know but I had to do a plea bargain, I had to say I did it." She was very upset. It was what she had gone through so much to avoid. She had always said she wouldn't go back to prison. Either she would win the case or she would kill herself.'

So in the end, the jury of twelve was never sworn in to make those decisions and both sides remain, publicly at least, convinced that their experts' testimonies would have prevailed. Neither side could claim to be entirely satisfied with the outcome: Marjory Fisher had originally intended that Caroline should serve more time inside, Michael Dowd had originally hoped that the evidence he had assembled would prove his client's innocence. But however the verdict had gone, perhaps Professor Brockington's belief that no one – not even Caroline – would ever truly know exactly what had happened inside suite 101 was the most accurate.

But for now the trial was over. There were parties at both Meg's and Margaret's houses. The combination of tension, weariness, booze and anti-depressants took its toll. Caroline crashed into bed and immediately out of it. When Clare came up to her room there was no one to be seen. Caroline was spending her last night in America the way she had spent her first night in Riker's Island – fast asleep on the floor.

Chapter Nineteen

A simple granite cross bearing the words 'He calleth His children by name' marks the entrance to the place on Hart's Island where 750,000 unclaimed and often unnamed Americans lie. It is known as Potter's Field, a name derived from Aceldama, the 'field of blood' below the south wall of the Old City of Jerusalem, where a potter's field was supposedly purchased by the chief priests with the thirty pieces of silver that Judas had thrown down before he hanged himself. It is referred to in the Gospel according to St Matthew as a place for the burial of strangers. It is used generically in America to refer to a paupers' graveyard.

And it was here that Olivia Ann Beale, or 'Baby Girl Beale' as she was described by the authorities, was buried. Caroline, who had carried her with her to the airport to bring her home to England, had always been assured that the body was being kept safe so that a burial or cremation could take place later. Both Michael Dowd and Marjory Fisher also believed this and it was some comfort to Caroline to know that at the end of the trial she would be able to lay the baby to rest. But a bizarre series of events had already removed the body.

The medical examiner's office had responsibility for the baby. Because there had been a dispute about how the child had died, it was assumed by both prosecution and defence that the body would be kept until the time of trial. However, due to a bureaucratic oversight, this did not happen. A spokeswoman for the medical examiner's office said that because the body was not claimed after a number of months it was sent to City Burial for interment. She added that 'Baby Girl Beale' was placed in a simple pine coffin and buried in Potter's Field in November 1995.

'We repeatedly told them to keep the baby,' says Marjory Fisher. 'We telephoned every month to make sure. At that stage we thought we might need the baby for the DNA tests. It was certainly an error that she was buried. Something got screwed up.'

'It was the result of incompetent bureaucracy,' says Michael Dowd. 'Caroline had been assured by me because I was assured by both the DA and the British Consul that the body was being held. They had put in a request to get the body of the baby early on and they were told that the baby was kept at the request of the DA. I was dumbfounded when I found out the body was no longer there in the medical examiners' office. Caroline was constantly concerned about the body.'

Hart's Island, which lies between Manhattan and Long Island, east of the Chimney Sweeps Islands, is the largest Potter's Field in America. Its inhabitants are buried there now by volunteers from the Riker's Island prison population, and in the past by the inhabitants of the long defunct reformatory on the island that housed vagrants and physically disabled prisoners before slinging them back to Hell's Kitchen or the Bowery. It was sold to New York City in 1869 and the first person buried there was orphan Louise Van Slyke who had died in the Charity Hospital. Now the mortuary department ships 170 unclaimed bodies every week to the island for burial in pine coffins and around fifty bodies are reclaimed every year by relatives or friends who had not been contacted at the time of death.

So it was to Hart's Island that the search for Olivia Ann came. Father Tony, like Caroline, had become aware that the baby had been buried only two days before Caroline left. Father Tony made his own inquiries and found that he knew the funeral director who had handled the interment. He assured him that the body had been that of Olivia: 'He said, "Father, I wouldn't fool you, if I didn't know I'd tell you. You have Miss Beale's child."' The baby was cremated and the remains were taken to the Rectory of the American Martyrs and then to Margaret's house where they were kept in the room where Caroline had stayed.

In the summer of 1996 when Father Tony and Margaret came to London Margaret brought the remains over in a small box wrapped in a scarf belonging to Margaret's late mother. 'I decided to carry her in a knapsack round my neck like her mother had done,' she said. In the Beales' front room in Chingford the remains were laid on the table and Father Tony read from the Book of Wisdom and the story of the disciples on the road to Emmaus in St Luke. 'It struck me that Caroline was a stranger when we met her and the baby was a stranger to all of us, we'll not know her for a long time.'

They went to the church of St Peter and St Paul in Chingford. It was Suffering Sunday and there was a sermon about suffering – losing someone close, death, loss of a friend. Almost every reference seemed applicable to Caroline, Father Tony noted.

Chapter Twenty

There were three empty seats in Club Class of the plane flying into Heathrow from New York. The other seventeen were occupied by journalists and camera crews. Aware that the British media had discovered what flight Caroline, Meg Spinelli and Michael Dowd were taking, even though they were booked under false names, the British Consulate had executed a subtle manoeuvre with all the discreet cunning that one would expect from career diplomats.

The Consulate had been asked by the doctors who would be treating Caroline in England to try to ensure that she was exposed to as little pressure – and press – as possible. The Consulate was able to assist the request to give a final body swerve to the media.

Flight BA 127, the plane on which Caroline was travelling, flew into Gatwick airport where it was met by Ken Dwyer, the brother of the British Consul, who happened to be a taxi-driver and could be relied on to keep quiet about Caroline's movements. There had originally been plans for her to hold a press conference when she returned, which she dreaded, but on advice from Channi Kumar it was agreed that others would talk on her behalf.

Caroline felt ambivalent about the sudden return: 'All the time I had been longing to come back in some ways but, when it finally came to it, I thought of all the friends I had made and all the people I wouldn't be seeing any more. Half of me was wanting to come back and the other half was wanting to stay in New York. It had been eighteen months since I was home and I didn't know what to expect, where I would live, whether I still had a job.'

Part of the plea-bargain deal was that she would receive treatment from what Marjory Fisher had described as 'one of the preeminent psychiatric institutions in the world', and thus her first stop was the Maudsley Hospital where she arrived exhausted. The doctors who were to care for her were asked by the press about her treatment.

Professor John Gunn, one of the team, put into context the still simmering row over the argument between Judge Hanophy and the Beales which had been followed up in the press: 'We in this country have nothing to be crowing about and shouting across the Atlantic about how things should be.' A country that shackled pregnant women in hospital, he said, in reference to a recent high-profile case where a woman prisoner had been taken for treatment and handcuffed to the bed, had nothing to teach other countries about the treatment of prisoners.

Professor Channi Kumar said he believed that Caroline was perfectly capable of making a full recovery and, anticipating a question that was on many journalists' lips, said: 'And if it's in anyone's minds, the chance of such events recurring are virtually nil.'

At the Maudsley, Caroline found herself swamped with flowers from well-wishers, both people she knew and strangers who had followed the case since her arrest. 'One of the other patients asked if I was a film star,' she said.

Her friends were conscious of the adjustment she was now having to make. Clare Webb had arrived in New York just as Caroline finally knew that she was coming home. 'She was elated. She ran up to me at the airport and said, "I'm going home!" Then it was seeing people and saying goodbye and all the farewell parties. Then the realization hit her that she was going home to nothing – Where was she going to live? What was she going to do for money? – so for the last week she was quite low. The night before, she said, "Do you think I'm doing the right thing?" I said, "Going home has got to be the right thing. Whatever they say doesn't mean anything in England." But she was like a rag doll, she didn't know where to turn. She had all these new friends and people who had become her family in America and she didn't want to leave. Everywhere she went she was adored and she was coming home to grey skies and not a lot else.'

For her close friends and family, there was delight that she was home. Caroline Two still recalls the news: 'She phoned up and said, "Guess what, I'm coming home." She was a bit shocked. She said, "I've got to plead guilty but then they said I can come home." We wanted to shout it from the hilltops but we couldn't tell anyone at first. Then it was on the news and it was lovely – people were driving past and waving.'

Lesley Warren went down to see her in the hospital: 'She kept saying, "I want to go back to New York." She didn't belong there, it was like going backwards for her. When we went out for a walk she didn't want to be recognized so she would always put on a hat or glasses and kept her hair down.'

Araminta Thorne found her quite sedated and disoriented and also went for a walk with her outside the grounds. 'She was frightened of being recognized. We were out together and three teenage girls walked towards us and one did a double-take and turned round to look at us. But she soon became more relaxed. She became a friend to the other patients and helped other people there, in particular, a very depressive woman. Caroline responds very well to people who are in trouble.'

Mandy Goff saw her shortly after she returned: 'We'd gone out for a walk in the forest and we came back through North Chingford and she said I'm not getting out of the car. She wouldn't venture out because she thought she might be recognized.'

A Stranger and Afraid

Caroline was recognized, albeit obliquely, when she went with her work colleague Kevin Mansell to a West Ham v. Newcastle United football match at Upton Park. At half-time a spectator turned round and said to her: 'I've seen you on the telly. You're an actress, aren't you?' He thought she had played a part in *The Bill* or on *Brookside* in which someone was killed. Five minutes into the second half, the spectator passed her a note. It read: 'I'm ever so sorry. I know who you are. I wish you all the best for the future. God bless you.'

For Peter Beale, whose life had been taken over by the events of the previous two years, it was confusing to find his daughter almost reluctant to be home after all the energies that had been invested in bringing her back. But he and Daphne were still overwhelmed with the support they received from the public. Of all the hundreds of letters sent to them only two had been hostile: one had suggested that they must be mad to support their mad daughter, the other enclosed pictures of ladies' underwear. After Caroline left the Maudsley she returned to King's Head Hill and her old room.

For Caroline it was also a confusing time. She gradually made contact with her old friends, made appointments to see her probation officer, as she was required to do by the terms of her plea bargain, and started to see a psychiatrist three times a week. Initially, she was shy about going into the street although she heeded the advice that few people remembered for more than a day or two someone they had seen in the newspapers, and especially in her case since the image of her with which they were most familiar was of a distressed, unmade-up person with untidy hair and a face distorted by tears and the drugs she was being given, rather than the svelte, elegant woman who had returned to Britain.

Chapter Twenty-one

The first contact that Caroline had had with the media was a shouted question from a woman reporter as she was frog-marched, her hands cuffed behind her, by two male police officers into a squad car. 'Why did you kill your child?' The police gave her a blanket to put over her head but nothing could protect her from the public's fascination with her story, which attended her right up to the conclusion of her case.

In the eighteen months between her arrest and the trial, the media played a crucial part in the story. From a very early stage, those in Caroline's corner on both sides of the Atlantic had decided that the press and television had a vital part to play in deciding what would happen to her. Her parents were adamant that she should not be lost from view in Britain and her attorney and psychiatrist in America both believed that favourable publicity could only aid her case in a country that was used to trials being conducted on their TV screens before the jurors had even been sworn in. In addition, the money that the media could provide made it possible both for the Beales to keep in touch with their daughter and to pay for the medical and psychiatric experts whose opinions they believed might help to acquit her and who were essential for the mounting of a proper defence.

Under American law, through the First Amendment, if a prisoner wants to be interviewed by a member of the national media, the authorities are obliged to honour that desire; in the United Kingdom there is no such constitutional right, although

216

a recent judicial ruling has upheld the right of a prisoner to see a member of the media.

Inside prison, the first contact that Caroline had with the media was when the BBC journalist Nick Catliff of *Inside Story* came to visit her. Although being filmed was an ordeal, she liked the crew, who gave her hugs and illicit packets of cigarettes. Catliff had seen a tiny item on the case on the news, had looked up the Beales in the phone book and had telephoned them. They had already been contacted by two other interested television companies and, inexperienced in the media world, were perplexed as to what was the honourable course to take. Eventually the Beales decided to go with the BBC rather than an independent Channel Four company.

A total of 6.2 million people watched the *Inside Story* on Caroline, 38 per cent of the viewers at that time on that night, and the film had a major effect on the way in which Caroline was perceived. What was striking about the film was that people remember two specific images: the shaking, tearful Caroline in jail and the ice-cool Marjory Fisher announcing, 'You don't get many points for killing babies in this country.'

Throughout the programme, Fisher is resolutely unmoved by arguments advanced on Caroline's behalf: 'I'm not sure I understand what she's a victim of.' Asked if it was not odd that someone should be carrying a dead baby out of the country with her, Fisher says: 'It may be the ultimate in concealing evidence, to take it out of the country where the trail and what happened is going to be completely erased ... She was trying to conceal it.' She brought the case constantly back to the baby: 'I represent the baby and the people of New York ... one million people in this state would have given anything to have this child.' And, in response to the Beales' plea that what Caroline had done did not make sense: 'There are several cases where crimes don't make sense but they have to prove that she was suffering from a mental disease or defect because what she did that day didn't make much sense. There are defendants who rob people, take all their property, there's nothing left to take, they could just disappear into the night at that stage and they take a gun out and they stick it in the head of the victim and blow their brains out. That doesn't make any sense either but it doesn't make it any less a crime.'

Catliff said that talking to Fisher 'was the most bizarre interview. We did it in nine minutes, we did it in less than a roll. She knew what she was going to say and she just said it. From a television producer's point of view it was just great because she was so clear, so precise. That became the bedrock of the whole film.' Marjory Fisher was delighted with the film, says Catliff, as were most of the other participants, including the Beales, Michael Dowd and Meg Spinelli. Paul Faraway declined to participate.

Matthew Norman, reviewing the programme in the *Evening Standard*, described Fisher as 'a creature whom a saint would enjoy seeing stretched on a rack'. He concluded that 'If the jury who will shortly decide whether Caroline Beale is a murderer were to see it [the programme], they would laugh the case out of court.'

Caroline had qualms about participating despite the advice she was receiving. 'I remember I was shaking, I couldn't keep my legs still. It was so daunting being faced with it at the time and I've not been able to watch it since. I felt – when this is all over how am I ever going to walk down the street without people recognizing me? But Michael Carter, the British Consul, said that people had a very short memory and wouldn't remember. He told me, "Just go for it."'

The reluctant media star soon found herself having to answer the same questions again and again and, once released on bail, having to walk down streets and stand at stations so that television crews could film her. She hated it. Both she and her parents found it hard sometimes to act out the scenes the cameras required. GMTV had paid for the Beales to come over and they wanted a grand reunion in the hotel room and to film them all together in the Rockefeller centre. 'Michael said it was important to get the Americans interested in the case,' said Caroline. Through Meg Spinelli's husband, Bob Reitano, who was a friend of the writer and journalist Nora Ephron, contact had been made early on with ABC's *20/20* documentary slot. This was a prestigious programme to appear on and one that would guarantee a high response. Indeed, for many of Caroline's friends in America, it was the first time they had learned the details of the case. 'I had a very heavy session with them up in the attic with all the cards [from friends and supporters] on strings. They filmed us going round New York at places where we would never have gone – my poor mum and dad up the Empire State Building.'

A year after Caroline's arrest, the programme went out. It was introduced by anchorwoman Barbara Walters, the doyenne of television broadcasting in America, as 'the haunting case of Caroline Beale, a mystery that spotlights a bizarre disorder ... one of the strangest journeys you'll ever take – inside a mother's troubled mind'. The story, which was entitled 'A Mother's Madness' and presented by Lynn Sherr, was a broadly sympathetic treatment of the case, coupled with a tacit suggestion that the United States had much to learn from the United Kingdom in terms of how Caroline should be treated. To give the issue greater topicality, the co-anchorman Hugh Downs reminded viewers that the Princess of Wales had just admitted to suffering deep post-natal depression. Of Caroline, the programme asked: 'Is she evil or is she sick?' and added that 'She could spend the rest of her life behind bars.'

The footage of Caroline, some of it taken immediately after her arrest, was harrowing. Throughout her interviews with Lynn Sherr, she is almost constantly in tears and stuttering uncontrollably as she relives what happened and talks about Alison's death. Marjory Fisher declined to be interviewed by *20/20* who instead used some of the BBC footage when she remarks, in referring to the British law on infanticide:

'In the United States you don't get extra points for killing a baby as opposed to an adult.' Marjory Fisher said later that her mother had seen her on television, thought she looked terrific but told her that she had come over as the Wicked Witch of the West.

At the end of the programme, Barbara Walters asked rhetorically: 'Is American justice blind?' and concluded that 'It does seem that England is so much ahead of us.' For Caroline's supporters, the programme was what they had hoped for: it showed that Caroline was deeply distressed, devastated by what had happened and was in no way a sinister or callous criminal.

Neither Detective O'Donnell nor Marjory Fisher, who both watched the programme with interest, felt that it was fair. Both believed that it heavily favoured the defence and did not give the full picture. 'They didn't have the full facts,' said O'Donnell. 'They were constricted by time.' Marjory Fisher said, 'I thought that *20/20* was completely one-sided. It was very close to the trial and and I thought that it was something that, as the prosecution, we couldn't do so close to the trial. The defence may have different views.' Her boss, Greg Lasak, also said he was opposed to the prosecution taking part in a documentary in advance of a controversial trial.

But any potential juror or member of a juror's family who might have come across the programme between the ads for Frank Sinatra's eightieth birthday bash or Elizabeth Taylor's latest excursion into perfumery would surely have been left in little doubt as to what the case for Caroline Beale now was. It even contained footage of Professor Ian Brockington talking at his Birmingham clinic to English mothers who had experienced their own panics after the birth of a child or who had refused to accept that they were carrying a child that might survive.

Nick Catliff was unimpressed with the behaviour of the *20/20* team. 'I thought they behaved appallingly badly. They turned up at the airport when the Beales arrived and they repeatedly asked the same question until Daphne cried. You could see it happening. It was this question about Caroline and the baby – Daphne cries. "Cut. Let's do it again." Same question was asked. Then it was "Cut. See you at the hotel," and they just walked out. There was no "Gosh, Mrs Beale, I'm terribly sorry." I disliked *20/20*, they were so relentless in their use of the Beales.' The BBC team moved the Beales to a different hotel so that they could dodge the *20/20* team.

Caroline never watched that film either. She said she had found the making of it much too painful to want to relive it. Indeed, she made this decision about all the media coverage of her case, deliberately avoiding articles about her on both sides of the Atlantic. She even abandoned reading most newspapers altogether because she felt they relied too much on personal tragedies. She was already aware, from the arranged visits to Riker's Island, that people were interested in her story although, as she recorded in her diary, performing for the cameras or even the most sympathetic of interviewers had become an ordeal for her. She became more aware of the continuing media interest when she was released: 'When I was first given bail, they were all there tripping over each other. I could hardly speak because I was so tired and they wanted to have me give a message to my mum and dad. It was like that all the time. People always seemed to want you to say something obvious, something that they already knew.'

Down in the East Village in a shop called Myers of Keswick, the Heinz baked beans tins sell at $1.85 (£1.13) and Bird's Custard at $3.50 [£2.15] but to the visitors over the years – including some of the Beatles, the Rolling Stones and Princess Margaret, who wanted their Robinson's Barley Water – the price for the taste of home is clearly worth it. Everything from Branston Pickle to Fortnum and Mason tea is there, beside the Donald McGill seaside postcards and photos of the Queen. It was to Myers that Mick McGovern, veteran New

York reporter and former Chicago cabbie, went on the day that Caroline was released from jail.

Having worked with many of the British New York hands as a stringer for the *Daily Mail*, the *Daily Express*, the *Sun* and the *Mirror*, McGovern knew well the weaknesses of the Briton abroad. He went round the corner from his apartment to his English friends, the Myerses, who ran that little corner of the foreign field, and asked them to make up a wicker basket with all the delicacies – Cornish pasties and Scotch eggs, HP sauce, sausages and mushy peas – that he thought Caroline might appreciate after a diet of overcooked jail food. Adding some white roses of Yorkshire, and a note from the New York bureau of the *Daily Express* for whom he now worked, McGovern dispatched the hamper by limousine to Michael Dowd's Park Lane office addressed to Caroline, welcoming her back into the outside world and wishing her well. He attached a telephone number. 'I figured she could use the food to build herself up but, of course, she knew what I was wanting.'

It worked. Caroline agreed to talk to him over the phone with Michael Dowd listening on the extension to make sure that nothing untoward was discussed. She retained a soft spot for the burly six-foot three-inch newsman who covered many of her subsequent court appearances. Some of his English-born colleagues had not thought it much of a story at first, he says, as he nurses a glass of red wine in the Tavern on Jane Street near his home. 'They described it as a – what do you call it? a fish-and-chip murder,' he says.

McGovern is an experienced reporter: he had covered the trials of Charles Manson and Lieutenant Calley, the American Marine who took part in the My Lai massacre in Vietnam. He had quit school early and was making a living as a driver when he picked up a newspaper proprietor as a fare, told him about the stories he was writing in his spare time and found himself hired on thirty-seven dollars a week. He had been working for the *Daily News* in New York when he was approached by the *Express*. The first story he was asked to file, which gives an idea of how long he has been on the beat, was of the romance between American tennis player Chris Evert and the British John Lloyd.

'I thought it was a great story,' he says, and remembers that when he first saw Caroline, she had been 'a sad creature then', but she had gradually changed so that she was 'full of life and into high heels and everything. She had been in this hell hole with whores and killers and become friends with them.' Colour had been added to the story, he felt, by the performances of Dowd ('gutsy guy, up to all the police tricks'), Hanophy ('the most injudicious judge I've ever seen') and Fisher ('perfunctory and cold, every time she opened her mouth she put her foot in it; she said she was concerned about justice but if she had been concerned about justice she would have shown some concern to this woman').

To McGovern, Caroline came over as a 'non-malevolent, unsophisticated, tragic figure, shackled by chains at the hands and feet and waist and with these Supreme Court marshals who were just white bread taking her to the pen.' He liked the English, anyway, and was even working on a book about the English actress Joanna Pettet, who had been in *The Group* and *The Night of the Generals* and whom he had met in Hollywood.

Although McGovern maintained his and his newspaper's interest in the story, he conceded that Daniel Jeffreys, who had worked on the *Inside Story* documentary and for the *Independent* and the *Mail*, had the inside track on the story. 'She would talk to him. It was his natural British charm. He would talk to her about movies they had seen while all the others would jump in her face and ask her these stupid questions.'

Jeffreys was a former City whizzkid economist who had become a financial journalist with the BBC in England, had been unhappy there and had returned to the City before going

223

into journalism in New York. An elegant, self-assured English-man, he had spotted the story early on. At the time of Caroline's arrest there had been confusingly different reports: one television channel even suggested that because Caroline had been sharing an apartment with more than one man at the time she had been part of 'some kind of love triangle in a seedy SoHo hotel'. (One British reporter who jetted in to cover the case found himself staying in the very same room.)

Jeffreys wrote the first major piece on the case and, since journalists often rely on the first substantial and researched report that appears to have reached a conclusion on a story, his article became the template for much that followed. As he describes it: 'It was – British girl captured in the maw of unfeeling American judicial system. The British press saw her as mad and badly treated.'

He became more involved in the case: 'It was horrible to watch Caroline in court,' he says over bass and Chardonnay in a Manhattan restaurant. 'She would shiver, she would shake, she had a wild look, she was incoherent. She would start a conversation and then break it off.'

Jeffreys's article in the *Independent* on 18 April 1995 quoted Marjory Fisher as having said of Michael Dowd: 'This is Mike's comeback case. He is an interesting choice to defend Caroline because he's only just got his lawyer's license back ... He needs a high-profile victory.' Dowd was quoted as saying that 'Marjory Fisher is too ambitious for her own good. The way she is handling Caroline's case, I'll be able to paint her as the enemy of women. She's not prosecuting Caroline, she's persecuting her. When I play that card her career will come crashing down like a crystal chandelier.' Ms Fisher is quoted as having responded: 'Mike is so full of shit. If I won the lottery tomorrow I'd be home with my boys in a flash.'

Both Dowd and Fisher were unhappy about the quotes attributed to them: Fisher particularly denies having asserted that Dowd was 'full of shit' and says that he and she understood that they were talking off the record. Yet Jeffreys undoubtedly captured the flavour of the competitiveness between them. The acrimony was exacerbated when the same quotes appeared again verbatim in a feature a month later in the *Daily Mail*. The article came in the middle of the *Inside Story* filming and caused great friction because Jeffreys was acting as the New York fixer and associate producer for the BBC team.

The British press, almost without exception, found the story gripping. There was certainly an element of how-dare-foreigners-treat-our-women-like-this? to some of the coverage and this theme was familiar: newspapers had recently followed the arrest, imprisonment and eventual release of Karyn Smith and Patricia Cahill, the two West Midlands teenagers held in Bangkok on heroin-smuggling charges. As more than one commentator remarked, if she had given birth twenty-four hours later, after her arrival in Britain, she would have remained in hospital, not shackled in leg irons and locked up in a grim jail. Broadly, the press reflected that level of disquiet. In December 1994, when Caroline had been in prison for six weeks, the *Daily Mirror* headline read: 'Free Me Or I'll Kill Myself, Sobs Mum'. The story inside was headed 'My Ordeal in Hell Jail, by Brit Mum.' In May, the *Daily Telegraph* opened its report: 'The shackles and chains will be clamped on to British civil servant Caroline Beale again this morning.'

While Caroline made a point of never reading anything that had been written about her case, her parents studied the way she was portrayed in the media closely. They found the television coverage almost universally supportive of Caroline and were broadly happy with the press, although they remarked on the large numbers of inaccuracies in the stories.

One article that had upset them appeared in *New York* magazine. Peter Beale interpreted it as critical of him and Daphne for being 'normal' and 'ordinary', in a way, as he saw it, blaming all that had happened on that very ordinariness.

The article said that Caroline had come from a family 'that was, by all accounts, the Platonic form of middle-class ordinariness – a condition much prized in England . . . It wasn't the sort of house in which emotions were much discussed.' Later the article, by Rebecca Mead, concluded: 'One can't help but wonder whether if Caroline hadn't been expected to be so "normal", she might not have ended up doing something so extraordinary and so awful.'

Caroline had phoned her parents after she had given the interview and Peter noted her reaction in his diary: 'Caroline said the interview with *New York* magazine went well – Rebecca Mead was the reporter and Caroline said she was like Alison.' Caroline had mentioned this to Rebecca Mead who had in turn remarked on it in her article: 'Whatever the objective basis for the comparison, the fact that she made it is intriguing. I'm convinced that she hadn't considered at all how it might sound to me – a person who had been giving much thought to the notion of her psychotic identification of her baby with her dead friend – to find myself identified with that dead friend, too.'

To most of the New York press, used to a murder rate around ten times that of the United Kingdom, the story of one young woman accused of killing her child was small beer. Pete Donohue covered the case for the *New York Daily News*. A young man with three years on the paper, he works from a small press room in the bowels of the Queens court buildings on Kew Gardens with newspaper splashes – 'Woman, 102, Tackles Two Thugs' – stuck to the wall.

'It was a very striking case for me,' says Donohue, who was just about to start work on the Zucchini Robber case – a man who held up a store with a courgette which he pretended was a gun. 'It was very disturbing because it was so obvious that she seemed tortured. It was an upfront city-wide story but not huge.' It was only after the clash between Judge Hanophy and the Beales that intense interest developed: 'After Hanophy's remarks, they went nuts. But for us the story ended as soon as she got on the plane and would only be revived if she messed up in England.'

Certainly the American press that covered the final stages of the trial had a different take on it from the British press. *Newsday* reported Hanophy's remarks under the headline 'Brits Blasted in Baby Killer Sentence'. The paper recorded that the judge 'lashed out at her parents and blasted Britain's legal system'. The same paper headlined their summary of Hanophy's handling of the case: 'Tough On Crime, Rough On British'. Their report from Associated Press suggested: 'The overseas uproar notwithstanding, Hanophy actually gave the defendant a break.'

The *New York Daily Post* wrote, under the headline 'Judge's Diatribe Irks Brits', that 'A battle of words raged across the Atlantic yesterday as British officials fired back at a Queens judge who took potshots at their justice system – and the judge's supporters told the English to stuff it.' The *Post*'s London bureau had sought views from Conservative MP Jerry Hayes who responded: 'The poor fellow's either coming up for re-election or got up on the wrong side of the bed.' Manhattan lawyer Brian O'Dwyer weighed in on behalf of his fellow Irish-American: 'Hurrah for Judge Hanophy. The judge rightfully pointed out that the English system of justice is no justice at all, especially for the Irish.'

The letters columns of *Newsday* continued the controversy: 'Hanophy's derogatory comments were uncalled for. Before throwing stones he should concentrate on how to clean up our corrupted legal system,' wrote Rita R. Claridge from Whitestone. There were misunderstandings. When Caroline emerged from court after her final hearing she was asked what she intended to do on her return and replied, as a joke, that she wanted to learn 'how to speak proper English again'. It appeared in *Newsday*, in rather gnomic form, that she now wanted 'to learn how to speak properly'.

In some of the reports Hanophy was said to have referred to the film *In The Name of the Father*, the story of the miscarriage of justice involving the Guildford Four, but, in fact, he had not seen it. Closer inspection of the reports shows that the reference to the film was made by an aide.

Back in Britain as the case ended, the *Daily Mirror* headline read: 'I Did Kill My Baby, Admits Brit Girl'. The *Daily Telegraph* took a critical stance: 'So Just Why Did It Take Them So Long?' was the headline. Charles Laurence commented that there had been 'a sense that Miss Fisher was in no hurry to see Miss Beale freed into the care of British psychiatrists and probation officers'. Referring to Marjory Fisher's post-trial statement that Caroline had serious psychological problems that needed to be addressed, Laurence ended his article: 'To her critics, and to those who believe that the Beale case has left American justice tarnished, this is something that Miss Fisher could have concluded many months ago.'

Professor Ian Brockington said that he was angry about the coverage of the end of Caroline's case, which implicitly accepted Caroline's guilt. He complained about the ITN bulletin that referred to Caroline's guilty plea: 'I went to a lot of trouble and rang a lot of people to say that "You've got to understand that there are a lot of international experts who don't believe that she did anything whatever, that she is totally innocent. It's very important that you say that in your reports." I complained and they never replied.'

He also tried to have an article published in the American press and wrote to the *New York Times*, which eventually decided not to use it. Had they run it, the American public would have read that

Although our laws differ, we have respect for American accomplishments in the area of the psychiatry of mothering – it was New York, in 1874, that pioneered the protection of abused children, a proud achievement that

Britain cannot match . . . Mental illness should not confer exemption from justice. Psychiatric patients have a right to both prompt diagnosis and care and a full and fair trial. Otherwise, we are left with the outcome of this case: Miss Beale back from 'holiday' with a criminal record. She was welcomed with open arms – in the eyes of many British people, not a felon, but a victim.

He completed an article for the *New York Daily News* but was told that they had been unable to run it because coverage of the death of the veteran American comedian, George Burns, had to take precedence. 'It is not a good reflection on them that they were not prepared to publish them [the articles]. It seemed important to get something into the press there that threw doubt on her conviction.'

He and Professor John Emery, Emeritus Professor of Paediatric Pathology at the University of Sheffield, who had also been instrumental in preparing Caroline's defence, wrote thus to the *Guardian* in response to the newspaper's story: 'Your report on Caroline Beale's repatriation included the words "that led her to kill her child". This is wrong. A large body of international experts on pathology and psychiatry were ready to testify in her defence. All agreed she was suffering from a psychiatric illness. There was no evidence of unnatural death. If the case had come to trial, we feel confident she would have been acquitted.'

Daniel Jeffreys wrote, in a concluding article in the *Independent*, that 'The New York prosecutors who handled Caroline's case have got their pound of flesh, the district attorney will be able to add another guilty plea to his statistics.' He also asked the question as to why no one had realized that Caroline was pregnant.

Above all Caroline Beale and her baby were victims of 'British reserve' – that insidious sickness which makes us all reluctant to intrude or even inquire about the emotions of others ... Unless the British learn to talk more about their emotions, there will be other Caroline Beales and similar tragedies. Psychiatric illness has social as well as biological causes and the often suffocating nature of British relationships did much to trap Caroline Beale inside her own sickness.

Michael Dowd, of course, was very familiar with his hometown press, both from his own experience at their hands and through his friendships with a number of prominent journalists. Peter Maas, the author of *The Valachi Papers* and *Serpico*, was a good friend. On one occasion before the trial, Maas, who knew about the case from Dowd, had seen District Attorney Richard Brown in Elaine's restaurant in Manhattan and had remarked that he was glad that the case was in Brown's hands because it was clear that it should not lead to jail and that Caroline should be going home. Dowd believed that media pressure could have been one of the factors in the final agreement that Caroline should not serve time: 'Even though you live in Queens, you don't want the people in Park Avenue laughing at you.'

The Beales gradually became familiar with the whole media game: the names on Peter's contact list read like a Happy Families of the world of television – Richard and Judy, Eamonn and Anthea, Anne and Nick, Oprah. Magazines from *TV Quick* to the *Observer*, *Take a Break* to *Bella* dot the pages of his diaries. The various pleas and wheezes used by reporters to gain access to him or his family and the excuses offered as to why the promised fees had not arrived would make most journalists cringe with self-recognition. Peter Beale had found his first dealings with the press extraordinary, with journalists on the doorstep trying to thrust envelopes of money into his hand 'and they always gave you the impression that if they didn't get the interview they would be sacked'.

Not that they ever felt completely at home with being recipients of the media's largesse. When they were in New York, filming a documentary, they were taken out for a meal. He noted in his diary afterwards: 'Had steak and wine. Seems wrong for us to do this but we tell ourselves it's for the cause.' In March, Peter Beale met Daniel Jeffreys and his wife: 'Daniel is good company, his wife is called Debbie and she is very charming. She managed a plate of oysters and a huge lobster all by herself.'

By the spring, they were real media professionals. When Caroline was released from jail, a television crew was at the Beales' home in Chingford to record their first telephone conversation. Peter Beale noted in his diary: 'She is at Mike's and is going to have a hot bath – I said not to use too much hot water. Joke! They gave us a bottle of champagne, chocolate and flowers. It ended very nicely and they all got what they wanted.' Later he noted, almost with surprise: 'We saw ourselves on the tele last night on a trailer . . . It doesn't seem to make us embarrassed to see ourselves on the screen any more.'

But by July 1995, Peter Beale was obviously starting to have second thoughts about all the media coverage. After news of plans for yet another documentary had emerged he confided in his diary: 'I am not sure about whether we should let Caroline be exploited or whether it is to her advantage to keep in the public eye. I feel it is in her interest to be seen just in case she does go to prison and she won't be forgotten if she is a media figure.'

For her part, Marjory Fisher felt bruised by her encounter with the British media. 'I never said that Michael Dowd was full of shit, in fact it was a very amicable relationship. I was appalled that someone would write that. I have a lot of respect for him, he's an excellent attorney. He was quoted as saying that it would damage my "feminist credentials". I wasn't concerned about that and whether he really said that or not, I don't know. I was most concerned about the kid who died. The English media was totally unfair. I believe Caroline was treated very fairly. We agreed to bail. The medical evidence was very strong. For her parents to call me barbaric was outrageous.'

Judge Hanophy felt equally aggrieved at his treatment in the British press. 'I had a niece in London who told me it was on the front page every day and that it was a big story.' One British newspaper said that the judge was 'reported to drink beer chased by whisky – Scotch, by repute, rather than Irish or its American descendant, bourbon'. This upset Hanophy: 'I think the English papers did a very poor job of reporting what was going on. It was highly inaccurate and there was a lot of stuff that was completely untrue about me and about the case. They said that Michael Dowd and I used to drink beer and whiskies in a bar together on Queens Boulevard but we had never met before this case. I drink very little hard liquor as it happens and as for drinking beer and whisky together . . . Well, I drink a little wine with a meal.'

He had been unhappy, too, when the BBC crew started filming in his court, even though they had been granted permission. 'He went berserk,' says Nick Catliff, 'and hauled me to the front of court and treated me like I was a little boy and told me he could have me thrown in jail. I was petrified. All the English tabloid journalists were there, sniggering in their grubby macs. I had never come across a judge behaving like that before. Clearly he has a temper.'

Mary de Bourbon, who handles the press for the DA's office, was also critical of some of the coverage. Sitting in her office drinking a Diet Coke from the can and smoking a Marlboro – 'Only the old dames smoke any more' – she elucidates: 'It was unusual to have so much interest from another country but because we have JFK we do have a lot of foreign cases. Forty-three per cent of the city's Asian population lives in Queens and there is a big Arab, Senegalese, Latino,

Iraqi, Irani, Pakistani and Indian population. I understood from friends in England that Caroline's case was a *cause célèbre*. But there was a lot of misinformation flying around. The infanticide laws in England were misinterpreted here to suggest that you weren't prosecuted at all. The whole case was very strange. There was no question in my mind that she killed this baby but to strap the baby to her and go to the airport she was obviously showing not very good judgement and that's putting it charitably. The job of the prosecuting counsel is to represent the interests of the state of New York and they have an interest in seeing that people who are believed to be criminals are prosecuted. Obviously the duty is not only to prosecute but to do so in a fair way and a just way. People believe that people should face the music, face the bar and face the accusation. Justice and fairness have to be satisfied.'

She said that she understood why the Beales complained so vehemently: 'How would you feel if your daughter was arrested for the murder of your grandchild? I still feel sorry for them, they were obviously salt-of-the-earth type of people, small wonder that they had bitter and strong views. No one in this office was surprised that they were angry and upset because that is what loving parents would do. You love your child, you don't want to see them prosecuted in a court of law.'

Paul Faraway hated his experience with the press. 'I was under extreme pressure and forced into unpleasant corners,' he said. With his family's backing, he stayed as far away as possible from the media.

But even after the end of the trial, interest remained intense. When the Beales arrived back in London, the *News of the World* made an offer of £20,000 to £25,000 for Caroline's story.

Chapter Twenty-two

Many people sent Caroline books in prison and, as she remarked, they seemed particularly enthusiastic about Dickens and Austen. Perhaps there was a subconscious feeling on the part of the donors that these writers might be uplifting or perhaps they just felt that as their tales had withstood the test of time they might be more reassuring to read in prison than twentieth-century novels – although she also was sent and enjoyed George Orwell's *1984* and *Homage to Catalonia* and John Steinbeck's *The Grapes of Wrath*. A search through the classics would have provided possibly more pertinent material in Sir Walter Scott's *The Heart of Midlothian*. The story was based on that of a young woman called Isabelle or Tibby Walker, which had taken place almost a century earlier, in the 1730s. Isabelle was a strikingly beautiful young woman who had become pregnant, had delivered her baby in mysterious circumstances and no one knew whether the child had lived or died. Because there had been a number of such incidents at that time the law had recently been changed to make a woman liable to a charge of murder if she was unable to prove what had happened to the child and could not show that she had told anyone about the birth.

Isabelle Walker had been charged with murder and sentenced to death. Under Scottish law, a period of six weeks had to elapse between a death sentence and the execution. On the day that she was condemned to death in Edinburgh, her elder sister, Helen, had set off barefoot for London to seek a pardon.

She arrived, with her simple petition, having walked much of the way and taken lifts with carriages and carts, dressed in 'tartan plaid and country attire', before John, Duke of Argyll who represented Scottish matters at court. He arranged a pardon from the Queen and Helen Walker returned to Edinburgh just in time to save her sister's life. It was suggested to Scott by a woman friend that this would make a marvellous story and *The Heart of Midlothian* was published in 1830. (Many years later, Scott wrote the inscription for the tombstone for Helen Walker in Irongray churchyard in Dumfriesshire.)

It is a remarkable tale, with the feckless Isabelle transformed into the comely Effie Deans, and her sister Helen into the more homely Jeanie. It ends with the discovery that the child, a boy, survived, became a brigand, and was sold to a slave owner in Virginia whom he killed before joining a tribe of Indians. It is written with perhaps more compassion and understanding than 'Effie' or the real character might have found in some quarters 160 years later. As one of the characters in the novel describes it, Jeanie had to save her sister 'from the bloody fangs of an unjust law', a view not dissimilar to that held of the American criminal justice by some of Caroline's supporters. Scott makes the point that a woman is being charged with murder when perhaps no killing took place. 'If the law makes murders,' says another character, Mrs Saddletree, 'the law should be hanged for them.' Scott quotes the controversial law under which the death penalty could be required: 'By an act made in the second session of the first parliament of our most high and dread sovereigns William and Mary that a woman who shall have concealed her condition and shall not be able to show that she had called for help at birth in case that the child shall be found dead or amissing shall be deemed guilty of murder thereof.' It was, indeed, as one of the magistrates in the novel described it 'a cruelly severe statute'. In the court case, the judge who sentenced Effie Deans to death said: '"It is my painful duty to tell you that your life is forfeited under a law which, if it may seem in some degree severe, is yet wisely so to render those of your unhappy situation aware what risk they run by concealing out of pride or false shame their lapse from virtue and making no preparation to save the lives of the unfortunate infants whom they are to bring into the world."'

George Eliot addressed the same subject in *Adam Bede*,* which was published in 1859 and became a best-seller. She, too, chose a true story of a woman convicted and sentenced to death for the murder of her infant child. In her journal about the genesis of the book, she records that her Methodist aunt had told her the story almost twenty years earlier. Her aunt had accompanied the woman, Mary Voce, to her execution at Nottingham gallows in 1802.

Mary Voce had been only eighteen when she was convicted by a jury of poisoning her six-week-old child with arsenic after being abandoned by her husband; she had earlier had an adulterous affair and the baby was not her husband's. As the rather lurid account in a contemporary broadsheet recorded: 'She had embraced the allurements of infidelity and unable to withstand the resentment of an injured husband, she said she had expedient to the dreadful expedient.' The jury deliberated for only ten minutes before returning their verdict of 'guilty of wilful murder'. As the broadsheet reported: 'His Lordship and the Court were deeply affected, on beholding a woman in the prime of life and comeliness of person, stand before God and her country, a guilty creature unable to live any longer in this world, and not sufficiently prepared to enter that of another, "where the worm dyeth not".'

Her 'confession', committed to writing by a 'friend', doubtless a predecessor of those many helpful but anonymous 'friends' who talk to the press today, was as purple in its prose as the newspaper:

---

* I have referred to the world classics paperback edition of *Adam Bede*, with an introduction by Valentine Cunningham, Oxford University Press, 1996.

The dominion of Lust seized my soul, I quitted the protecting partner of my virgin heart and rambling after new delights became intoxicated with a succession of carnal pleasures, nor did I awake from my reverie, till my husband became so exasperated by my conduct that he left me prey to remorse . . . In a fit of revenge I sought the deadly poison; with a view at first to destroy myself, but Satan, always watchful for our destruction, dictated to me the infernal spirit of murdering that sweet innocent.

Another broadsheet used the occasion of her conviction to deliver a warning: 'May every such awful occurrence as has now been recorded operate as a powerful warning to all those Persons who find themselves tempted to evil.' A third broadsheet account of Mary's execution was even able to entitle her end as 'The Experience and Happy Death of Mary Voce' because she had been persuaded to confess her sins just prior to her death. 'Before her soul was set at liberty, she was much concerned at being made such a public spectacle, but ever after, all shame was banished from her mind.' She was even reported to have greeted her executioner with a smile and to have told him, 'Bless you, I have nothing against you, somebody must do it,' while she assisted him in placing the rope round her neck. The report concluded: 'She desired the people at the gallows to take warning by her and assured them that she was happy and that she was confident she should be in Glory directly.'

George Eliot turned the wayward heroine into a beautiful young woman: in *Adam Bede* the dairymaid, Hetty Sorrel, whose 'cheek was like a rose-petal, that dimples played upon her pouting lips, that her large dark eyes hid a soft roguishness under their dark lashes'. She was seduced by young Captain Arthur Donnithorne of whom Eliot wrote: 'We don't inquire too closely into character in the case of a handsome, generous young fellow, who will have property enough to support numerous peccadilloes.' Their romance was described in equally rosy terms: 'Such young unfurrowed souls roll to meet each other like two velvet peaches that touch softly and are at rest . . .' The child is abandoned under a nut-bush. Hetty is said by one of the witnesses at her trial to have looked 'a bit crazy' and in court is described as 'visibly trembling'. The jury in the novel were as swift as in real life and returned after a quarter of an hour with a guilty verdict: 'Those who were near her saw her trembling.' She falls into a fainting fit and is carried from court. In fiction, the young woman is spared the gallows with Captain Donnithorne arriving at full gallop with a pardon – at least from the death penalty – in his hand and Hetty is, like Scott's heroine, banished rather than hanged.

What is notable both in the factual and fictional accounts of the time is that the young women are condemned as much for giving in to Lust and Temptation as for being responsible for the deaths of their infants. In fact, the death penalty is interpreted as much as a punishment for promiscuity as for any crime against the child, and a grim satisfaction is taken by the law-abiding members of the public and commentators in the suffering of the women concerned, a sense of relief that 'sinners' can be seen to be punished and righteousness rewarded, however pitiless the punishments may seem a century or two later.

Both Scott and Eliot ensure that the young women, although portrayed as victims of men of privilege and position, are the ones who pay the penalty and there is no sense of redemption for them or for other young women whose similar exploits are recorded in ballads of the time. As long as illegitimacy remained such a shame on a family, such tales made for riveting fiction, especially when the young women facing the noose had the requisite number of ringlets and dimples and dark lashes. Other writers addressed the theme tangentially. 'Infanticide is practised as extensively and legally in England as it is on the bank of the Ganges,' wrote Disraeli in his novel, *Sybil*. The heroine of Mary Wollstonecroft's *Maria, or The Wrongs of Women*, published in 1798, confesses to having committed infanticide.

The themes may seem outdated now but the trembling figure in court and the refusal of the authorities to listen to Effie Deans' protestations of innocence or to take notice of the terrified Hetty Sorrel might strike a chord with those who saw Caroline Beale in the courtroom on Sutphin Boulevard.

Chapter Twenty-three

In 1778, Sarah Sant was executed for the murder of her child. She had insisted that the baby was stillborn but medical evidence was produced by putting the lungs of the child in water and finding that they floated, thereby indicating that a breath had been taken. The weekly *Cumberland Pacquet* described the outcome of her trial: 'She was attended at the place of execution by a Divine but, in the most pathetic manner, she denied the least intention of destroying the child. And we hear that the [her] Mother, on her return home, being received into the neighbourhood with a coolness she did expect, hung herself.'

The lung test, whereby it was deemed that a child had been born alive if the lungs floated in water and stillborn if they sank, became an increasingly controversial method of proving innocence or guilt. Mark Jackson, a research associate and lecturer in the Wellcome Unit for the History of Medicine at Manchester University, referred to Caroline's case in the introduction to his book *New-Born Child Murder*, a study of how women were charged with murdering their newborn children in the eighteenth century. As he pointed out:

All writers on the subject accepted that if lungs swam in water, they must contain air. However, the presence of air in the lungs was not conclusive evidence that the child had respired. The lungs could have been inflated by respiration, by putrefaction, by efforts to resuscitate the

240

child, or, according to Erasmus Darwin, a physician from Lichfield writing in 1767, by the child simply falling on its side at delivery.

More than two hundred years later, similar arguments of proof were being advanced in Caroline's case.

But, as Jackson makes clear, the unusual feature of Sant's case was not that she was prosecuted, which was common throughout the eighteenth century, but that she was convicted and executed. In the study that Jackson carried out, using the records of the Northern Circuit, of nearly two hundred women indicted for the crime, only six were convicted and only two hanged. Judges and juries were looking for ways to exercise leniency and to give the women the benefit of the doubt on whether a child had been stillborn or not. Thus two hundred years ago, the sides were lined up against each other in much the same way as happened in Caroline's case: one side, with the technical backing of the law, sought capital or at least severe punishment for women deemed to have killed their babies, while the other side argued for mercy or at least a presumption of innocence rather than guilt.

In a case in 1773, Margaret Hedley testified that her pain and labour was so intense that she took leave of her senses so 'that she knows not nor does she now recollect whether the Child was born alive or dead but she remembers that as soon as she came to her senses she found the said Child lying dead upon the ground'.

What they were doing was interpreting the Stuart Bastardy Act of 1623, which had been introduced to punish women who gave birth to illegitimate children and then tried to disguise the fact. The statute ran thus:

Whereas many lewd Women that have been delivered of Bastard Children to avoid their Shame and to escape Punishment do secretly bury or conceal the Death of their

Children, and after, if the Child be found dead, the said Women do alledge that the said Child was born dead ... for the Preventing therefore of this great Mischief, be it enacted by the Authority of this present Parliament, that if any woman ... be delivered of any issue of her body which being born alive should by the laws of this Realm be a Bastard, and that she may endeavour privately, either by drowning or secret burying thereof, or any other Way, either by herself or the procuring of others, so to conceal the Death thereof, as that it may not come to Light, whether it were born alive or not, but be concealed: in every such case the said Mother so offending shall suffer Death as in Case of Murther, except such Mother can make proof by one Witness at least, that the Child (whose Death was by her so intended to be concealed) was born dead.

The James Statute was acknowledged at the time to be severe but no more so than similar provisions in the contemporary legal codes of France, Denmark and Sweden.

Effectively, the burden of proof was thrown from the prosecution to the defence in that the woman had to prove that the child had been stillborn and, if she could not, was liable to the death penalty. There were exceptions. A case recounted by Sir Mathew Hale in *Pleas of the Crown* is reported in 1668 where a married woman was accused of murdering her newborn child but pleaded 'temporary phrenzy'. The jury accepted that she was of good character and suffering from insanity and acquitted.

Daniel Defoe made a lengthy contribution to the debate in 1731 in *The Generous Protector, or A Friendly Proposal to Prevent Murder and Other Enormous Abuses by Erecting an Hospital for Foundlings and Bastard Children*. What angered Defoe was that he felt that jurors were being fooled by midwives who gave evidence by 'ready rote' for the defence that a child had not been full-term and was therefore likely to have been stillborn. Defoe had the backing of the Church and public – as opposed to private – morality in that it was felt that women who had illegitimate children were by nature lewd and criminally inclined and therefore it did not matter if the justice was rough.

William Hunter, a surgeon, anatomist and 'man-midwife', writing in 1784, concluded that women pregnant with illegitimate children were often deprived of 'all judgement and rational conduct' at the time of delivery. He continued: 'Surely the only crime is the having been pregnant, which the law does not mean to punish with death.' Hunter, a fascinating, enlightened man, physician extraordinary to the Queen and a member of the Royal Academy of Sciences in Paris, allowed his findings to be used in trials of young women for child murder and his attitude is in stark contrast to those present two hundred years later. In his address to the Medical Society, in which he referred to some of the cases he had observed, he said: 'Often they are overtaken sooner than they expected; their schemes are frustrated; their distress of body and mind deprives them of all judgement and rational conduct; they are delivered by themselves wherever they happened to retire in their fright and confusion; sometimes dying in the agonies of childbirth and sometimes being quite exhausted they faint away and become insensible for what is passing; and when they recover a little strength find that the child, whether still-born or not, is completely lifeless. In such a case, is it to be expected when it could answer no purpose, that a woman should divulge the secret? Will not the best dispositions of mind urge her to preserve her character? She will therefore hide every appearance of what has happened as well as she can; though, if the discovery is made, that conduct will be set down as part of her guilt.'

Hunter recounted one case of a young unmarried servant who had given birth to a child in her room. The child had been found in a box wrapped in wet clothes and the woman was charged with murder, the lung test having been carried out and having indicated that the child had taken a breath. She had intended to have the child at a midwife's and to return immediately to work having heard that soldiers' wives were able to give birth in such a way behind a hedge and still travel with their husbands. But before she could carry out her plan she had been taken ill and fainted and had recovered consciousness 'in a deluge of discharges and with a dead child lying by her limbs. She first of all attended to the child and found that it was certainly dead. She lay upon the bed some time, considering what she should do and by the time there was a little day-light, she got up, put all the wet clothes and the child into her box, put the room and bed in order and went into it.' Hunter found her tale credible, arguing that the floating lungs was far from being conclusive of life. 'She was acquitted,' he concluded, 'and I had the satisfaction of believing her to be innocent of murder.' The case has many echoes of Caroline's so perhaps it is not surprising that Peter Beale kept Hunter's address close at hand and would refer to it for comfort at times of despair. 'Whenever I felt down, I would read it and felt that someone understood,' he said.

Hunter concluded his address with the 'facts, which I know from experience to be true and which will be confirmed by every person who has been much employed in midwifery'. The 'facts' included: that a child who took one gasp and instantly died would 'pass' the lungs test just as if it had breathed far longer and had then been strangled; that a child may breathe as soon as its mouth protrudes from the mother and may 'lose its life before its body be born ... and if this may happen when the best assistance is at hand, it is still more likely to happen when there is none; that is, where the woman is delivered by herself'; his third assertion was that 'we frequently see children who are but barely alive and after breathing a minute or two or an hour or two die in spite of all our attention. And why may not that misfortune happen to a woman who is brought to bed by herself?' He concluded that a strong child may be born perfectly alive but may die in a pool of natural discharges or wet clothes: 'An unhappy woman delivered by herself, distracted in her mind, will not have strength or recollection enough to fly instantly to the relief of the child.'

In 1772, Edmund Burke, Charles James Fox and others argued for repeal of the law on the grounds that 'Nothing could more strongly prove the absurdity and inexpediency of the law than the impossibility of putting it in execution, under which the judges found themselves; that laws were made to be executed not dispensed with.' Others were unhappy that such cases could still attract a death sentence and urged the transportation of women to America instead of hanging.

The Act was the subject of fierce debate and attempts to repeal it finally succeeded in 1803. Lord Ellenborough, who introduced the Bill as the Lord Chief Justice of the King's Bench, said that the reason for the change was that judges were 'straining the law' on the side of leniency and allowing the slightest evidence that the child might have been stillborn. The new statute meant that women charged with the murder of their infants were now subject to the same rules of evidence as for any other type of murder but a separate offence of attempting to conceal the birth of what would, if born alive, have been an illegitimate child was introduced with a two-year maximum prison sentence attached.

In the meantime, as Mark Jackson describes: 'Disputes about the character, conduct and responsibility of single women accused of murdering their children at birth captivated the writers of ballads and broadsheets in this period.' He adds: 'While persistent prosecutions and occasional convictions appeased local demands for some form of public retribution, frequent acquittals, legitimated by medical opinion, satisfied humanitarian concerns (and the claims of accused women themselves) that suspects were guilty of little more than concealing their pregnancies.' By the mid-nineteenth century it was estimated that as many as three hundred infanticides were carried out annually in London alone and that up to five per cent of all illegitimate babies were killed at birth.

In the revised version of 1880 of the Draft Criminal Code of 1878 a section stipulated that every woman should be guilty of a crime who being with child and about to be delivered of it, neglected to provide for reasonable assistance in her delivery, if the child was permanently injured thereby or died just before, during or shortly after birth, unless she could prove that the death was not caused by such neglect or by any wrongful act to which she was a party. If the offence was committed with the intent that the child should die, it was proposed that the woman be punished with penal servitude for life; if the intent was to conceal birth, the punishment was to be penal servitude for seven years.

Jurors, however, remained sympathetic to women charged with the killing of their children, as was illustrated by the case of a young woman called Sabina Tilley in Brighton in 1888. She had become pregnant by a soldier and had given birth to twins whose month-old bodies were found in a basket under a seat in a third-class railway carriage at New Cross station in south London. She had been impoverished and in despair and her case aroused great sympathy in the local press. At her trial, her counsel argued that the children could have died from the cold, from her inadequate lactation or congestion of the lungs, and she was acquitted. Stephen Plaice, who wrote about the case in *The Printer's Devil*, concluded that it 'may well have begun a sea-change in public thinking about infanticide which eventually led to a reform in the law early in the twentieth century'.

Certainly, reforms followed not long afterwards. In 1908, during a debate in the House of Lords on the Children Bill, the Lord Chancellor, Lord Loreburn, argued that the law regarding the deaths of infants should be changed because passing the death sentence in such cases had become a 'mockery' in that no one had been executed for the crime since 1849. As the *Lancet* reported, in an article on the subject twenty years later, 'He thought that public opinion was shocked at the idea of the death sentence being passed in cases where it was manifestly inhuman to carry it out, and, on the other hand, it was very much to be regretted that the death penalty should be nominally inflicted when there was no reality behind it.'

The Infanticide Act, 1922, enacted that any woman found to have caused the death of her newborn child could be convicted of infanticide, which was treated as a form of manslaughter rather than murder. She had to prove that 'the balance of her mind was disturbed by reason of her not having fully recovered from the effect of giving birth to the child or by reason of the effect of lactation'.

The Act referred to a newborn child and an early Court of Appeal decision ruled that a thirty-five-week-old baby was not covered by the Act. In 1927 a waitress in a London hotel was sentenced to death for killing her illegitimate child five weeks after the birth. In her signed confession she stated, 'I had nobody to mind him and had no money.' This was not accepted as a valid defence under the Act and although the death sentence was not carried out she was condemned to penal servitude for life. The period under which the Act operated was finally changed in 1938 to a year. The lesser charge was seen as appropriate for crimes that did not create as much public concern or social insecurity as random killings.

As the *Modern Law Review* noted in 1937,

The widespread dislike of the application of the law of murder in all its severity to cases of infanticides by mothers led to such a divorce between law and public opinion that prisoners, witnesses, counsel, juries and even many of HM's judges, conspired to defeat the law. The resulting breakdown was in many ways more serious and complete than that witnessed earlier in the nineteenth century when the public revolted against the severity of punishments for larcenies or forgeries of bank-notes.

There have been considerations of the law since. The 1975 Butler Committee on mentally abnormal offenders pointed out that the effects of childbirth or lactation were often remote at the time of a baby's death and the Royal College of Psychiatrists, in evidence to the Criminal Law Revision Commission, said that some mothers might feel impelled to kill a newborn child not because of a chemical imbalance but because of the 'overwhelming stress from the social environment . . . with the emphasis on the unsuitability of accommodation'.

In sentencing terms this allowed for leniency, whereas a murder conviction meant an automatic life sentence and, of course, until 1964, the possibility of execution.

Dilemmas still arise in the interpretation of laws relating specifically to women. Helena Kennedy, QC, the barrister and commentator on women's rights and the law, wrote in her book *Eve Was Framed*:

The idea that women can be subject to their hormones was the traditional way of explaining otherwise inexplicable behaviour in women . . . the workings of the female body and its potential for child-bearing are sometimes justifiably used in special pleading for women but it does have the double bind of being used to shackle women to very confining roles. Biology is commonly assumed to determine women's lives and there are times when it feels as though it does.

Chapter Twenty-four

On 21 December 1996, at the Old Bailey, Emma Gifford, aged twenty-two, pleaded guilty to infanticide and was sentenced to three years' probation with a condition that she receive psychiatric counselling. The story, like Caroline's, made the front page of many newspapers. The *Daily Mail* splashed with the headline: 'How I Hid My Baby In Freezer.' The *Daily Telegraph* reported: 'Daughter of Millionaire Gave Birth Alone to Secret Baby.'

Emma Gifford was, again like Caroline, an attractive, intelligent young woman, but after that their stories and the consequences of their actions differed greatly. She was the child of a broken home, the daughter of a former chief executive of the Rank Organization and a mother who was described in court as an alcoholic – a description she contested. She had been privately educated and had been studying English and drama at Edinburgh University, although she did not complete her course. She had suffered from depression since her teens and had previously attempted suicide. Two years earlier, she had had a pregnancy, which she had concealed, and had given birth to a baby, which was given up for adoption with the agreement of both her family and her boyfriend, a Portuguese architecture student.

In February 1996, she realized she was pregnant again and told her boyfriend, with whom she had just split up, that she would have an abortion. But in May, alone in the bathroom of her flat in Kensington, she had given birth to a boy. She tried to breast-feed him but had been unable to do so. She fell asleep with the baby and the following morning rang the florists' where she worked to say that she would not be coming in because she was unwell. In a statement read out in court, she told the police: 'I was bleeding quite heavily and did not feel well. I felt I had no option. I did not know what to do.' She put a flannel over her son's face, a pair of her boyfriend's pyjama bottoms round his neck and a pillow over his face. 'Then I went away and was physically sick.'

She then went in to work and when she returned could not bear to look at the baby. She considered suicide but phoned an older brother who took her to the family home in Kent. She carried the body of the child with her and brought him back with her to the flat the following day, again telling no one what had happened. She put the baby's body in a plastic bag in the freezer. She continued to go to work until four weeks later when her brother found the baby where she had hidden it. She later made a confession to the police in which she told them: 'I was afraid. I didn't want people to know. They didn't know I was pregnant. I didn't know what to do . . . It's in my head. There's no connection between what's in my head and what's in my mouth.' She pleaded guilty to infanticide and not guilty to a charge of trying to conceal the birth, a charge that was left on the file.

Her experience in court was very different from Caroline's. The judge, the Recorder of London, told her: 'This birth could not have been more lonely for you and what occurred immediately afterwards, although it must, of course, cause you great remorse, is not something that should be allowed to cloud your life for the whole of the future.' He added: 'It is entirely inappropriate that you should get into a situation where another pregnancy might occur. That cannot be a condition of the order but is a matter I trust you will bear in mind throughout the period of supervision.' The court was told by her defence counsel that she had been fitted with a coil.

Broadly Emma Gifford was regarded, both within and without the court, with a large measure of sympathy. The *Daily Telegraph*, for instance, a newspaper that had recently hired Ann Atkins as an agony aunt with a strongly anti-abortion and anti-pre-marital sex agenda, quoted Alison Hadley of the Brook Advisory Centre, which gives advice on pregnancy to young people: 'We usually have a few cases every year where young people deny or conceal their pregnancy and have their baby alone: sometimes abandoning it or feeling they simply can't cope. The fear and trauma they go through cannot be overestimated.'

While Caroline had been kept in prison for eight months and threatened with the possibility of a fifteen-year jail sentence, the police investigating Emma Gifford's case had made it clear that they knew they were dealing with a disturbed young woman and, until she made her full confession, there was even a possibility that she would not have been charged at all. Both young women experienced the full spotlight of publicity but there was a stark contrast between their treatment within the two legal systems. A proponent of the American system might argue that Ms Gifford was treated too leniently, that she had killed a defenceless child and hidden his existence but, despite a climate in Britain in which judges were being increasingly attacked for light sentences, there was little noticeable sense of public dismay.

In a way, what was remarkable about Emma Gifford's case was how unremarkable it was. Babies of less than a year old are the most likely murder victims in Britain – four or five times more at risk than any other age group – and are most likely to have been killed by one or other of their parents.

Professor Channi Kumar, who had come so speedily to the aid of Caroline, published research in 1996 based on Home Office statistics between 1982 and 1988 which indicated that an infant is killed in Britain every twelve days. Around 20 per cent of the deaths occurred within twenty-four hours of birth.

Professor Kumar's research also showed that almost all of the day-of-birth deaths were committed by the mother, while after that the parents were equally represented.

'There is a huge amount of interest when an adult is killed in the community, say, by a schizophrenic,' he said, at the time of the publication of his research. 'This is a problem which might happen every month, every two months. There is a crisis and we are told we must target the risk. But an infant is killed every twelve to fourteen days, that is thirty homicides a year.' It was possible, he said, that some deaths attributed to sudden infant death syndrome – cot death – had been infanticides but without the proof necessary for a prosecution. There are now around 100,000 abortions a year yet infanticides continue at a static rate, in contradiction to theories that young women who are too frightened to seek advice are the likeliest to kill a child.

It is worth looking at other recent cases in the United Kingdom where women admitted to having killed their child, sometimes without anyone else having known they were pregnant, and comparing them with Caroline, who had been adamant from the moment of her arrest that her daughter had been stillborn.

On New Year's Eve 1993, a nineteen-year-old local government officer from Greenwich in south London gave birth to a baby boy while sitting on the toilet, a case that received little publicity except in the local press. She told Southwark coroner's court that she had not realized she was pregnant. After the birth she said that the baby had cried once and then not moved and she had assumed that he was dead. She had then wrapped him in a towel and concealed him between two mattresses under her bed. When she started bleeding heavily later and screamed out in pain her parents had arranged for her to be taken to hospital where she had initially denied she had been pregnant. Staff at the hospital told police of their suspicions and they had found the baby. The pathologist, Dr Vesna Djuravic, told the court that the child had been alive at birth and concluded that death was due to lack of care and the cause of it was asphyxiation. The detective inspector who handled the case said that a file had been passed to the Crown Prosecution Service but a decision had been made to take no action.

It is worth looking, too, at a dozen cases of women convicted of killing their children, which appeared over the last decade in the British courts.

In March 1986, a woman, aged twenty-five, who strangled her fifteen-day-old baby, was put on probation for two years for infanticide at Birmingham Crown Court. She had locked herself into a toilet at the maternity hospital where she had been readmitted after suffering from stress.

In June 1986, a mother who smothered her nine-month-old daughter because she felt she could not cope on her limited income was put on probation for three years at Winchester Crown Court after pleading guilty to manslaughter. She had told the police: 'I could not cope. I thought she was better out of it.' Mr Justice Tudor Evans told her: 'This is a tragic case in which you are in need of medical treatment and other help rather than punishment.'

In January 1988, a mother who killed her eleven-month-old son in a fit of depression was put on probation for three years at the Old Bailey. A former accountant from Caterham in Surrey, aged thirty-six, she had originally claimed that the child was a cot-death victim. She had tried to commit suicide immediately afterwards and the court heard that she had left the residue of her estate in her will to the National Society for the Prevention of Cruelty to Children. Judge Hazan told her: 'You are in need of help and not of punishment.'

In March 1989, a nursery worker from Birmingham, aged twenty-two, was put on probation for two years and agreed to twelve months' psychiatric treatment after pleading guilty to infanticide. She had hidden the pregnancy – the result of a casual affair – from her family and had given birth alone in an attic bedroom. She had cradled the baby for half an hour, given him a name and then wrapped him in a blanket and shut him in a suitcase. The suitcase was found a week later dumped in rubbish. Mr Justice Owen, sentencing her, said: 'You need help, not punishment.'

In August 1989, a mother who had strangled her four-month-old baby daughter was placed on probation for two years at the Court of Criminal Appeal in Edinburgh. She had initially been jailed for twelve months after admitting culpable homicide but was freed after the court heard that she had been suffering from severe post-natal depression.

In March 1991, a schoolgirl aged seventeen, who had strangled her newborn baby, was put on probation at Oxford Crown Court after agreeing to psychiatric help. She had not realized she was pregnant and had stuffed tissues in the baby's mouth and tied a shoelace round its neck. The court was told that her parents had not approved of her boyfriend.

In April 1991, a mother, aged thirty-eight, was put on probation after pleading guilty to infanticide at Sheffield Crown Court. She had squeezed her three-day-old daughter so hard that seventeen ribs were broken. Twice previously she had given birth to children who had died after suffering from similar injuries. In both cases, the cause of death had been diagnosed as pneumonia with the fractures seen as the result of vigorous attempts to revive the child. Mr Justice Judge told her: 'This is a very sad case. You are a loving mother of five children and a lot of people like you.' The court was told that she had suffered from depression for many years.

In June 1993, a young woman, aged nineteen, who stabbed her baby daughter to death after giving birth, was given three years' probation. She was said at Newcastle Crown Court to have been too frightened of her father's anger to admit she was pregnant.

In September 1993, a mother, aged twenty-seven, who battered her six-month-old son to death with a television remote control, was put on probation for three years after admitting manslaughter. Judge Bruce Laughland said he was taking the 'exceptional course' because she had been suffering from severe depression for many years.

In February 1995, a woman was given a three-year probation sentence after admitting that she had suffocated her baby with a pillow. It had originally been believed that the child had died of cot death but she had confessed to her boyfriend a year and a half after the death. At St Albans Crown Court her defence counsel, David Burgess, said that she had felt 'isolated and abandoned'. Her probation order was conditional on her spending six months in a clinic.

In July 1995, a mother from Swindon in Wiltshire who admitted the manslaughter of her baby by drowning was freed after the judge heard that she had difficulty in telling right from wrong.

In September 1995, a widely travelled secretary and linguist, aged thirty-seven, was sentenced at the Old Bailey to two years' probation on the condition that she receive psychiatric help for depression after admitting infanticide. She had killed her eleven-day-old son by swinging him by the legs and hitting his head against a stair. The court heard that she had been suffering from depression and had been in a 'black fog' of despair, unable to cope with having an unplanned baby. She had initially told her partner, an international quantity surveyor, that the death was an accident. Judge Gerald Gordon concluded: 'The question I have to decide is whether the loss of the child, and the public horror at what you did, deserves punishment. This was a tragic event. You are a woman of hitherto impeccable character.' On that basis, he decided that the public interest would be better served by her receiving treatment.

The women convicted are of a wide variety of ages and from all social and educational backgrounds: a schoolgirl and a former accountant, a mother of five children and a girl who did not know she was pregnant. The courts passing judgments span the country and two legal systems: Winchester and Edinburgh, London and Sheffield. The ages of the babies vary from the newborn to children of almost a year old, the cause of death from suffocation to strangulation. In Scotland, where there is no infanticide law, women have tended to be treated in the same way as they would be in England: given probation although convicted of culpable homicide. Crucially, the thread that runs through the hearings is that, although many of the women initially denied any involvement, the cases are treated as tragedies and the defendants as in need of – in the phrase that is repeated almost ritually by every sentencing judge – 'help not punishment'.

Caroline had not been accused of killing a child that had been demonstrably alive and known by others to be so; neither was she accused of any violent act, which confirms the assertions of her family and legal team that she would have been treated differently if she had been arrested in the United Kingdom. After the first major article on Caroline appeared, in the *Guardian*, a woman responded with her own experience of post-partum psychosis. Judith Harper, from Cardiff, wrote of how she had been convinced four weeks before the birth of her son that he was dead and she had attempted to convince her husband and family of this. 'My son was born perfectly healthy but, at the time, I thought I knew he was dead or, at best, horribly deformed . . . I lived in a nightmare world where I thought I was being asked to dress and feed a dead child.' She added that her son was now a healthy eleven-year-old.

In passing, it is perhaps worth noting that the psychiatrist, R. D. Laing, author of such seminal works as *The Divided Self, Sanity, Madness and the Family* and *The Politics of Experience*, was born in Glasgow in 1927 to a mother who concealed her pregnancy right up to the day of his birth and who insisted, as did his father, that they had ceased sexual activity years before his birth.

But what is the pattern in the United States? Because each state has its own interpretations of the law, there is no clear trend. Take, for instance, the following two cases both of which occurred after Caroline's case had been heard in court.

In November 1996, an eighteen-year-old first-year art student at the University of Delaware gave birth to a son in a motel with her boyfriend, also a student from a comfortable background, present. Within the hour the baby was dead, his head crushed by blows. The body, in a plastic laundry bag, was found stuffed in a dumpster at the back of the motel. The case took on a high profile in the United States, with the couple described, because of their ages, as Romeo and Juliet. 'How Will The Liberals Justify This?' asked the headline in the *New York Post*, suggesting that that derided breed had been able to explain away such deaths when the perpetrators were poor and under-privileged.

In New York, in November 1996, the Brooklyn District Attorney said that he would not prosecute a fifteen-year-old girl, Keisha Simmonds, who had been initially accused of murdering her abandoned baby. She had been found unconscious in her apartment after giving birth earlier in the day and police had then found the child's body in a garbage bag at a sanitation depot. The baby was deemed to have been alive and to have died of asphyxia. The DA's office was quoted in the *New York Times* as saying that no charges of murder or manslaughter would be brought because of 'legally insufficient evidence'.

But not everyone sees the British system as necessarily the better of the two. In an article on Caroline's case in the *Sunday Telegraph*, the writer Yvonne Roberts asked:

So which is better? A law of infanticide unevenly applied? Or the American system in which the prosecutor assumes a woman is bad unless proven otherwise? In my view, American rules are clearer, unmuddled by prejudices or

unproven beliefs about biological destiny. They caused
Caroline Beale pain but that might be the price to be paid
if justice is to be extended not just to the increasing
numbers of women who fail the test of conformity but
also to those babies who otherwise have no voice: the
victims of murder committed by a rational hand.

Chapter Twenty-five

Few people connected with Caroline's story were untouched by it. We started our account with Alex Velez, the police officer who arrested Caroline at JFK. He was awarded a 'meritorious medal' for doing so, his only previous such award being for catching a bag thief. His local paper, the *Staten Island Advance*, 'gave a beautiful account with my name and my department mentioned just as it was'. Driving down to the Staten Island ferry in his van, he remarks: 'I feel sorry for her. I don't know what the story is in London. Is it a disgrace to have a baby and not be married? If I felt in my heart that she did it intentionally I think she should go to jail for life. But I figure she was so emotionally disturbed she's not aware of what she was doing. You can't blame someone for being sick.'

Detective O'Donnell is shortly retiring from the NYPD to his home in the blue-collar suburb of Bethpage in Nassau County. He has no doubt that he took the right course and still feels that diplomatic pressure played its part in the case.

Zayed Ali, in whose hotel the birth took place, discussed the case later with his wife, a doctor. 'We had a little debate. We thought a murder charge was too harsh. I didn't believe it was a cold-blooded murder, the way the District Attorney was suggesting. There was obviously some mental deficiency. It should have been a lesser charge. I didn't think it was fair she should be held here. She should have gone back to her own country and been tried there.'

In Marjory Fisher's office a Second World War poster

shows a woman with her hair caught up in a scarf and her arm flexed, her face determined and self-confident. The slogan reads, 'You Can Do It!' Another, hand-drawn, poster says, 'Thank you for showing us how to be safe – Class K106'. She has no doubts about her conduct in the case. 'Caroline stood up in court and admitted her guilt which I thought was really important.' But does she not accept that someone might do that in a plea bargain rather than run the risk of a long jail term? She says that Caroline was specifically asked if she had been under any pressure to plead guilty and had denied that she was. But surely a defendant has to do that for the deal to be accepted? Again she refers to the words Caroline used in her guilty plea. 'I was satisfied with the sentence and I was most satisfied that she stood up and said what she did. She said that she knew that what she did at the time could end the child's life. She knew that and the people in Queens and the people in England knew that.'

But did the people in England really know that? 'Sometimes I got the impression that people were more concerned about the defendant than about the victim. The prosecution had concern for the life of the baby and you could say that it had lived a very short amount of time so it had been deprived of more life than someone older. I believed that any system that treats the death of a child with a broad brush is lacking in compassion. I didn't treat her differently because she was English. I believe she would have been treated just the same if she had been American and had not had access to the same lawyers. She certainly had some very good psychiatric experts – not all of them, I don't think, but some of them. I hope she is able to move on with her life and contribute something. I hope something like this never happens to her again. I doubt that it will.' She is clearly conscious that within the British media she is regarded as more Cruella de Vil than Hollywood DA and she resisted four requests for an interview before she finally agreed. Her parting words are: 'Don't make me out to be the Wicked Witch!'

The plea bargain as a tool of justice continues to be a subject for debate in America. Professor George P. Fletcher of Columbia law school wrote in his book *With Justice For Some*: 'Though roughly 90 per cent of all cases are disposed of consensually, without trial, there is something unseemly about the prosecution's trading a lower charge in return for the defendant's cooperating and waiving his right to trial. The very idea that the authorities cut special deals with certain defendants offends the rule of law.'

Michael Dowd has just been representing a young woman who had been arrested after attending a function at Brown University at which Baroness Thatcher was speaking. The young woman had accused the former prime minister of being responsible for the death of IRA hunger-striker Bobby Sands. Dowd had just been to see the film *Michael Collins* and liked it very much.

He and Irene keep in regular touch with Caroline, who looked after their daughter, Lauren, when they came over to Britain for a golfing holiday in St Andrews in 1996. He believes that the case will have ramifications for other women facing similar charges, that it has finally raised the debate on the issue in the United States, both in the legal and the medical professions, and he reiterates his belief that Caroline would have been acquitted if she had stood trial – and if she had been able to survive that trial psychologically. He also believes that the way Caroline was kept in prison 'as if she was a contract killer for the Mob' was indefensible.

At the entrance to Judge Hanophy's office in the Sutphin Boulevard courthouse is a large shamrock with a record of how many days there are left to St Patrick's Day. A miniature Irish tricolour flies alongside the Stars and Stripes on his desk. After a hearty handshake, he expounds on his views with a frankness that would be highly unusual in a British judge: 'The thing that had got us here was that this baby had died when she was minutes old. Now in England it's a slap on the wrist, you go and see a shrink a couple of times but it's treated differently in the United States. We bent over backwards to give her probation so she could return to England. The court extended itself and it was our initiative that had made it possible.' That was, he said, the reason he had called Peter Beale a Ralph Kramden character.

'What he said could have jeopardized what we were doing. The people could have said they were no longer going to accept the deal and she could have been facing twenty-five years to life if she had lost. I let her out. What we did was something that is almost never done, then her father comes out with this stuff about the American system. I would have loved to have had them [the Beales] in but they had gone home.

'Afterwards I got all this hate mail, letters from people in England saying that they wanted to kill me and dismember me. One said that in America you have the blacks who are on the dole, refuse to work and commit crime and in England we have the Irish who are on the dole, refuse to work and commit crime. We had a lot of that sort of stuff to put up with.'

In April 1997, Hanophy was reprimanded by the Commission on Judicial Conduct for his 'undignified and disparaging remarks'. The Commission concluded: 'Out of pique over critical remarks that Ms Beale's parents had made to the news media, respondent retaliated with angry and vituperative comments, referring to the family's homeland as "primitive and uncivilized" and calling the defendant's father "Ralph Kramden – the guy with the big mouth..." In open court, respondent engaged in hyperbole about the British legal system in ways which he knew misrepresented the law there, even though he was aware that his remarks would be broadcast abroad.

'His gratuitous and irrelevant reference to defendants from Northern Ireland who had been sentenced in British courts was mean-spirited and political in nature. By these comments and his insistence that the Beales apologize to the prosecutor and the police, respondent failed to act at all times in a manner that promotes public confidence in the integrity and impartiality of the judiciary.'

Meg Spinelli, like the Dowds, remains a friend of Caroline, visiting her in London when her work and research bring her over. After the 20/20 programme was broadcast, she received many calls on the issue. 'For better or worse, I tend to get very involved and I felt this burning need to do something for Caroline. It was not necessarily all altruistic, we do things for many reasons. I've now been first-hand involved with these women who have been wronged by our legal system. It seems so preposterous that they're mentally ill and punished for it.' She is now working on a book, provisionally entitled *Those In Shackles*.

'We're in a double bind in the States especially: you've got one faction of the feminist movement saying we don't want to hear what hormones do and don't do. They don't want to hear that mental illness has any kind of parallel with femininity because the suffragettes used to be force-fed in psychiatric hospitals. And that's worthwhile to remember. But the bottom line is, that if we don't recognize these things, then a lot of women are going to suffer and that's a bad alternative.'

Professor Brockington understood the reasons for accepting the plea-bargain deal but was scathing about the confession that Caroline had been obliged to make: 'I would not attach any credibility whatever to any statements she made in court. It was a charade.' He said that a formal complaint about Caroline's treatment in New York has been lodged with the World Psychiatric Association.

Gary Jacobs, the first lawyer contacted by the Beales, has written about the case on the Internet. 'The United States promises justice for all, which is a joke,' he says. 'The plea-bargain system is disgusting. It's a means of getting innocent people to plead guilty by putting them into fear.'

Sister Marion remains busy with her penal-reform work and her campaigning to change the drugs laws. She has taken part in a video called *Drugs Mules*, which detailed the way in which women couriers ended up spending long periods in jail while the drug traffickers escaped. She hopes that what happened to Caroline will have some effect: 'Caroline got tremendous support. If you could have Margaret Spinelli and Michael Dowd, those heavy hitters, on every case and the publicity and *20/20* then there might be a change. But it's an evil system and in an evil system you have to do what you have to do. So many women who are innocent plead guilty because if they go to trial they're risking a long sentence. I would never advise a person charged with drug trafficking to plead innocent even if I knew they were innocent. The fact that Caroline had to do that was deplorable but that's what she had to do.

'If they had allowed Caroline to go free of this they would have to do this to all the other women. The prosecution want to win their cases and the prosecutor in this case took a very strong line. A child had died and she was going to represent the child. I'm sure she believed in her position and the law is on her side in this country. What I think is so cynical is that you can have an abortion up to six months and nothing is ever made of that so that if Caroline had come here and had an abortion that would have been fine but one minute after . . .'

Margaret Brower, who now has a new lodger, a student from Ecuador, says that she learned much from what happened to Caroline, not least that the way in which unconvicted prisoners were treated was wrong: 'Once you are picked up the assumption is from the guards, the populace and the media that you would not have been picked up unless you were doing something wrong.' On mental illness, she says, 'We are still in the dark ages, we are still treating people as criminals rather than recognizing that there can be a chemical imbalance triggered by stress, genetics whatever. We're all very fragile and only well because we're lucky to be well.'

Her youngest daughter, Barbara, who is still in touch with Caroline, says: 'When she was here, she wanted the freedom to go back to England but now she's back there she feels just as much a prisoner because she would like to come back to New York.' She, too, says she learned much from the way Caroline dealt with everything.

Tony the Priest keeps in regular touch and has been over to visit Caroline. 'There have been one or two snide comments from foolish people. Someone asked after Caroline was freed, "Do you need another cause now?" He meant it to be light. We had a wonderful time together, the joking, the kidding. I do miss her.'

He knew that Judge Hanophy had spoken at the Holy Name Society, a men's fraternal organization in the neighbouring St Kevin's where Father Tony ministered, and he accepted a request to do the same. 'I gave a talk there on the death penalty – against it, of course, well, not "of course" because many priests are in favour of it. I spoke about my feelings about Caroline, the case. I said if you had met her you would have loved her. She was a wonderful young woman who found herself in a situation that was terrible. I have a feeling that her case would have been much more of a leaven in our society if it had gone to trial. It would have created much more awareness. It could have been a precedent if it had gone to trial and it might have saved one more woman from going through it. But I understand why the decision was made: you want to get her out of here, you want to get her home.' He thinks she would have had a terrible time if she had been jailed but would have survived: 'After all the trouble she'd been through, who could sell her short? And there are good people in prison.'

Velma, Caroline's fellow inmate who had killed a man

who raped her, was sentenced to five years for manslaughter. Sherain Bryant, another friend in prison, now serving twenty-five years, has just been joined in Bedford Hills prison by a third friend of Caroline, Venisa. Caroline corresponds with them regularly, sending them books and clothes. Of her other fellow inmates, she believes at least one is now dead.

Her friends in England find her changed. Jenny Bloor said: 'She has been through hell and survived it and it shows. She has become a very strong, independent woman.'

Mandy Goff says she is much quieter. She remains convinced of Caroline's innocence: 'You might say that's because I'm a friend and my loyalties are with her. She must have been living two lives in parallel – the normal Caroline exterior and the inner Caroline that was going through all this turmoil that no one knew anything about.'

Lesley Warren noted other changes: 'Before, Caroline was happy to be the centre of attention but since it all happened she wants to be out of the limelight. She's a different person now, more caring, a better person.'

Araminta Thorne also emphasizes the positive: 'It sounds like a terribly twee thing to say but so much good has come out of it – she's met such incredible people, who were all there willingly.'

Paul Faraway still lives in the house that he and Caroline bought and now shares it with his younger brother, Sam, who was with them on that journey to New York. He still finds the case painful and does not like to talk about it. He feels that the Beales disapprove of the way he behaved and does not feel that anything he says will now make any difference. He has not seen Caroline since she was arrested at JFK airport.

'It has been a hard two or three years for him. He's a reasonably private person but he's honest and genuine. He has been another victim, it's been the worst two or three years in his life,' says his friend, Colin Brosnan.

Nick Catliff, who had watched events unfold on both sides of the Atlantic as he made his BBC *Inside Story* documentary, concluded: 'I liked her a lot. I feel that all this weight of legal, emotional, political and above all psychological baggage had been placed on her by everybody. She seemed totally lost in the middle of it all. She's just been wafted around there. People were taking from her what they wanted to take and reading into her what they wanted to read into her.'

Daphne Beale said: 'You hear of so many people who have gone through these different traumas and the family splits up. I was determined from the start that this family wouldn't and if we do quarrel and split up I feel Marjory Fisher has won and at the moment she hasn't. She might have got a tick in the right box but she hasn't won.'

In March 1997, Louise Woodward, an eighteen-year-old from Chester, was charged with first-degree murder in Cambridge, Massachusetts. After completing her A levels in England she had been working as an au pair in America and was alleged to have shaken to death the nine-month-old boy she was looking after. She, like Caroline, protested her innocence from the start. The image of her on television, bewildered, handcuffed and shackled between two bulky American police officers clearly had echoes of Caroline's case.

'It's as though there is still a lynch mob there,' said Peter Beale, 'but now they get the law to do it for them. It seems that there has to be someone to blame, someone has to be punished for everything. They were like hyenas round a wounded animal.'

Caroline is back at work at the Department of Health in the Elephant and Castle. She also worked voluntarily for Prisoners Abroad, the London-based charity, which looks after the interests of Britons held in foreign jails. (The United Kingdom also holds large numbers of foreigners in its jails: 25 per cent of sentenced women and 8 per cent of men in British jails are from abroad.) She has bought a car, started working out in the gym, kept in touch with her 'family' in America, not given up smoking.

She reflects now on the case. 'I would have gone for trial even if they had said I would only serve another six months because I believed in myself. At the time all I wanted to do was come home. Looking back, it's easy to say I should have done this, done that. I knew that when I was back home in England and everything in the garden was rosy I would have wished that I could have fought it. But I was so ground down I couldn't take it – I contemplated doing myself in so many times and it seems that's the way they work.

'If I'm angry with anyone, I'm angry with Fisher. I know she was only doing her job but I have to hate someone. There's not many people I hate in this world but I hate her and I hate O'Donnell.

'In the end, I learned many things. Some people think that everyone in jail must deserve to be there but I have learned how wrong that is.

'In the end, I might have seen the worst of what people can do to other people but I have also seen the best.'

Perhaps for Caroline the quotation from Tennyson's 'Ulysses', which her father wrote in his diary half-way through the long battle to free her, remains most applicable:

> *I am part of all that I have met . . .*
> *Tho' much is taken, much abides . . .*
> *That which we are, we are.*
> *One equal temper of heroic hearts,*
> *Made weak by time and fate, but strong in will.*
> *To strive, to seek, to find, and not to yield.*

Much was taken, much abides.

Chapter Twenty-six

A few years ago the American journalist Joe McGinnis wrote a book about a prisoner called Jeffrey MacDonald who was serving a sentence for a murder of which he claimed to be innocent. While working on the book with MacDonald's full co-operation, McGinnis became convinced of his guilt and produced a book that portrayed MacDonald as a monster. When the book appeared, MacDonald sued for breach of contract and won. This saga led to another book, *The Journalist and the Murderer*, by Janet Malcolm in which she referred to the relationship of journalists and their subjects as 'invariably and inescapably lopsided'. A number of journalists on both sides of the Atlantic asked me, when I started work on Caroline's story, if I was familiar with the story and how I would deal with such a dilemma if it presented itself. What if Caroline had been lying over crucial parts of the story? What if I discovered, as I went through all the documents in the police, DA, defence and psychiatric files, that she was telling one story to someone and another to someone else, or that she had deliberately obscured the facts?

I hope that if I had discovered such inconsistencies that I would have confronted Caroline with them and, if dissatisfied with the answers, would have abandoned the book or written one in which the full story was told. I know that she embarked on this book with the encouragement of Michael Dowd and Meg Spinelli, who both hoped that it might help other people who found themselves in a similar predicament and might lead to a greater discussion of the laws and medical research in that area as well as the penal system in which Caroline became enmeshed. I know, also, that Caroline wanted to clear up the puzzlement many had felt when, after months of claiming her innocence, she had admitted her guilt. I know, too, that, for Caroline, having to relive parts of her life that were so painful has not been easy and that, in her heart of hearts, she may well have regretted agreeing to co-operate on the book. To have carried on with it required great gallantry on her part. However, I can say that nothing I have discovered from talking to more than seventy people, both hostile and sympathetic to her, who have been involved in one way or another with this case, and from the many hours I have spent with her has made me doubt in any way her story.

The phrase 'miscarriage of justice' is often bandied about without much thought as to what it means. In Caroline's case it can hardly have been more apposite. None of the statements she made to the police, the DA and the psychiatrists have differed as to what happened that night in suite 101 from the moment when she was first arrested to the present day. It would seem that the only lies she told were those when she admitted in court that she had knowingly taken the life of her child.

In the course of the last three years, Caroline has had to deal with the death of her child, the death of one of her closest friends, the end of a long and loving relationship, a lengthy jail term in a foreign prison and near-suicidal depressions. Remarkably, she has survived and in doing so has won the friendship of many who had never met her before as well as the admiration of those who were unaware of her personal strength. She has also stood by the women she met in prison who had supported her when she was first incarcerated. I hope that the last chapter of this book can represent the first chapter in what should have every chance of being a rich, fulfilled and generous life.